BUSINESS CYCLES

AND

BUSINESS MEASUREMENTS

THE MACMILLAN COMPANY
NEW YORK · BOSTON · CHICAGO · DALLAS
ATLANTA · SAN FRANCISCO

MACMILLAN & CO., LIMITED
LONDON · BOMBAY · CALCUTTA
MELBOURNE

THE MACMILLAN CO. OF CANADA, LTD.
TORONTO

BUSINESS CYCLES

AND

BUSINESS MEASUREMENTS

Studies in Quantitative Economics

BY

CARL SNYDER

"Almost all the great discoveries in science have been but the rewards of accurate measurement, and the patient, long continued labor in the minute sifting of the numerical results."

LORD KELVIN.

New York

THE MACMILLAN COMPANY

1927

To
WESLEY C. MITCHELL

AND

WARREN M. PERSONS

Pioneers in the Quantitative Study
of Business Cycles

"The Method I take to do this is not yet very usual, for instead of using only Comparative and Superlative words, and Intellectual Arguments, I have taken the course (as a Specimen of the Political Arithmetick I have long aimed at) to express myself in Number, Weight, and Measure."

Sir William Petty,
"A Discourse of Trade," *1683.*

INTRODUCTION

This volume embodies the results of an extended research carried on with the object of obtaining broader and more detailed measures of trade, production and business activity in the United States, and their fluctuations throughout the last half century or more; to provide a standard for the measurement of business or trade of the country from month to month from 1919 to date, by means of a new Index of the Total Volume of Trade, derived from 56 separately computed series; and to make comparison of this with other new indexes of business derived from bank debits corrected for changes in the general price level; from variations in the rate of turnover of bank deposits; from railway traffic, iron production, and production in basic industries; establishing from these a basis for the measure of business activity and its variations throughout the last fifty years, derived, first, from bank clearings corrected for price changes, and, secondly, from deposits turnover; and comparison of these findings with corresponding indexes from iron production and general industrial production.

These new measures offer a basis for answer to the question as to just what are "business cycles," what is the extent and regularity of trade fluctuations, and the time relations between various phases of business activity, such as production in basic industries, distribution of goods, wholesale and retail trade, and other phases of finance and business; likewise for a discussion of the influence of Interest Rates, Credit Supply, Business Insolvencies and of Price Changes. There is also description of a new index of the General Price Level or average of all payments as contrasted with special price indexes, as of commodities at wholesale, and the like.

With this is given a review of the evidence tending to establish the view that the cyclical fluctuations in trade, with their concomitants of crises and depression, reached the peak of intensity in the latter half of the Nineteenth Century, perforce largely of the rapid expansion of railways and the wide distribution and interchange of products thereby made possible; and that these cycles in the last thirty years have tended to decline in intensity and probably also in duration, with the gradual integration of the country's industry, more capable and enlightened management, and the establishment of a coherent and co-ordinated banking system for the nation.

The volume endeavors to substitute definite measures for the chiefly descriptive material which has hitherto been available for long term comparison. The validity of these measures is based upon the wealth of new material which has become available since the War, covering almost every field of industrial and commercial activity; and upon the relations and correspondences therein established between such a composite measure of total trade and its several components; and especially bank debits, or clearings, when corrected for price changes.

All this meant, necessarily, the establishment of some kind of a norm, or base, by which the condition of trade may be determined, alike in the present and in the past; that is to say, a scale of business measurement; to know, in brief, how the high activity of 1925 and 1926 compared with similar periods in the last half century; what, for example, was the extent of the prostration of business in 1921, in 1908 and previous periods; how far production and trade were stimulated by the War, and in other boom periods; and from these to gauge how far the canons of business guidance of past years are applicable to the present time.

This norm of business conditions was found in the measurement of that persistent growth and expansion of industry which has been so notable and characteristic of the last century. The country has grown enormously in population; and this growth has been at so sure and even a pace that it could have been at almost any time projected to a reasonable degree into the future. This growth of population has meant, necessarily, a corresponding increase in our needs for food, for shelter and for the other necessities and comforts of life. And along with this growth, discovery, invention, a continuous improvement in the means of production and transport, and the general diffusion of well-being have implied a corresponding expansion of trade. And so we find, in all the lines of industry for which adequate data are available, the same sure evidences of persistent growth, and, viewed in the large, something of the same even pace and the same element of reasonable predictability.

The result of this was to establish in a large number of instances, at least, a kind of actuarial expectancy, for any given year, from which the variations from prosperity to depression might be measured. What would have been a phenomenal product of industry twenty or thirty, to say nothing of fifty or sixty years ago, might easily represent the extreme of business stagnation at the present time. What might be regarded as a huge increase over ten years ago, measured simply in tons and barrels and bushels and bales, might represent a serious decrease in the rate of growth from preceding periods. The standard in such a country as ours is never static; it is a moving base; so that the selection of any given period, for comparison, rapidly loses its significance and value.

The especial aim of these studies was to obtain from all this more definite knowledge of the relations of business activity, or volume of trade, and the extension of bank credit; and with this in view the volume includes also measures of deposit activity or the rate of turnover of average deposits. These measurements unexpectedly reveal that deposit activity tends to vary closely with the fluctuations of trade, and in itself forms a fair measure of business activity.

New York, Oct. 1, 1926.

ACKNOWLEDGMENTS

Much of the present work was planned out some years ago, as the background for a volume then in prospect. But time and opportunity were lacking, and in 1913 came Wesley C. Mitchell's masterly summation of the then available material. Since then have come the publication of the original and pioneering investigations of Warren M. Persons and his associates, and especially Edmund E. Day, of the Harvard Committee of Economic Research; much valuable work by the statistical organization of the American Telephone & Telegraph Company, under M. C. Rorty and his successor, S. L. Andrew; the mathematical correlations of Henry L. Moore and Irving Fisher; the establishment of the National Bureau of Economic Research, with W. C. Mitchell, W. I. King, Frederick R. Macaulay, and Oswald Knauth heading its staff; a series of publications by the Pollak Foundation under the initiative of W. T. Foster and Waddill Catchings; a number of illuminating studies by Walter W. Stewart, Leonard Ayres, Holbrook Working, Alvin H. Hansen, W. A. Berridge, W. F. Ogburn, Henry A. Wallace, and others; and, especially for Canada, H. Michel, of the University of Toronto.

The substance of the present work has been reported in various articles listed in the Bibliography appended, and in a course of lectures at the Summer School of Columbia University in 1925. The manuscript has been edited and prepared for publication by Dorothy Swaine Thomas, the proofs read by Lucile Bagwell, and the tables checked by Chas. Kayser. Toward various phases of the work so many have contributed valuable counsel that adequate acknowledgment is difficult; an especial debt is due

Messrs. Mitchell, Macaulay and King, of the National Bureau of Economic Research, for their friendly interest. The work herein presented has been very largely a composite production and W. Randolph Burgess, especially, has been constantly and closely associated with it from the beginning. So also have Alice Carlson, Lucile Bagwell, and, at one time or another, J. H. Riddle, George B. Roberts, Harold V. Roelse, Irene Sheehan, Hazel Reilly, J. S. Meiklejohn, H. E. Niles, Frederick C. Knote, B. P. Chambers, Nancy Mac-Leod, and Victor von Szeliski. To all of these the writer's debt is deep.

In view of my connection with the Federal Reserve Bank of New York, it should be said that the views expressed herein are in no sense official and that responsibility for these is wholly the writer's own.

CONTENTS

BUSINESS CYCLES

AND

BUSINESS MEASUREMENTS

BUSINESS CYCLES AND BUSINESS MEASUREMENTS

CHAPTER I

THE NATURE OF BUSINESS CYCLES

WHEN in April, 1789, George Washington, fifty-eight years old, left his home in Virginia to become the first president of the new republic, he did not have the means to pay for the journey. Though he belonged to one of the wealthy families of Virginia and possessed thousands of acres of land there and beyond the Alleghenies, he had difficulty in borrowing, first, five hundred Virginia pounds, and then an additional £100 to pay off his debts and defray his travelling expenses. During his term of office he had frequently to receive advances from his pay as President, so little was the return from his own estates. His first Secretary of the Treasury, Alexander Hamilton, a successful lawyer and one of the ablest financiers this country has ever known, received a salary of $3,500 a year, and apparently had no other income while he remained in office. It is evident that the per capita income in the United States at this time must have been on a very small scale indeed.

Banking operations were of slight importance, judged in terms of the twentieth century. The first Bank of the United States, which Hamilton organized, had a nominal capital of only ten million dollars, of which two millions represented a Government subscription in Government bonds, at that time of slight value. Sumner [1] says: "The

---

[1] William Graham Sumner: "A History of Banking in the United States" (edit. by Jour. of Commerce, N. Y., 1896), p. 28 and p. 33.

Bank might go into operation when $400,000 had been paid in in gold and silver . . . (and) the belief at the time, and subsequently, was that no more than the specie part of the first installment ever was paid into the Bank in specie." Yet, on so slight a foundation, the Bank proved a tower of strength to the new Government and established branches in each of the principal cities.

When Washington came to New York, then the capital, it had a population of a little over 30,000. The largest city in the country was Philadelphia, with a population of 42,000, and Boston ranked third with 18,000. In all the cities and towns of the new nation there were probably not more than 150,000 persons, and the rest of the population of three million whites gained its livelihood directly from the plantations and farms.

Of domestic trade there was little, and the bulk of that was carried in sailing vessels. Express riders on horseback could make the distance from New York to Boston in ninety-six hours, but the stage coach took six or eight days.[2] The usual journey from Albany to New York was accomplished in "safe, fast, and commodious river sloops."[3]

"A few good roads led from Philadelphia into the interior, and from Boston to Worcester there was one of the best highways in the country. Elsewhere, when water routes could not be made to serve, progress was painful and slow. It took three weeks or a month to bring a wagon load of flour or tobacco from the Valley of Virginia or from Lynchburg to Richmond, and as much more to carry back the supplies for the plantations whence came the flour or the tobacco. Two trips a year were about the only communication that planters living fifty miles from Virginia's commercial town had with the storekeepers of that place whence came everything consumed in the household that

[2] Edward Channing: "A History of the United States," Vol. IV, 1920, p. 4.
[3] Channing, op. cit., p. 5.

was not produced or made on the plantation."[4]   These facts are even more striking when it is remembered that Virginia was then the richest and most populous State of the Union.

Even communication was slow and expensive.   Channing says[5] of this that "the poor transportation facilities were due in great part to the lack of demand for better means of communication in the years before the establishment of a strong Federal Government, in those days when each colony or state lived a life of its own and a very simple life at that."   In 1789 there were only seventy-five postmasters in the whole country and the total receipts of the postal service were some twenty-five thousand dollars.[6]

The great bulk of the population produced its own food, built its own houses, spun its own wool, made its own clothes, tanned its own leather, and cobbled its own shoes. "With the exception of flour and a few tropical commodities and some manufactured goods," says Channing,[7] "the New Englander bought almost nothing that was not produced or made within five miles of his own house.   The case was even truer of the farmer of the Middle States or the planter of the South."

Nor was the position of Great Britain or the other chief nations much different.   The population of London then, it is true, was approaching a million, but there was little to indicate the familiar industrial England of today.   The coal mines were just beginning to make use of the newly invented steam engine, and the smelting of iron with coal was in its infancy.   The use of cotton for clothing had scarcely begun, and the great manufacturing centers of Manchester and Birmingham were practically unknown. The entire population of the island did not exceed eight millions; and the great bulk of these were cotters and peasants, living by tilling the land.

[4] Channing op. cit., p. 5.
[5] Loc. cit., p. 6.
[6] Loc. cit., p. 7.
[7] Loc. cit., p. 11.

The trade of the nations, that is, the barter or exchange of goods, could then represent but a slender part of the total subsistence or consumption of the population. In this country, at least, nineteen out of twenty derived their subsistence almost exclusively from what they themselves harvested or made. Beyond the slight exchange of luxuries, like silks and tobacco and snuff, some flour and a goodly quantity of wines and rum, the commerce of the country was of the most meagre sort. Possibly a single freight train of the length that one sees flying by on one of our great railway lines could have carried the entire annual traffic in goods between New York and Boston or New York and Philadelphia. The industrial organization of this new country, and, for that matter, of the most advanced nations of Europe, did not vary much from that which had prevailed on the plains of Asia Minor for thousands of years. Wealth consisted largely of land, flocks and slaves.

Such an economy would scarcely produce the violent ups and downs of commerce, trade, production and unemployment with which our modern industrial order is unhappily so familiar. For the average man who tilled his own fields and worked twelve or fourteen hours a day to gain enough for the subsistence of himself and his usually large family, there could be slight danger of enforced idleness or starvation. The most he could fear was the wrath of the gods and the failure of his crops. He could not face ruin from the failure of the firms with which he did business, for such exchange of goods as took place was little more than local barter, and there were no banks in existence until just before the Republic was founded.

In less than a century and a half the whole world order has changed. There has been an increase in population, especially of Europe and America, of a degree unequalled in all the history of mankind. Today, in New York City alone, dwells a population twice as great as that of the straggling colonies along the Atlantic seaboard which drew together to form the new American Union. In London alone is a population now nearly as great as that of all England when the Colonies broke away. In that former day the whole of the English speaking peoples equalled scarcely more than 10 or 12 millions, while today it is nearly twenty times that number.

But it is not the mere increase of population that has distinguished this modern time; it is the transformation in the whole economic order. The native population of North America, when the white man came, probably did not exceed that of the smallest of our forty-eight states now. Yet the larger part of the 120 millions that dwell north of the Rio Grande have comforts and luxuries such as were unknown to most monarchs in the days of Columbus. Alike in Europe and America the spectre of famine, from which few of the nations of former days were wholly free, has almost disappeared.

If population has increased in these parts of the earth ten-fold and twenty-fold, production, trade and wealth have increased a hundred-fold. In the first year of our existence as a nation our total exports reached in value about 20 millions of dollars; very recently they exceeded 8 billions of dollars. And while this latter figure was in part the result of a great rise in prices, and while today food and many commodities are far dearer than in the times of Washington, there are thousands of articles that are much cheaper; so that, on the whole, there is little question that the average man today can obtain far more of the necessaries and even the luxuries of life than was possible in those days.

This continent now exports more grains, flour and meats than were consumed by the three or four largest nations then and these exports are but a minor part of the immense production and consumption at home. In addition, from all over the world we import vast quantities of silk, sugar, coffee, tea, tobacco, rubber, tin, wool, hides and the like, exchanging these for still greater values of our great basic products of cotton, wheat, copper, lumber, oil and the like. Yet, before the dislocations occasioned by the War, the United States stood only third among the great exporting and importing nations of the world.

But our internal trade probably exceeds that of the next largest three or four nations of the earth combined. This trade is the product largely of modern machine organization and the peculiar distribution of our population. About half of our people dwell in a narrow area not more than a fifth of the whole national domain, lying east of the Missouri and north of the Ohio Rivers. In this area is to be found three-fourths of our manufacturing and seven-eighths of our product of coal and iron, on which is based our modern industrial supremacy. By contrast the food supplies and other basic materials of this industrial area are drawn largely from other sections hundreds or thousands of miles distant. And so specialized has this organization of industry become that this area, like that of England or Germany, if cut off from these external supplies, would find its industries paralyzed, and its population would starve. It is probable that in Washington's day the average movement (from producer to consumer) of food and other raw products in the country did not exceed a mile. Today it would be a hundred times this. And even the per capita product must now be more than ten-fold, with scarcely two-thirds of the average hours of labor.

What is true of the United States has, of course, been more or less true of the other commercial nations. A hundred years ago the trade of the world was still carried in sailing vessels, among which a vessel of more than three or four hundred tons burden was regarded with the same admiration that we today bestow on a *Homeric* or an *Olympic* of fifty thousand tons burden. And where the whole trade of that time might have been stowed away within the holds of half a dozen of our modern liners, today the international trade of the world commands the services of thousands of steam vessels of aggregate burden exceeding fifty million tons, to say nothing of sailing vessels that alone far exceed the combined fleets in the early days of Watt and Fulton.

It is sometimes said that the huge congregations of population in the great cities today are parasitic growths; but only in some respects is this true. New York, for example, is by far the greatest manufacturing area in the known world, and industrial centres like Chicago, Pittsburgh, Cleveland and Detroit, are far more than mere centres of exchange or of parasitism. London, it is true, is largely a vast depot of exchange, a colossal world ledger, but Manchester, Liverpool and Birmingham are great both as manufacturing and trading centres. This concentration of industry and trade has, however, brought about great concentration of the population—and the urban aggregations have tended steadily to outstrip in growth the agricultural areas. It has recently been shown that a narrow strip twenty-five miles in width, covering the valleys of the Hudson River to Albany and of the Mohawk extended to Buffalo, supports eight of the ten millions of population of New York State. There are only two millions in all the rest of the Empire State. And while the population of these two narrow valleys has expanded eight times since 1840, the rest of the population has remained stable, and the farm population has declined by one-third. What is true of New York State has been equally true of New England and other areas. The dispersion of population which the incredibly wide distribution of the automobile, the telephone, the trolley car, electric power, and all the modern creature comforts, was so widely expected to bring about, has not appeared; nor does there seem any prospect now.

I have set forth these things in some detail to give emphasis to the definite fact that the last hundred years have been a period of unexampled *change*. The essential nature of this change has been a huge increase in the human power of production and a still greater increase in the transport and exchange of goods produced; that is, a vast expansion of *trade*. It has involved a corresponding division of labor, first as between artisans of different types, and second as between distinct sections of the country and of the world. To take but a single example of the latter tendency, America could produce all the wool it needs for itself and vast quantities for export as well; but it has been cheaper and more advantageous to produce other things and obtain the greater part of its wool from other sections, some of them distant by half the span of the earth, a tendency which has implied a corresponding growth of transportation and exchange.

This profound new development has almost inevitably brought with it conditions which were previously non-existent. Among them are those fluctuations of supplies of and demands for goods, the disturbances of the even flow of trade, the crises, depressions and booms which, following Prof. Mitchell, we have come latterly to group under the name of business "cycles." In considering their nature and origin, the first fact to establish is that they have a definite history and date, that previously they were unknown in the present-day sense, and that they are the product of a new order.

All this has not, hitherto, been overly clear. It is held that records of periods of plenty and of dearth, periods of prosperity and of famine, run back even to Biblical times; and this is true. We are all familiar with the seven fat and the seven lean years of Egypt. But these were essentially conditions that grew out of the relative yields of the fields. They derived almost wholly from agrarian conditions. The organization of industry and manufacture was largely of the local or patriarchal type, such as was characteristic of our own Colonial days. Of large scale manufacture, save in a few notable instances, there was little and, therefore, relatively little of "trade."

This does not mean that a wide system of barter and exchange had not existed for thousands of years. Archaeology shows more and more how ancient were the beginnings of human intercourse and the exchange of products. Trade routes ranging the length of the Mediterranean, and to India on the east and to the Baltic on the north, probably existed for thousands of years before any written history. But the tiny dimensions of Columbus' caravels indicate how slight was the amount of goods involved in these exchanges.

The population of the Roman Empire, however, has been reckoned as high as 50 millions and there is little reason to doubt that a large population subsisted upon this area for many millennia. The volume of trade then, in relation to the total product of the population, was almost negligible, and it follows that such things as "industrial depressions" and booms had little fuel to feed upon. It was not until the development of steam power, the wide use of coal and iron, and the extraordinary burst of mechanical invention which followed, that modern industry, and therefore modern trade, could arise. It was from these that the business "cycle" was born. And we may pretty definitely date its beginning and plot the curve of its growth and tendency to wane.

It is in America that these relatively wide fluctuations have been manifest in their most acute form and in a pathological sense the United States offers the most instructive clinical "case." Data from which we can study these fluctuations, furthermore, though leaving disconcerting gaps, are unusually full in America, and so, in these measurements of the business cycle I shall confine myself to American conditions. Though the population of the new Republic, like that of the Colonies before them, grew rapidly, it is quite notable that in the earlier decades its wealth or income did not apparently expand in a corresponding degree. The foreign trade of a country like ours, and especially its foreign purchases, are a fair index of this growth, and for our imports the records go back to the first year of Washington's administration. Even then the value of our imports had risen as high as 81 millions for a single year, and in each of the three years of 1805, 1806 and 1807 the average was 125 millions. But for the period from 1820 to 1830, and even well into the 40's, the average was only about 75 millions per year. Then came a remarkable leap. By 1851 our imports had doubled, by 1856 they had tripled, by 1873 they had sextupled and by '91 they had risen above 800 millions of dollars. In other words, after a period of extremely slow growth they suddenly began to increase by leaps and bounds.

Another example of the phenomenal growth of income and wealth in the nineteenth century is found in the records of traffic on New York State Canals; for, it has recently been established that indexes of trade, industry and employment in New York State are highly representative of conditions in the whole country, and it is probable that New York was an even better "sample" a century ago, when it included more than one-seventh of the total population of the country. The opening of the Erie Canal, which then represented a tremendous project, and was the first real effort at establishing an extensive system of transportation, occurred in 1825. For eighteen years thereafter, the total traffic of all New York State canals had risen in only one year as high as a million and a half tons. Then, from 1843, came the same amazing change that we have noted in imports. In the next seven years the traffic had doubled; in ten years it had tripled; and by the late 60's it had reached four times the traffic of 1843. In spite of the enormous growth of rail transportation it continued to maintain this traffic as late as the early eighties.

Practically the same history is revealed by the records of the iron and coal trades. It is quite remarkable that before the American Revolution, and in spite of competition with the mother country, the Colonies were producing considerable quantities of iron and even enjoyed a good export trade in this commodity. Eckel [8] calculates that "during the middle of the eighteenth century the Colonies were making almost if not quite as much pig iron, bars, and blooms as Great Britain." But for many years after the Revolution, the growth in this industry was extremely slow in this country, and it was not until more than a century later that the two countries again returned to parity. For forty years after the Revolution our total iron product seldom rose much above the amounts reached in the War, and in 1820 it was actually less. "Fuel, furnace operation, product and methods of after-treatment were all much the same in 1823 as they had been in 1783," that is, it was for the most part produced in small charcoal furnaces making a few tons per week. Then began a rapid advance which, however, had only carried the total product up to a little more than 300,000 tons annually as late as 1840, and in 1843 it was scarcely more than 200,000 tons. In 1847, the total product was more than 800,000 tons. It had doubled this by 1860—and then doubled again in 1880, 1890, and 1903. Pictorially, we find a long plateau, slightly sloping, prior to the 40's, and then a mountainous rise.

So also with coal. "Of the 10 millions of people who inhabited the United States in 1820," says Eckel,[9] "there was probably not one person in a thousand who had ever actually seen a piece of American coal, and perhaps not as much as one in ten thousand was mad enough to dream that it would ever be of any service except as a convenience to the housewife or the blacksmith." As late as 1812, in the then leading city of Philadelphia, a reputable citizen was nearly arrested as a swindler for attempting to sell

[8] Coal, Iron and War," 1920, p. 20.   [9] Loc. at p. 33.

"stones" as fuel. This was long after the discovery of anthracite.

The entire amount of coal produced by 1820 was estimated at only 15,000 tons. In ten years this had risen to 300,000; in another ten years to 2,070,000, and by 1850 to over 6 millions. Today it is annually above 500 millions. Coal is the very foundation of our industrial development; virtually its history is the history of modern industry. It would be difficult to put the story more vividly than in the records of this single product.

Hardly less dramatic was the rise of the cotton industry. In the first year of Washington's administration our total product was under 3,000 bales. When we made the Louisiana purchase it had risen to nearly 100,000 bales. In 1815 it was 200,000; by 1836 it had reached a million; in 1842 it was 2 million; and when the Civil War opened it was 4½ millions.

Railway construction, afterwards to give the United States a steel network of transportation almost equal in extent and in carrying capacity to that of all the rest of the earth, was still more delayed. Up to 1840 the entire amount of railway in existence did not equal the mileage which was to be constructed in the single year of 1856. Even when the gold rush to California had begun, the whole amount did not equal the mileage laid in a single year of the eighties. But, once under way, the increase was swift. By 1845 the amount of railway in existence was double that of seven years previous; by 1850 it had quadrupled; and at the opening of the Civil War it was ten times the extent of twenty years before. For a few years, in the fifties, the increase of railway mileage was at about the same fabulous rate as the increase of automobiles in the last fifteen years.

Parallel to all this was the oncoming of that vast tide of immigration to America, which was to become the most momentous trek of population in the history of the globe. Its beginnings were exceedingly small. It is estimated that in the first two centuries of Colonial growth the entire number of colonists who ever reached these shores probably did not exceed 200,000. Sometimes as many as half of them died on the way. Yet, so rapid was the natural increase of this population that by 1790 their number had increased to about 4 millions. It is curious to reflect that the people who fought the Revolutionary War and established the new Republic were to a far greater extent native born stock than has ever been true since. Even in the next thirty years the total immigration scarcely reached a quarter of a million. In the next thirty years, from 1820 to 1850, it was ten times this number, from 1850 to 1880 thirty times this number, and in the thirty years from 1880 to 1910 it exceeded seventy times. Of the total of 30 millions or more who have come to America as colonists since the days of Columbus, more than 95 per cent have come since the great burst of industrial development which began here in the early forties.

Up to the forties this country had only rudimentary experience with what we now call the business "cycle." It is true that there was a violent panic in 1837, often referred to as our first great economic crisis. But it is clear that this was rather a financial and banking episode than the beginning of an industrial depression, for our major industries showed but slight perturbation. For example, few things could then have been more sensitive to financial conditions than the new venture of railway construction. But this appears to have been scarcely affected by the panic, as is clear from the amount of railway construction in the years just preceding and following, as given below:

1833	235	miles built
1834	281	" "
1835	177	" "
1836	175	" "
1837	224	" "
1838	416	" "
1839	389	" "

We have much the same kind of evidence from the traffic on the New York State canals, which was singularly varied and representative in character, products of the farm being only about one-third of the total. The tonnage had risen so rapidly in 1835 and 1836 it exceeded 1300 thousand tons a year. This was cut down by about 11 per cent in the panic year of '37; but the traffic of 1838, '39 and '40 was each year greater than in any previous year.

Still less is there any disclosure of serious disturbances in the records of our registered merchant marine. The tonnage registered rose continuously from 1191 thousand tons in 1830 to 2180 thousand tons in 1840 without a single break. There was, nevertheless, during these years no falling off in the total tonnage of new vessels built, as is evident from the following table:

1834	118,000	tons
1835	75,000	"
1836	116,000	"
1837	115,000	"
1838	125,000	"
1839	125,000	"

The same tendencies occurred in very sensitive industries like coal and iron production, which in later years of depression have undergone devastating slumps. The early figures we have as to iron are untrustworthy, but for coal production they compared as follows:

1833	734,000	tons
1834	600,000	"
1835	824,000	"
1836	984,000	"
1837	1,253,000	"
1838	1,355,000	"
1839	1,560,000	"

Since these are precisely the types of industry which have, in later years, given us such an exaggerated idea of the nature and importance of the business cycle, it seems clear that, in an industrial sense, the panic of '37 was

merely a passing financial flurry and was chiefly confined
to the collapse of a large number of mushroom banks.
Since this is the first of the great crises or "panics" for
which we have any real and extensive quantitative measures, it is clear that prior to the unprecedented industrial
expansion begun in the "Roaring Forties," such waves of
prosperity and depression as this country had known were
very largely either years of plenty or dearth in the yield of
the farms, or, as in 1837, epidemics of failure in wildcat
banking.

The next formidable panic was that of 1857, following
the California gold boom, and here again the evidence
seems clear that it was essentially a financial and banking
convulsion and not the beginning of a serious industrial
depression. Consider the evidence. From the plateau-
like levels of the preceding thirty years, our imports in
the middle forties began to rise at an accelerated rate, and
by 1857 were above three times the average of the three
decades from 1820. In the panic year there was a brief
decline amounting in money value to about 24 per cent.
But the totals were back again in the following year, and
in 1860 had reached the previous high point.

Much the same thing occurred with the traffic of the
New York State canals. This, too, had shown a rapid
rise to 1855-'57, and a brief decline in 1857. The decline
amounted to only 19 per cent and traffic was increasing
steadily again through the next three years.

Railway freight traffic showed the same lack of any decline. By 1857 our railway system was already among
the greatest in the world, with over 25,000 miles of rails,
and an annual freight traffic of more than 2 billion ton
miles. It was growing at such a prodigious rate that
traffic did not fall off during the panic nor did Postal
receipts show any decline.

In coal production, too, there was practically no let-up.
That amazing increase which went on with scarcely a

break through more than half a century continued through and after the panic of '57. We have reliable data for iron production from 1854, and here there was a brief decline extending over two years, but amounting at the extreme to only 20 per cent. The years of '59 and '60 were again at the previous high levels.

Railway construction was one of the few series for which we have data showing a heavy and continuous decrease. After the rapid rise from the forties there had been a sharp falling off in '54 and '55, but a new bound of activity carried construction to a peak in 1856 which it was not to reach again for another ten years.

Then came the Civil War, and the available evidence indicates that that momentous struggle produced about the same effect upon industry and commerce as other wars, for example, the recent World War. In the available quantitative data the effects of these wars were scarcely observable. It is a singular fact that there were few business indicators save the violent rise of prices, the inflation of bank clearings, bank deposits and other data in dollars to suggest any unusual disturbance at all.

With the exception of the cotton industry, by far the larger part of the industry and commerce of the country was in the Northern States, and, for the most part, save in the cotton mills, this went on almost without interruption. Postal receipts, which seem an excellent indicator, rose through the War at just about the normal rate. And railway traffic continued its amazing increase year by year.

Imports, it is true, fell off rather sharply in the first two or three years, but they were back to near the normal rate of growth by 1864 and much above it in '66. The traffic on the New York State canals was scarcely disturbed at all, but continued to grow at much the same rate as through the previous thirty years, just as if nothing was happening.

The same is true with regard to coal. The product of

the coal mines continued to rise without a break from 1860 to 1873. In iron production there was a slight decline in 1861 and again in '65, and after that a steady rise to 1873.

In other words, up to the time when the Pacific railroads had been completed and a band of iron stretched across the Continent, when the ancient activities of our wide system of canals had begun to decline, and the new West was being opened up at a prodigious rate, this country had never known such deep and prolonged periods of industrial stagnation as were to characterize the next thirty years. What depression there had been was very largely obscured by the continuous and irresistible growth of the country and its industries.

The advent of the unmistakable business "cycle" in the sense that it has been so extensively used in our own day, appears to date from about the late sixties. Following the Civil War there was a post-war boom, resembling in many ways the post-war boom that has come since the World War, with the difference that there was no such intervening collapse as that of 1920. It reached its height in three highly prosperous years, ending in the summer of '73. Actually for the full year of '73 none of the four indicators which have been available for the previous periods showed any material declines. Railway traffic, in ton miles, showed a slower but continuous growth, straight through to the eighties, and postal receipts showed similar tendencies.

But for the next three or four years most forms of industry suffered a drastic setback. Yet here, as long before and ever since, there has been the impulse towards sensational exaggeration of the decline. Picturesque incident and vivid description have always had far greater vogue than exact measurement. In money value, from the peak of '72 to the low year of '76, our imports fell off by 35 per cent, but a part of this decline was due to a general decline in commodity prices which occurred throughout Europe as well as in America.

The decline in New York canal traffic was from 6,365,000 tons to 4,172,000 tons, or 34 per cent for three years. Pig iron production fell off from a high point of 2561 thousand tons in 1873 to a low point of 1869 thousand tons in 1876, a decline of 27 per cent. Coal production was reduced from a high point of 58 million tons to 52 million tons, or 10 per cent.

Again, in money values, New York City bank clearings fell 40 per cent, but according to our estimates, making due allowance for the lowering of price levels or the general average of all payments, the decline in trade and commerce as a whole amounted, on the annual figures, to not more than 10 or 12 per cent (much more, of course, in the monthly extremes of high and low).

Yet in many ways the depression, running from '73 to '78, appears to have been one of the two worst which this country has ever known. There is a story that business, even in New York, was so dull that grass and rye began to sprout between the cobblestones of Wall Street and lower Broadway. And railroad construction, which throughout the generation that followed the Civil War was one of the most potent influences affecting the ups and downs of trade, fell off from a peak of 7,379 miles in 1871 to a low point of 1,711 miles in 1875.

Almost as if in recoil from this period of prolonged stagnation, came the half fabulous expansion of the eighties, in some ways the most amazing boom that this and probably any other country ever enjoyed. It brought in ten years the construction of 60 thousand miles of railway and the opening of what remains today the most fertile agricultural empire of the New World. We shall never see its equal again for the reason that there is no comparable new and undeveloped territory to be expanded.

It seems scarcely possible in human affairs that such a

prodigious effort could continue indefinitely without a severe reaction; and when it came it was accentuated by the fact that something of the same sort of development had been taking place in other parts of the earth, especially in Australia, and the Argentine, in the opening up of new tracts of fertile land. The result was a glut in the food markets and in consequence a world-wide depression in agricultural prices. The panic of '93 and the ensuing depression was to an extraordinary degree the replica of '73-'79. It lasted about the same length of time and fully equaled if it did not exceed the earlier period in severity. And then, precisely as in the previous peak, there came an exuberant rebound with rapidly rising prices, a heavy resumption of building and construction; the era of great consolidations. With a brief interim in 1903-1904, this cumulative prosperity marched swiftly forward to the panic of 1907.

There had been—previous to the great depression in 1893—a sharp break in prosperity in 1884, with an equally sharper and almost immediate recovery in most lines. The panic of 1907 bore a close resemblance to this earlier panic, with its spectacular failures and sharp recoveries.

Just before the World War, there was evidence of a marked decline in the volume of business and industrial production, beginning in the latter half of 1913, and continuing into 1914. But in the War, we now have abundant evidence, the expansion of trade and production, with a few notable exceptions, was no greater than in certain peacetime expansions; e.g., from 1900 to 1907, 1880-1890. An opinion seems to prevail that the monetary inflation, or debasement of the currency which has been the accompaniment of almost all wars, means a corresponding disturbance of the industrial and commercial life of a country. But the evidence of quantitative measurements shows this to be often untrue, as seen by the fact that in railway traffic, iron production, or the volume of exchange as measured in bank clearings, the depression of 1914 was actually sharper than after the panic of 1907. But there was one decisive difference between the panic of 1907 and the slump of 1914 on the one hand—and the panics and slumps of the '70s and '90s on the other hand—and that is, that these later crises were not followed by the long, grinding depressions so characteristic of the last decades of the 19th century.

Now the available evidence which we have reviewed leads to the conclusion that nothing like these two periods of prolonged stagnation had previously been experienced in this country. From this, and the fact that nearly a full generation has passed since the '93-'98 era, the idea readily emerges that these two exceptional crises were the evanescent product of our industrial development, a phenomenon rising in intensity as the full sweep of this development broke into the post Civil War boom, and the railway building boom of the eighties, and waning in violence with the more effective integration and organization of industry, characteristic of the present day.

In evidence to be reviewed in the following chapter, we find, in all the series representing our industrial life, a curiously insistent and characteristic rate of growth. There seems to be no measure of the intensity of the fluctuations in business save in terms of variations from the line of characteristic growth. And from this method of measuring the deviations from the "normal" or customary it becomes clear that alternating waves of prosperity and depression have proceeded with a certain irregular but notable rhythm for at least the past eighty years, waxing and waning most notably in the period for which the evidence is most trustworthy and most extended.

In the chapters that follow, this evidence will be reviewed in detail. New measures of the volume of trade will be discussed. The measurement of cycles in the volume of trade as variations in the deviations from the persistent and characteristic rate of growth may offer a clue to the nature of business cycles; that is, that prosperous periods represent over-expansion beyond the rate of growth to which that industry has been geared up, and that this results in a breakdown in the balance of production, leading to the phenomena of stagnation and depression.

Whether from all this new knowledge it will be possible to find the one true "cause" of business cycles, if one true cause exists, is a matter of the future. We have had a multiplicity of theories, owing to the paucity of accurate measurement. Here, as in all scientific investigations, he will be the discoverer who proves. But this much at least seems clear; no industry can long remain widely out of balance with other industries. None can absorb too much save on the penalty of later having too little. Not even the most favoured trade can expand indefinitely, for every boom, as every depression, has come to an end. Now that we can measure every phase so closely, we shall be able better to calculate, in each industry, the probable demand, and automatically to regulate production to this demand. When we do, to all intents, the business cycle will have disappeared.

CHAPTER II

ECONOMIC GROWTH

IF the reason for the number of fanciful ideas about the business cycle has been the paucity of facts, and the lack of adequate and trustworthy measurement of existing facts, the last few years have brought a wonderful increase in new statistical material, by which it has been possible to check and make use of older data and thus to build up a solid foundation of new knowledge. And now we can use this rapidly growing body of information about our economic life to *measure* the business cycle.

When we look at a chart of any of the most representative economic and industrial phenomena, especially in this country, for a period of, say, fifty or a hundred years, we are impressed by the tremendous *growth* which all of them show over this period of time. Before we can approach the measurement of the ups and downs of business, we must get an adequate picture of the long-time growth factor.

A prime factor of importance has been the astonishing growth of population, especially in countries like the United States. The curve of population (Chart 1), for this country, for the last hundred and thirty years has shown an increase at a rate unheard of before in the history of the world. And this growth of population has in itself been a decisive factor in causing a consistent increase in our national product. It is obvious, for instance, that crop production must increase in proportion to the increase in population in order merely to sustain the population.

Again, if we divide the curve of population into two

component curves (Chart 1), one representing urban and the other rural population, we note further the extraordinary rate of increase of urban population, which in the past eighty years has grown at an average rate of 4.3 per cent, whereas the rural population has grown at a rate of 1.5 per cent, and the general population at a rate of 2.3 per cent. We have here another decisive fact in that urban population does not sustain itself, for it does not produce its own goods, and therefore, this growth of town and city population has had a tremendous influence on the economic development of the country.

It has meant, first of all, a reorganization of agriculture. It has been necessary for farm production to expand at a greater rate than the rate of increase of the farm population, in order to take care of the needs of the expanding urban population. This has necessitated a large increase in per capita production of farm workers.

An even more important effect has been its influence on the growth of trade. The urban population functions not only as consumer, but as manufacturer and converter of goods produced by the farms. These goods must be brought to the factories, which are largely in the cities, and a part of them carried away in the manufactured state. Hence, the chief reason for the enormous growth of the movement of goods, and for the development of trade facilities.

Yet another factor of importance in the growth of trade has been the increasing division of labour as between different sections of the country. It has been found an economic advantage for certain localities to specialize quite narrowly in their types of production or manufacture. This specialization has been made possible only through the development of an amazing network of railways, waterways, etc., and, as specialization proceeds, this in turn, acts as a further stimulus in developing transportation.

One result of this division of labour and specialization

CHART 1.

POPULATION, U. S. A.

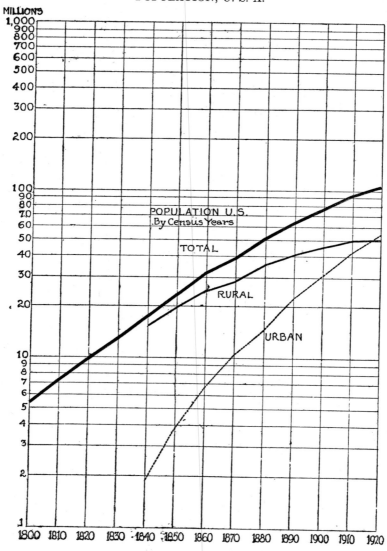

Sources: Total population, U. S. A., 1790-1920. U. S. Bureau of Census Monograph "Increase of Population in the United States, 1910-1920," p. 21.
Urban and rural population, 1900-1920, *loc. cit.,* p. 75.
1880-1900, Abstract of XIII Census, 1910, p. 55.
1840-1880, estimated. From 1880 the census data for urban population includes all towns of over 2500 population. From 1840-1870, data are given (U. S. Bureau of Census Monograph "A Century of Population Growth, 1790-1900, p. 15) for towns of over 8000. Estimates of urban including towns of over 2500 population were made by link relatives, giving the following estimates for rural and urban population in the United States, 1840-1870.

	Rural	Urban
1840	15,186,000	1,883,000
1850	19,426,000	3,766,000
1860	24,836,000	6,607,000
1870	28,070,000	10,488,000

of trade has been an extraordinary concentration of population and wealth. In the northeastern corner of the United States, in what I have called Industrial America, we find, in less than one-fifth of the total area, over one-half of the population, with two-thirds of the wealth and income of the country. In this area are three-fourths of the manufacturing and seven-eighths of the coal and iron production of the country. It is the very backbone of our industry. It is obvious that this concentration could not have been possible without a vast development in transportation facilities, and that it must lead to a tremendous growth in the movement of goods. The curves show this phenomenon clearly. In the last half century the population has increased 2.6 times, total production has increased a little less than four times, iron production has increased fifteen times, but freight traffic has increased twenty times. Pushing our comparison back to 1850, when we were already the premier railroad country in the world, the statistics are even more remarkable. In 1852, our railway traffic had reached a billion ton miles, which was considered an astonishing achievement in that day. Today, the movement of goods on the railroads is much over four hundred billion ton miles, a growth of four hundred fold in three-quarters of a century.

But of even greater moment for our purpose here, let us turn again to the charts showing the year-by-year movement of a large number of these economic series over a period of time and note the impressive *stability* of this growth. Population (Chart 1) has grown steadily and consistently for the past hundred or more years. The rate of increase has changed, but has changed so consistently as to make prediction from one decade to another quite feasible. The chart of urban and rural population (Chart 1) decade by decade, likewise shows perfectly even and consistent rates of growth. Rural population shows a more sharply decrescent rate than does general

CHART 2.

CROP PRODUCTION, U. S. A.

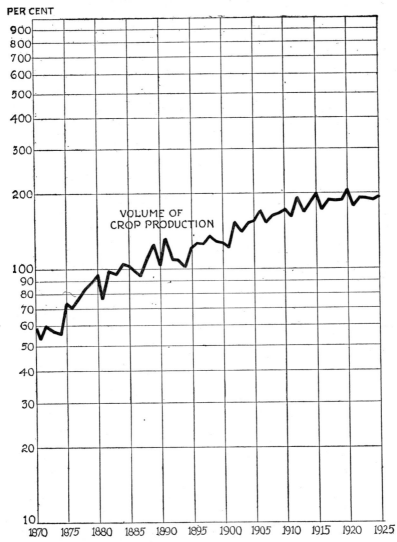

PER CENT

VOLUME OF
CROP PRODUCTION

Index of volume of crop production. Ten crops, each weighted by its average price for period 1909-1918. Base period 1880-1889. See Appendix, Table 1, p. 237.

population; and the rate of increase of urban population shows less of a decrescent tendency than either.

The line of growth of crop production (Chart 2) lies between the lines of growth of urban and of rural population, and is greater than the one and less than the other. Although the year-to-year movement is jagged and irregular, due to variations in the harvests, the line of growth persists, and shows the same tendency to bend as was observed in the population charts. Although bearing a close relation to the growth of population, it should be noted that crop production grows at a characteristic rate of its own.

So also with the other series showing our industrial development. Railway traffic reveals the same even rate of growth and always with the diminishing rate of increase that is characteristic of most of these series. Iron, coal, steel, and cotton, all show the same general picture in this regard. There is a period of rapid increase, but, after a point, a persistent tendency for the rate of increase to diminish. Each series has its own distinctive features. Some increase much faster than others and show a much slighter bend. There is also a dissimilarity in the time at which the rate of increase begins to fall off and in the degree of stability which it maintains. All of these characteristics depend on factors internal to the industry.

Let us consider in detail the characteristics of the long-time growth element, the so-called secular trend,[1] in certain

[1] The secular trend of a time series may be determined by any one of a number of mathematical formulae. The simplest concept is one of "moving averages." If there were no growth element, the average over a long period would approximate the averages for sub-periods comprising similar cyclical elements. But where there is a strong element of growth, the average of each successive sub-period tends to be consistently larger than that of the preceding one. A trend may, therefore, be successfully computed by a line of moving averages where the sub-period of the average is approximately equal to the length of the cycles. There are, however, certain objections to the use of the moving average. It may have many minor irregularities inconsistent with the idea of growth which we generally assume to be a regular movement subject to longtime forces and not responding to minor

of the more important economic series. The cotton industry, for example, as shown in chart 3 has an interesting growth. The growth in cotton consumption from 1826 (the first year for which data are available) up to the Civil War was at a higher rate than for the years following the Civil War. Since the Civil War caused such a complete disruption of the cotton industry and put it on a basis so different

fluctuations. Furthermore, if the series is convex or concave, the trend obtained by a moving average will not fit the area of convexity or concavity.

Most of the series which we have used have been found to approximate a straight line or a parabolic trend, usually a second degree parabola, fitted by the method of least squares. That is to say, the secular movement is represented by the equation $y = a + bx + cx^2$ . . . where y is a function of time. The constants are solved by the condition that the sum of the squares of the deviations of the actual values from the values of y be a minimum. Parabolas of higher orders may be used where the direction of the trend bends more than once, but these involve labour disproportionate to the validity of the results, (and in such cases we have generally resorted to a moving average).

These trends are obviously empirical. The determination of the true or ideal trend is not possible, and the trends which we have used are to be regarded only as a matter of interpolatory convenience. As further data are added year by year the computed trend may change somewhat, but it is improbable that any but the later years are affected much by these recomputations, and the differences have not been found to be great.

We have found it necessary to extrapolate our trends for a year or so beyond the given data, in order to compute current indices. Extrapolation of parabolas is open to the difficulty that a parabola will eventually turn down, and will give a forecast of the trend which our general knowledge of the behaviour of economic series tells us is likely to be absurd. We have found that, in all cases, we can safely extrapolate for one year, and frequently for several years ahead, without deviating greatly from the trends computed as the later data come in.

It is possible, of course, to fit the data with curves other than parabolas. The Compertz curve ($y = ab^{cx}$) and the Pearl-Reed curve $\left(y = \dfrac{b}{e^{-ax} + c} \right)$ are satisfactory in fitting data which correspond closely to the growth of population in their general trends. These curves do not decline from an apex as do parabolas, and give often a probable forecast which is not logically absurd. It is, however, doubtful whether they actually forecast the movement of economic series any better than do parabolas, and, as far as interpolation is concerned, a parabola is quite as satisfactory and much simpler to compute.

The secular trend may be computed either in terms of the amount of increase for any given time unit, or in terms of the rate of increase per unit. In the former case it is computed on the actual data and in the latter case on the logarithms of the data. We have found it more satisfactory to use the logarithms because we are primarily interested in rates of growth, and also because the process is often simplified by the use of a logarithmic trend (e. g., a parabolic trend on actual data may become a straight line on the logarithms.)

CHART 3.

COTTON CONSUMPTION U. S. A.

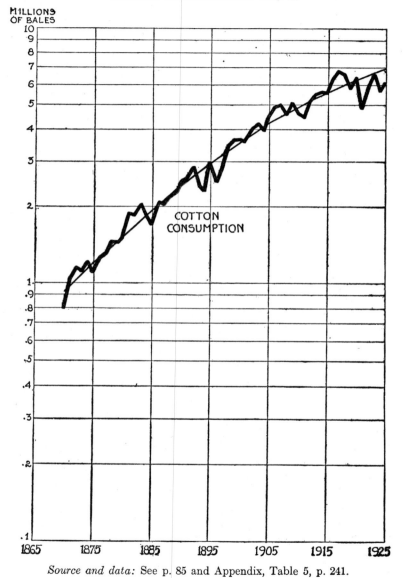

Source and data: See p. 85 and Appendix, Table 5, p. 241.

from that preceding the War, we have computed a trend [2] for the data extending only from 1870 to the present (Chart 3). This trend shows a period of rapid increase following the Civil War—the average rate of growth from 1870 to 1885 being 5 per cent per year. But this rate of increase has shown a constant tendency to slow up. From 1885 to 1900 the average annual increase persisted at about 4 per cent—falling off steadily to an average of 3 per cent per year from 1900 to 1915 and averaging only 2 per cent from 1915 to date. Furthermore, the actual data of the last three or four years have been so far below the line of growth as to lead to the supposition that the computed trend does not show the whole of the normal decrease, and that, as more data come in, we may find the growth not merely slowing up but becoming zero or negative. Cotton consumption grew faster than population up to the beginning of the twentieth century but from that point it has not managed even to keep pace with the growth of population.

Coal production in the United States (Charts 4 and 5) grew much faster up to the beginning of this century than the average rate of growth of world production.[3] There was a tremendously rapid production in the years following the Civil War, averaging 9 per cent per year in the sixties. This rate of increase has, however, shown a constant tendency to diminish, and we find that the annual average rate of increase was 8 per cent in the seventies, 7 per cent in the eighties, 6 per cent in the nineties, 5 per cent in the first decade of this century, 4 per cent in the second decade, and latterly an almost negligible rate of increase.

Looking at the charts for United States coal production (Charts 4 and 5), it is interesting to note the differences in

[2] The formula for the line of secular trend, computed on the data for crop years from 1870 to 1921 (origin of trend at 1895) is $\log y = 3.4712835 + .0166725x - .0001419x^2$.

[3] World production of coal increased at about 4% per year from 1864 to 1914.

CHART 4.

ANTHRACITE COAL PRODUCTION, U. S. A.

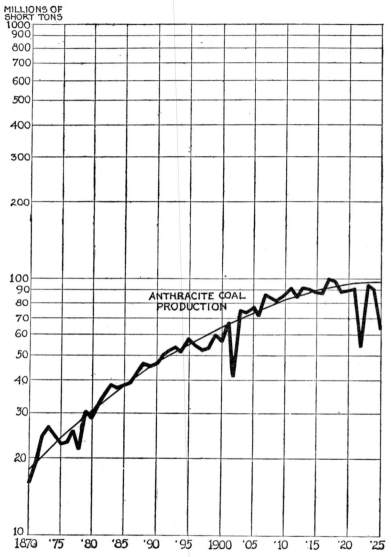

Source and data: See p. 91 and Appendix, Table 5, p. 260.

CHART 5.

BITUMINOUS COAL PRODUCTION, U. S. A.

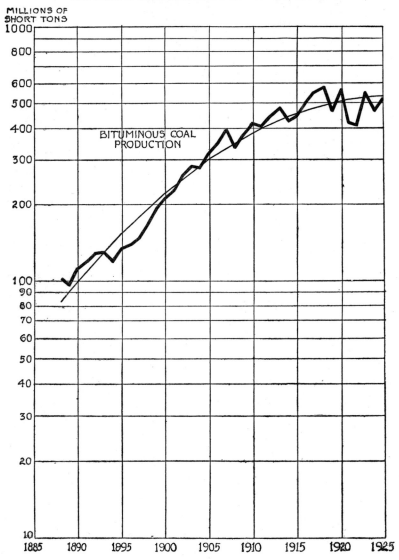

MILLIONS OF
SHORT TONS

BITUMINOUS COAL
PRODUCTION

Source and data: See p. 88 and Appendix, Table 5, p. 249.

the growth of bituminous and anthracite coal.   Anthracite coal has shown much less of a spectacular increase than has bituminous.   It has shown a marked tendency for the rate of growth to decrease since 1870.[4]   At that time the annual rate of growth was about 5 per cent and that rate has decreased each decade until it is now a little more than one-half of one per cent per year.

Bituminous coal increased at a tremendous rate up to the beginning of this century.   In the eighties and nineties it was increasing at a rate of 9 per cent to 10 per cent per year.[5]   Since that period, however, it has shown a rapidly decrescent rate of increase.   The actual rate has diminished by about 2 per cent each decade, until the normal rate of growth of bituminous coal production is now under one-half of one per cent per year.

The development of the iron and steel production represents the basis of the growth of modern industry.   For the machines by which this era has become industrially great are largely products of iron and steel, and their production in turn has been dependent upon coal.   So these series give an historical perspective of the development of our modern industrial system.

Iron and steel show the same tendency to a decreasing rate of growth as coal production, but they do not show the levelling off characteristic of coal in the later years.   The iron and steel industry is growing, if not at the spectacular rate of earlier years, at least at a pace great enough to care for the still growing needs of industry.

Pig iron production (Chart 6) had received a mighty impetus in growth by 1870, and, at that time, was increasing at a rate of about 11 per cent per year.   This high rate of increase in production has, however, fallen off quite

[4] The formula for the line of secular trend, based on the data from 1870 to 1924, omitting the strike years 1902 and 1922, with the origin at 1870, is $\log y = .259413 + .0247292x - .00020893x^2$.

[5] The formula for the line of secular trend, based on the data from 1888 to 1922, with the origin at 1905, is $\log y = 4.478883 + .0235387x - .0005594x^2$.

CHART 6.
PIG IRON PRODUCTION, U. S. A.

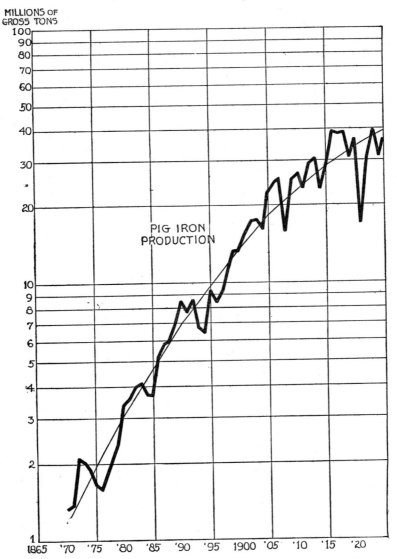

MILLIONS OF
GROSS TONS

PIG IRON
PRODUCTION

Source and data: See p. 85 and Appendix, Table 5, p. 242.

CHART 7.

STEEL INGOT PRODUCTION, U. S. A.

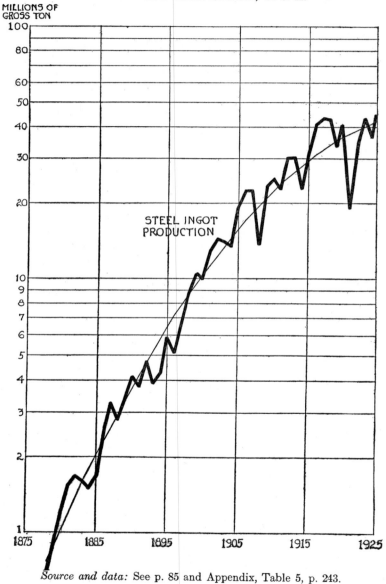

Source and data: See p. 85 and Appendix, Table 5, p. 243.

steadily from that point. By 1900 production was increasing [6] at 6 per cent per year, by 1910 at 5 per cent, and at
present by about 3 per cent per year.

Steel production (Chart 7) showed an even more spectacular growth. In the eighties it was increasing by 15
per cent per year, and by 1900 it was still increasing at the
very high rate of 10 per cent per year, by 1910 at 7 per
cent, and latterly at the same rate of increase as pig iron
production, i.e., 3 per cent per year.[7]

If iron and coal production are indexes of the growth
of a new type of industry, freight traffic is no less truly an
index of the consequences of this modern industry, of its
geographical specialization and its tendency to concentration which have led to the development of an intricate
and extensive system of distribution facilities. Freight
traffic, in ton miles, is an excellent indicator of the growth
of our internal trade.

The chart of the curve of freight ton miles (Chart 8)
is indeed impressive. From 1852 to 1870 freight traffic
was increasing at a rate of 14 per cent every year. From
1870 to date the rate of increase has slowed up, but it is
still considerable. In the nineties, the railroads were carrying 7 per cent more ton miles of freight each year than in
the preceding, and now they are carrying about three and
a half per cent more each year. Truly this represents an
extraordinary and significant growth in trade.[8]

The development of the automobile industry is very
recent, and the rates (Chart 9) of increase are incomparable
with any past experience, unless it be the very early development of railroads. From 1900 to 1905 passenger car production increased 38 per cent per year, 47 per cent per year

[6] The secular trend for pig iron production based on the data from 1870 to
1922, with the origin at 1896, is expressed by the formula $\log y = 4.0229831 + .0286644x - .0003084x^2$.

[7] The formula for the line of secular trend based on the data from 1878
to 1924, with the origin at 1901, is $\log y = 4.062592 + .037566x - .000587x^2$.

[8] The formula for the line of secular trend, based on the data from 1889 to
1923, with the origin at 1906, is $\log y = 3.3364207 + .0239141x - .0002909x^2$.

CHART 8.

RAILWAY FREIGHT TRAFFIC.

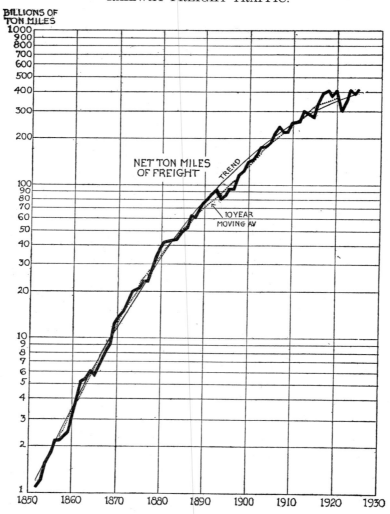

RAILWAY FREIGHT TRAFFIC: Net ton miles of freight (revenue and non-revenue) carried on Class I railroads in the United States.

Sources: 1888 to date, "Railway Statistics of the United States" prepared by Slason Thompson (1924 edition, p. 96). From 1852 to 1887 inclusive, total freight traffic was estimated from the principal lines as reported in Poor's Manual of 1881 and 1888. For 1852 and 1853, one railroad only was used: N. Y., Lake Erie, and Western. The following additions were subsequently made:

1854—N. Y. Central.
1855—Pennsylvania.
1857—Pittsburgh, Fort Wayne and Chicago.
From 1865 to 1882, the 13 roads listed in Poor's Manual of 1888 (pp. XXVIII-XXIX) were used—and from 1883-1887 "all roads"—as listed in Poor's Manual of 1891.

Data: See Appendix, Table 2, p. 238.

from 1905 to 1910, and 35 per cent per year from 1910 to 1915. The rate of increase averaged 18 per cent per year from 1915 to 1920, and although the production itself seems to be keeping up at this tremendous rate still, the indication is that the normal rate of increase has declined to about 5 per cent per year.[9]

This really stupendous development of a new industry has, of course, had its repercussions in many other fields. It has, for instance, stimulated greatly the production of oil and rubber, and these, in turn, have affected the development of other industries.

Petroleum production (Chart 10) had been showing quite a steady increase up to the beginning of this century. This increase had been very marked from the Civil War up to the eighties, averaging about 14 per cent per year. This rate of increase was showing a marked tendency to fall off after that point, however, and in the nineties the average rate of increase had declined to about 4 per cent per year. With the tremendous development of automobile production from the beginning of this century, however, petroleum production was given an entirely new stimulus, and the trend [10] shot up again at a rate twice as fast, and more than half as great as in the early development of the industry. The normal increase of production has been 8 per cent per year since 1900, with no evidence of any bend. In fact, the abnormally great automobile production of recent years has sent the petroleum production far above its line of secular trend.

The series which we have examined up to this point have been, with the possible exception of automobiles, basic features in the development of modern industry, and their growth has been highly representative of the

[9] The line of secular trend is a Pearl-Reed curve passed through the logarithms of three annual figures taken as normal, 1910, 1915, and 1920, with the origin at 1900. The equation is $\log y = \dfrac{.9027}{e - .1929x + .2545}$.

[10] Secular trend, 1906-1920, origin 1913, $\log y = 4.3931607 + .0330744x$.

CHART 9.

PASSENGER AUTOMOBILE PRODUCTION, U. S. A.

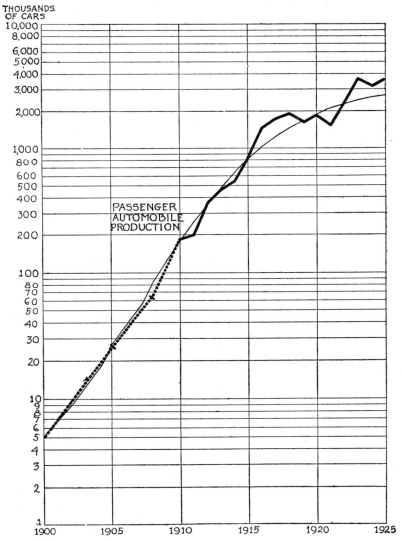

Sources and data: See p. 95 and Appendix, Table 6, p. 261.

CHART 10.

PETROLEUM PRODUCTION, U. S. A.

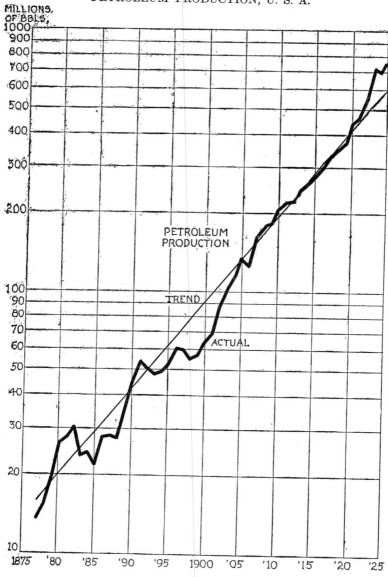

Source and data: See p. 87 and Appendix, Table 5, p. 247.

CHART 11.

RAW SILK IMPORTS INTO U. S. A.

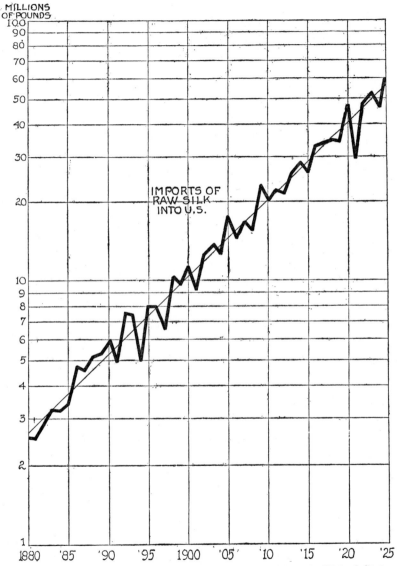

Source: Quantity of unmanufactured silk imported into the United States, 1880-1925, U. S. Department of Commerce, "Statistical Abstract of the United States," 1918, p. 821 (ibid.), 1923, p. 836, and "Monthly Summary of Foreign Commerce of the United States," December, 1925, Part I.

industrial expansion of the country. It will be interesting to consider also the development of luxury consumption during the same period.

Silk imports (Chart 11) are a very good index of the consumption of luxuries, and, as the chart shows, silk imports have shown a constant rate of increase since about 1880. The imports of raw silk have increased, year in and year out, with only minor interruptions, at a rate of 7 per cent per year.[11]   This is, indeed, an interesting commentary on the persistence of growth of a purely luxury consumption.

A series representing fashion as much as does cigarette consumption would scarcely be expected to show a persistence of growth, but rather to fluctuate in waves. Yet cigarette consumption (Chart 12) has shown an amazingly straight and steep line of growth for the last quarter of a century. The rate of growth has been 17 per cent per year since about 1900.[12]

There are very few economic series, indeed, in which a persistent growth is not characteristic. There are, however, certain exceptions to this general tendency. Grain exports is one of these few exceptions. The chart showing data for grain exports extending from 1899 to date (Chart 13) gives no evidence of the even growth observed in the others. It is difficult, indeed, to determine a "normal" trend, and the simplest solution has been to consider the average of the whole period as the "normal" towards which any particular year approximates.

It is evident, from this detailed analysis of many economic series that there is a persistent and characteristic rate of growth in many different forms of industry, trade, commerce, and finance. The actual rates of growth have, of course, varied from one series to another, but the broad characteristics of the lines of growth have tended to approach a norm, and this fact suggests that we may be

---

[11] Secular trend, 1881-1919, origin 1900, $\log y = 4.01731205 + .0294544x$.
[12] Secular trend, 1900-1920, origin 1910, $\log y = 3.9382543 + .0688852x$.

CHART 12.

CIGARETTE CONSUMPTION, U. S. A.

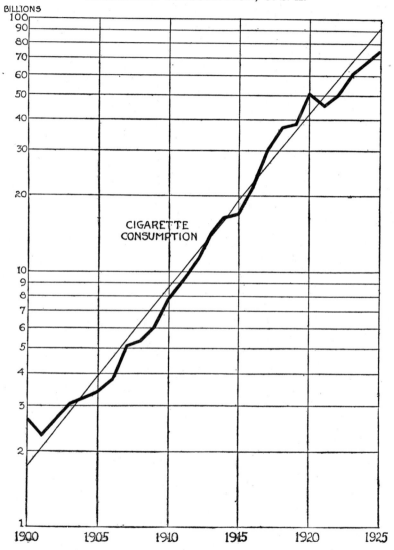

Source and data: See p. 90 and Appendix, Table 5, p. 255.

CHART 13.

GRAIN EXPORTS.

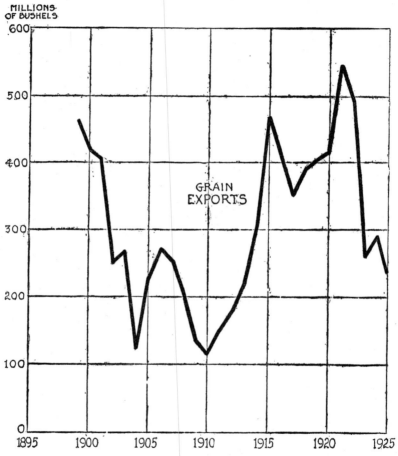

Source and data: See p. 129 and Appendix, Table 21, p. 283.

able to compute a line of growth which will represent the general industrial growth of the nation. This general rate of growth will be analogous to the rate at which a large army is marching. The separate divisions of the army will be marching at different rates and will, perhaps, join the army at different points, but if the relationships between the different divisions do not change too widely the army as a whole may be said to have a definite rate of marching. Similarly, if we take all the different types of industries for which we have the data, and combine them into a series, we get a curiously even "rate of march," which we may consider typical of industry as a whole.

There have been several attempts to combine the various types of productive activity into an index of general production as shown in Chart 14. One of the first of these to combine a number of representative series into a single index was that of W. I. King.[13]

Shortly thereafter similar indexes were constructed by Day,[14] and by Stewart,[15] and by Snyder.[16]

Kings' index extended from 1880 to 1920 and included some fifteen series, with weights "proportioned roughly to the relative importance of the different indicators." (op. cit. p. 5). The index included series representative of the leading fields of mining, agriculture, trade, and transportation. It was expressed on a 1914 base.

Stewart's index extended from 1890 to 1919 and included 91 different series (thirty-nine of materials, fifty of manufactures, and two of transportation). Weights were estimated by "the assignment to each commodity of a value

[13] W. I. King, "Is Production Keeping Pace with Population?" Bankers Statistics Corporation, Aug. 24, 1920. Earlier estimates had been made by Fisher (Irving Fisher: "The Purchasing Power of Money," 1911, p. 478) and Kemmerer (E. W. Kemmerer: "Money and Prices," 1909, p. 127).

[14] E. E. Day: "An Index of the Physical Volume of Production," Rev. of Econ. Stats., Jan., 1921, p. 19.

[15] W. W. Stewart: "An Index Number of Production," Amer. Econ. Rev., Mar., 1921, p. 57.

[16] Carl Snyder: American Economic Review, Mar., 1921, p. 70.

CHART 14.

PRODUCTION INDEXES, U. S. A.

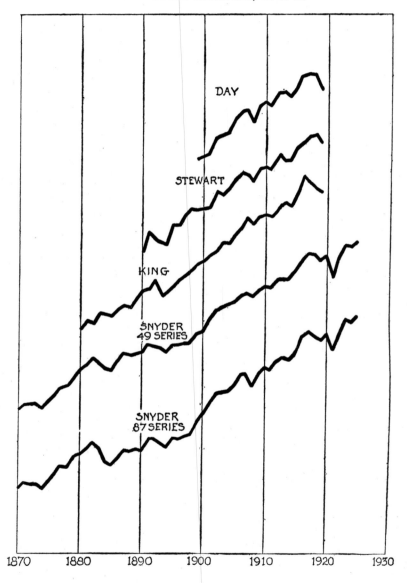

Sources of King's, Day's and Stewart's indexes, cited in footnotes p. 47.
Data for Snyder's indexes in Appendix, Table 3, p. 239.

The indexes of production shown on this chart have been plotted on
the same ratio scale, so that equal vertical distances measured upward
indicate the same percentage increase; and equal distances measured downward represent the same percentage decrease.

which when it was added to the values assigned other commodities in the same sequence would keep that sequence in proper proportion to other sequences." (op. cit. p. 61). This index was computed on a 1911-1913 base.

Day's index represented a combination of indexes of production for agriculture, mining, and manufacture. It extended from 1899 to 1919. The indices for agriculture, mining, and manufacture had been computed separately and weighted internally according to the value of their products. "An unadjusted combined index is secured by calculating a weighted geometric mean of the three separate indices for each year of the period. The weights employed correspond to the aggregate values of production in agriculture, mining and manufacture during the census year 1909." (op. cit. p. 19). "The adjusted index is a weighted arithmetic mean of the three separate indices." (op. cit. p. 20). The indices are expressed on a 1909-1913 average base.

Our indexes of physical production are based on the unweighted [17] average of a large number of series representative of many fields of productive activity. One series of 49 representative items extends from 1870 to 1924. A series of 87 items was carried back as far as possible, and many of the items as far as 1870. Both these indexes were on a base of the average of 1910-1914. The chart of the lines of growth of these several production series shows a remarkable similarity in growth. Our series of 49 items did not differ greatly from our series of 87 items. Furthermore, the results do not show any great difference in the rate

[17] The various attempts at weighting described above, being based on the value of the product, tend to over-emphasize certain basic industries, especially the iron and steel industry, and to give an inadequate picture of general production. We have, therefore, discarded our attempts at weighting, and have combined as many series of all sorts as were available into a single index on the theory that each one of the series was probably representative of a type of movement in other series not available. This is, of course, not pure random sampling but in the absence of evidence to the contrary we have accepted it as an approximation to randomness, and as preferable to a weighted average.

of growth from either Stewart's or Day's. From a wide variety of sampling by different methods, it is evident that we have come upon a quite accurate measure of the rate of growth of the industry of the country as a whole. It is evident, too, that this rate of growth has not changed substantially in the last fifty years. If we accept the rates of growth as shown by our 49 items, and by the Day and Stewart series, the average will be found to be about 3½ per cent per year as far back as the data go.

The persistence and stability of growth in general production is further interesting because it is apparently independent of the growth of total population in this country. The population rate has been steadily declining through the past fifty years, while the rate of growth of industrial production has remained constant. This is an indication of the steady expansion of the per capita production of the United States.

The tendencies of stability and persistence in growth might lead one to suppose that forecasts of the secular trend would be very easy.. The line of growth in so many series has approximated the line of growth characteristic of general production and population. We know the general tendencies of growth in such a large number of series, why can we not make a reasonable judgment as to the probable future growth of any particular series? We know that this is possible with a large number of series. If, for instance, we take the series for freight traffic (ton miles) from 1870 to 1890, and compute from these data the probable trend from 1890 to 1910, we will closely approximate the actual trend computed for that period. Similar tests could be made for other series. But mathematical projections will quite often give absurd results (see footnote on Secular Trend). Even when the result is logical, the growth forecasts may be rudely upset by some industrial change or other circumstances which were unforeseen and whose future course must be hypothetical.

Consider, for example, the possibility of forecasting the growth of cotton production. There has been a distinct tendency to a falling off in cotton production. This is partly traceable to the boll weevil, which has been a serious factor in causing under-production. But if a remedy could be found for the boll weevil, it is very doubtful whether the fall in cotton production would be checked. For, before the World War, cotton was almost undoubtedly being produced below an economic level; i.e., wages in the cotton industry were at a distinctly lower level than for other industries. With the War, there came an opportunity for the more energetic negroes to emigrate to the North, and this draining of labourers from the cotton belt has brought about further difficulties of under-production. It is possible that cotton will never again be produced at pre-war prices. So a forecast of the future of cotton production resolves itself into the solution of these difficult questions: First, how far can the boll weevil be controlled? Second, will the community be willing to pay permanently higher prices for cotton, or will the higher prices curtail consumption? Third, how far will possible substitutes, such as artificial silk, come into general use? It will be seen that prediction of the future trend of cotton production cannot be made accurately because of the uncertainty of the factors involved.

It is obvious how very difficult it becomes to predict the future trend of series such as this, and careful analysis will show that similar difficulties exist in a great many other cases.

Although it usually happens that these economic and industrial factors which broadly influence the production in an industry develop gradually over a period of time, it is not easy to predict their future. For example, the curve of coal production has tended to bend quite heavily in the past few years. This can be traced almost directly to the competition of oil. Now the trend of oil production, after pursuing a nearly straight line growth for a long period, turned suddenly upward and has shown no recent tendency towards a decrescent rate. In order to make an adequate prediction of the trend of coal production, we must consider the possibilities of prediction of the future trend of oil production, and this in turn will be found to depend largely on the growth of the automobile industry. The automobile industry has shown an amazing line of growth, which during the past decade has reached unprecedented heights. Since the close of the War this country has produced seventeen million motor cars and trucks, or about four times that of all the motor cars in all the rest of the world. This burst of enthusiasm has produced a corresponding demand for oil, and along with this has come a marked reduction in the average cost of oil production.[18] It seems probable that this tremendous growth is an abnormal occurrence in oil production and that it will not permanently continue, but the difficulties of prediction are obvious.

Another problem of prediction arises in regard to a series like chain store sales. These sales have shown a straight line growth at the very high rate of 13 per cent per year for the past twenty years, and this growth has not been markedly affected by either price changes or business cycles. The growth now seems to be limited only by the ability of the companies to establish new stores and to put more commodities on sale. This sort of growth cannot, of course, continue indefinitely because the point must be reached where all articles for which there is a constant demand will be sold from chain stores, and then their growth must be limited by the growth of the buying power of the population. But we cannot predict when

[18] The relative cost of oil has decreased, and oil prices have not advanced greatly. This is due to the fact that oil wells are now drilled nearly twice as deep as was formerly the case. Instead of drilling 1200 to 1500 feet, the tendency now is to drill 2500 to 3000 feet, which has proved profitable in spite of the increased overhead expense.

and how this point will be reached and hence we are unable to predict the line of growth of chain store sales too far into the future.

It is thus evident that long-time prediction of trends is unwise and likely to be inaccurate. In order to study the business cycle, however, this long-time prediction is unnecessary. All that we need to compute is the present "normal" in comparison with the "normal" of past years, and this can be done with a fair degree of accuracy.

CHAPTER III

THE MEASUREMENT OF BUSINESS CYCLES

THE preceding chapter has developed the idea of industrial growth. It has been found that production and trade, —as represented by many series—have shown a persistent and usually characteristic tendency to increase over a period of time. The line of growth has varied from one series to another. In some cases there has been a constant rate of growth decade by decade; in many others the rate of growth has decreased, and the trend describes a parabolic movement. In all cases, the growth factor has shown an amazing persistence and has not usually been deflected by wars, panics, or other disasters.

But wars, panics, and other disturbances have, nevertheless, occurred and their effects are measurable in terms of interruptions to, or deviations from, the line of growth. More important still is the definite wave-like movement which appears to be superimposed on the line of growth. The persistence of a regular and even rate of growth is our concept of normality in business,[1] and "business cycles" can be thought of as these recurring wave-like interruptions to the normal growth. That is to say, each particular industry is geared up to a certain rate of growth, to a steadily, almost predictable, increasing demand.

---

[1] This concept of normality is in a sense artificial, since, obviously, if the cyclical movement recurs again and again, a more realistic conception of the normal in business is a state of continual flux and reflux. There is, however, this other type of change, this long time growth movement occurring at the same time, and a separation of the two is essential to the measurement of the true cyclical element. See Mitchell, "Business Cycles," 1913, p. 86.

Something happens to disturb this demand—some favorable circumstance develops which produces a sudden upward spurt in demand, and the supply in this particular case adjusts itself by increased activity. But the conditions which have brought about this increased demand are removed and there is a slump, which has frequently a considerable impetus and carries the line of activity or production below that of normal growth.

Let us consider how this will come about in specific instances. Most modern industries use great quantities of machines. These machines must be ordered and manufactured in advance. If an industry meets with an unusual demand for its product, it will attempt to meet this demand partly by using the existing equipment to the utmost and partly by ordering new machinery. When the machinery arrives, it will turn out more goods, and the previously existing excess of demand will tend to be met by an excess of supply. Now as soon as the excessive demand in those lines is supplied, there is a prompt falling off in demand for further machinery, and that will tend to produce slack times in this machine industry. The industry has been geared up to a certain rate of growth, and variations in that rate of growth, with their repercussions, are what we call business booms and business depressions.

Our problem in measuring the business cycle then, is to measure the deviations above and below the line of normal growth. Of course, these deviations will not always represent business cycles uncomplicated by other factors. In most of the data we deal with there will be a regular seasonal movement, repeating itself every twelve months and generally unaffected by the cyclical movement.[2] This average seasonal movement can be measured and separated from the cyclical fluctuations. Our method of computing

[2] Mitchell has pointed out that the seasonal and the cyclical cannot always be isolated, that, e. g., a revival of business activity is likely to occur in any particular series at the season of generally high activity and depression is likely to begin at the season of generally low activity.

indexes of various series, designed to show as nearly as possible the purely cyclical movement is as follows:

(1) The secular trend is measured by fitting a smooth curve to the actual annual data,[3] and ordinates of the line of secular trend are computed giving a comparative value of "normal" for each value of the actual data.

(2) The average seasonal movement is measured, and a set of twelve "indices of seasonal variation"[4] is computed. These indices represent the relative importance of each month to the year's total.

[3] See footnote [1], ch. II, p. 28.

[4] Indices of seasonal variation are computed as follows:

a—A graphical test of the existence of seasonal movement is made by plotting the monthly data for a series of years, one year above the other. If a definite seasonal movement exists, it is readily followed by the eye, in the tendency of some months always to be high or low in relation to other months.

b—If a seasonal movement exists, it is usually measured as follows:

(1). Twelve months moving averages are computed, and centered opposite the seventh month of the actual data.

(2). Percentage deviations of the actual data from the corresponding moving averages are computed.

(3). A scatter chart, or frequency distribution, is formed of these percentage deviations.

(4) Some central value (the median, or the mean of the several middle values) is selected as representative of the normal seasonal movement of each month.

(5). The twelve central values are expressed in terms of their arithmetic average as a base, and the resulting twelve relatives are considered the "indices of seasonal variation."

The true seasonal movement is thought of as a regular increase or decrease from month to month, due to recurring climatic changes, customs of the trade, etc. This seasonal movement is often obscured in the indices by the action of what we may call calendar variation. For instance, total production in any series will nearly always tend to decline from January to February because of the fact that there are three less days in February, although February may actually represent greater normal seasonal activity than January. Leap Year by giving an extra working day to February further complicates this relationship. The most usual disturbing factor, however, is the phenomenon of five Sundays, which occurs in every month at intervals of about three years. This occasions the loss of a working day in this particular month, and this loss may cause a decrease of as much as 4 or 5% in the monthly total in series such as bank debits or retail store sales, a decrease which represents neither a true seasonal nor a cyclical decline. The difficulty is overcome by reducing monthly totals to an average daily basis before computing seasonal indices; i.e., by dividing the monthly totals by the number of working days in that industry for each month of each year. The ordinates of trend are also reduced to an average daily basis, and the monthly index will equal $\dfrac{\text{actual data (daily basis)}}{\text{Trend (daily basis)} \times \text{seasonal index}}$.

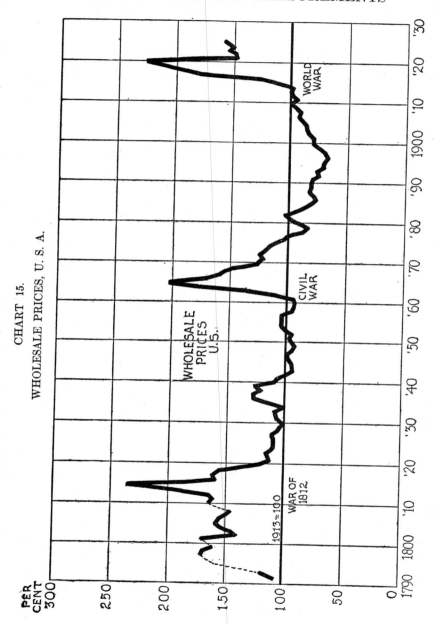

CHART 15.

WHOLESALE PRICES, U. S. A.

WHOLESALE PRICES, U. S. A.: An index on a 1913 base of wholesale prices
   from 1791 to 1925. The index from 1791 to 1865 is based on figures
   computed by Roelse and Hansen; from 1866 to 1889, by J. L. Snider;
   and from 1890 to date, the index of the Bureau of Labor Statistics.
   Source: "European Currency and Finance," Commission of Gold and
   Silver Inquiry, U. S. Senate, 1925, Serial 9, Vol. I, p. 436.

(3) The ordinate of secular trend for each month is multiplied by the seasonal index for that month. This gives a figure which shows what the activity in the series would be for that particular month if business were "normal;" i.e., if the estimated "normal" growth and the average seasonal movement had occurred, or in other words, if there had been no business cycle.

(4) Our next step, therefore, is to measure the cyclical movement in the actual data by allowing for the "normal" growth and seasonal. An index is computed by dividing the actual data by the product of the corresponding ordinate of trend and the seasonal index. The percentage deviations, then, of the actual data from the estimated "normal" show the relative cyclical position.

It is evident, then, that we have here a means of measuring business cycles which will enable us to get more and more exact knowledge of them. One further technical question in this problem remains to be discussed, and that is the measurement of the influence of price changes. Many of our important series such as exports, imports, wholesale and retail trade, and bank clearings are expressed in terms of the dollar. And the value of the dollar, as measured by its power to purchase commodities, has varied widely over periods of time, and often to such a degree as to distort any series expressed in its terms so as to confuse both the secular and the cyclical movements. The foregoing chart (Chart 15, p. 58) of the changes in wholesale prices for the past one hundred years illustrates the extent of this change. From the period of great inflation in the Civil War, there was a very gradual process of deflation over quite a long period, that is to say, there was a process of gradual improvement in the purchasing power of the dollar. There was a rising tendency of prices in the early eighties, but it was brief and the decline continued to the middle of the nineties. From then up to the beginning of the Great War, there was fairly steady inflation, or decline in the purchasing power of the dollar, a process evidenced by rising prices. So long as the inflation or deflation could be thought of as a slow, continuous movement over a long time, it formed no serious difficulties in the treatment of time series for the purpose of measuring the business cycle. But the violence of the price movements since the beginning of the Great War has been without precedent since the Civil War, a tremendous and sudden inflation and then a drastic deflation. This has been a world-wide process, and has had profound effects upon the course of business. We have to take it into consideration in all its relationships with the normal course of business, but we also have to measure it carefully to see if we cannot trace out of the tremendously complicated structure, whether business has followed anything like its usual course. All the series which we have used which are expressed in terms of the dollar have been reduced to a common standard; i.e., the dollar figures have been divided through by some price index with a fixed base, (usually 1913) thus eliminating the effect of the great price movements, and showing the real value of the series as expressed in terms of the 1913 dollar.

This, then, being the method we have used in our statistical analysis of economic series, it may be well to discuss at some length the rationale of these methods, particularly as to the choice of a base for index numbers of commerce and trade. A detailed discussion of the use of "deflated" dollar value series as measures of business is postponed to a later chapter. (Chapter IX.)

CHAPTER IV

THE CHOICE OF A BASE FOR INDEX NUMBERS OF COMMERCE AND TRADE

THE use of index numbers in the fields of economics was long limited to index numbers of prices. For almost a century after the earliest of these price indexes there were almost no other kinds. When, with the recent vogue of statistical investigation of business, attempts were made to reduce the various data of production, transportation and trade to index numbers, for quick comparison, it was natural, so strong is habit, that much the same methods should be followed as in the making of price indexes, and especially in the selection of a base for the comparison.

This method was almost universally the choice of some base year or series of years. It is the most convenient way; and it makes little difference what base is chosen, 1860, 1890, 1913, 1910-'14, or any other combination. For this country it made very little difference save, perchance, in war periods like 1812 or 1861-'5, or 1915-'21.

It made little difference for a very simple reason. Investigation has shown that, save in war periods, the variations in the broad levels of commodity prices have not been very wide throughout a period of more than three centuries. Following the great gold discoveries in America, in the sixteenth century, there appears to have been a remarkable rise in prices in Europe, bringing with it a great outcry against the increased cost of living, just as has been so familiar in our own generation, both before the World War and in the World War, curiously enough a far greater outcry before the War than in the War. But in the forty years before the World War, even in this country, the extreme variation in commodity prices appears to have been not much more than 25 or 30 per cent above or below the average for the entire period; and in England and other European countries somewhat less.

In other words, in the last three centuries there seems to have been, in the averages of commodity prices, no definite and persistent trend, and little evidence of secular or long-time change. Therefore, almost any period or representative year of relative stability, and freedom from the usual inflations which accompany wars, would serve equally well.

In the field of business indexes the situation is radically different. Let us take a case or two in point:

We have fairly good data as to the foreign trade of this country, and especially for imports, running back more than a century. In this period the variations in import and export prices have been at times (war times) quite violent, but for the larger part of the century the deviations from the common average have been relatively small. Supposing, then, we take the value of imports of one of the earliest available years, say something like 1819, as a base, with the familiar index number of 100. Where would this index be now? In 1926 it would be fluctuating somewhere around 10,000. In other words, we should have chiefly an index number of a prodigious *growth*. For practical purposes it would now, and for a long period backwards, be clumsy and useless. The difference between an index number of 8,791 and 6,244 might represent the extreme of the worst depression in half a century, but we should have to translate it into simpler numbers.

Or, take another case: We have been able to utilize early data to piece back an index number of railway traffic, measured in ton miles, running to 1852. In that year the total traffic of the railroads reached the prodigious figure for that time of over a billion ton miles. Today it is over 400 billions a year. In other words, if we took 1852 as a

base of 100, the index number now would be in the neigh-
borhood of 40,000; another needlessly clumsy and unusable
figure. As, for example: the slump in railway traffic in 1921
appears to have been, in percentages, about the worst that
we have known in nearly half a century. Measured in
index numbers, with a base of 1852 as 100, the extremes
from the previous high year would have been represented
by index numbers of something like 37,000 and 28,000.

The main use of a base number of 100 is that it affords
a relatively quick method of estimating percentages of
change. Such index numbers as those just quoted would
need a rapid fire calculator for everyday use.

In index numbers of business data covering any extended period, then, the chief element is that relatively
constant and even rate of change which is represented by
growth, the growth of production, of transportation and
of trade in general. And almost any fixed base, whether it
be a single year or series of years, therefore becomes rapidly out of date. If we take the year of 1913 for a base,
or the period from 1910 to 1914, or any other period, and
attempt to make close comparisons, the first thing we have
to do is to estimate this rate of change. Since, in the investigation of economic and business phenomena the main
centre of interest is in the short period changes which we
have come to call the business cycle, it is evident that from
our data this steady rate of change or growth must first be
eliminated in order that we may make quick and more
comprehensive comparisons of, let us say, the volume of
production and trade in 1913 and in 1926. What we call
the "business cycle" is very distinctly the variation from
this computable trend or rate of growth. In fact, any other
method of measuring these short-period, or cyclical, variations is most clumsy and roundabout.

For example, in the first quarter of a century for which
we have quantity data, in ton mileage of railway traffic,
(from 1852) there appears to have been only one single

year of actual decline. But the variations in the rate of
growth, in other words, the deviations from the computed
trend, were still of very much the same order, and even a
little more exaggerated than the deviations from trend of
the latest ten or twenty years. And very much the same
thing has been true in our own time of the amazing and
strikingly similar growth of production of automobiles.

If, then, we are to find a means for rapid and accurate
comparison in business data, and this is practically all the
value that index numbers have, over the actual figures, the
first and essential thing is to find a base of comparison that
will not rapidly become obsolete and out of date. And
here, obviously, the simplest and easiest method we can
discover is to use precisely this actuarial expectancy derived
from the measurable rate of growth in each line of industry and trade, that is, the deviation from the computed
trend.

The rate of growth in different series may vary widely,
and the rate of decrease in growth may likewise vary. But
with very few exceptions, any one is as easily computable as
any other. The trend of pig iron production, or of silk
imports, or what you will, offers no more serious problems
than the growth of population itself.

We have, then, in all business data of sufficient period, a
reasonable or actuarial expectancy, and in many instances
this expectancy is almost as precise and estimable as in the
case of population. True, in the latter case, the probable
error involved in projection has been reduced to a quite
astonishing minimum. We no longer have prolonged periods of famine, pestlience or wars, no sudden eruptions of
the Black Death or other scourges to sweep off huge sections of the population or give rise to great exoduses like
the famines of Ireland. In the field of business data we
have no such broad base of security. In industrial production, inventions, discoveries, new methods may bring
about very radical changes. Our railways almost destroyed

canal traffic; and now these, in turn, are being subjected to strenuous competition from the motor car and motor bus. The discovery of a means of giving to aluminium the hardness, durability and tensile strength of steel would make a prodigious change in the iron trade.   But as a matter of historical fact these changes are relatively slow and, to a considerable extent, calculable.   Moreover, we have no need to make our projections far into the future.   All we require is a reasonable expectancy as to the here and now.   What will be the probable output of steel or the traffic of the railways for the present year?   We cannot calculate the effect upon these of radical changes in general business, as from good to bad or bad to ordinary. But from the curve of growth through the last ten, twenty or thirty years, we can calculate very closely the ordinary, that is, what we may call the reasonable or "normal" expectancy.   And this we can go on doing, year after year, with no more trouble than that of taking due account of any clearly defined change of trend.

What, then, is simpler than to take this normal expectancy or, more briefly, the "normal" rate, as the base for our index numbers?   If, then, we wish to estimate or calculate those changes from boom to depression and back again, which are the chief object of our investigations, this normal expectancy, or calculable rate, becomes a base equally applicable to any year as far back as our data extend.   The year 1913, or the period 1910-'14, or 1907, or '93, or, if you please, 1860 or 1816, then takes its natural place in our index scheme, so that we may say with certainty and with precision whether the business of any one of these years was good or bad, whether production of iron or railway traffic was above or below this normal rate of growth; and, furthermore, and what is vastly more to the point, we may express in index numbers the precise degree of this variation.   In other words, by this method, for any kind of business data we may select, whether given in absolute figures or in percentages of a base year, we may establish a relationship to the trend or growth. For when we select a base year or fixed period for comparison, we must first establish the position of that year or that period in the historical sequence. Clearly it would be useless to take the present year as a base. We are little forwarder when we take last year, or the year before, or indeed any previous year, until we have established what was the position of that year. And if this base year be distant by more than perhaps five or six years, or even less, we have then to make either a mental or actual calculation as to what allowance we must make for the average expectancy of growth in the period.

When we select the normal expectancy itself as a base, of 100, all these needful calculations are ready made. Immediately, then, an index figure of 92 or 110 has a definite meaning, whether it be applied to steel production, or cotton consumption, or railway traffic, or any other data which we possess. We have no need to look further because the only valid base of comparison is precisely the base which we have chosen as 100.

The great advantage of this system is that by reducing every available series to a common denominator, and making due allowance, we may then make immediate comparison, month by month, or even week by week, one with another throughout the whole range. And not alone one with another, but the relation of each line of industry and trade to the whole. For practically only by this method has it been possible to put together into any adequate measure of the whole, all the varied and highly representative material which we now possess. And not until we have put together all the available series of basic production into a composite index can we have any clear idea of the relative position of one industry to the whole of industrial output.

In the same way it is only by combining all the available

series in some such fashion as this into a broad composite
that we can obtain any adequate idea or measure of the
real variations of the trade of the nation as a whole; or
know whether one of its major components, as, for example,
basic production, is running fairly well with general business, or above or below it.

It has been objected that it is impossible to compute this
normal expectancy, or trend of growth, with great exacti-
tude; and in many cases this is true. But it is usually of
importance only when the deviations from the trend are
relatively small, and it is precisely in such cases that, as a
rule, the trend may be fitted most easily. An error of 5
per cent in the calculation of the trend of postal receipts
which, even though measured in dollars, seem as indifferent
to booms and depressions as to wide changes in price levels,
would be serious; but it would be quite unlikely to occur.
A similar error in calculating the present position of more
difficult series, like pig iron production or building, would
be of little moment.

And when the percentages derived from these trends are
combined into a broad weighted composite, of 50 or 60 different series, the chances of a persistent bias are slight.
And if, further, it be argued that in all these percentages
we have only approximations and not astronomical precision, it is well to remember that this in general is true of
all price indexes. Practically without exception they are
merely wide samplings of quotations, not weighted averages
of actual sales; and, furthermore, weighted by rather du-
bious methods. For example, even the best of them, our
indexes of commodity prices at wholesale, may at times be
quite unrepresentative of the actual movement. Yet,
nowadays, we could scarce dispense with them.

So lengthy an argument as to the proper base for business measurements might seem superfluous were it not that
this easy and immeasurably valuable tool has met with
the same curious opposition as almost every innovation

probably from the beginning of time; so inescapable are mental as well as physical habits, and, in the present instance, so strongly ingrained the predilections established by long familiarity with index numbers of prices.

CHAPTER V

A NEW MEASURE OF THE VOLUME OF TRADE [1]

UP TO this point, our discussion has been concerned with the manifestations of business cycles in many different kinds of economic series: in series representing production, trade, commerce, and finance. Obviously there will be many differences in the cyclical movements of various series. They may not always synchronize exactly. Some may show cycles of very wide amplitude, rising to tremendous heights in booms and sinking very low indeed after a crisis, while others may show such a slight cyclical movement—so little interruption to the normal line of growth—that the cycles seem more like surface ripples than like waves.

Yet there is enough similarity both in the time movement, and the amount of displacement caused by business cycles, so that we can actually speak of *the* business cycle and can describe certain years as being years of crisis, recession, depression, activity, prosperity, boom, etc. But can we get a single accurate statistical index which will represent the general state of business of the country as a whole, and by which we can measure the different phases of the business cycle? It is improbable that any single series can adequately represent the general business of the country, because of the differences between series noted above. But if we get a wide sampling of all the various forms of busi-

[1] Descriptions of this index of the volume of trade were published in two articles in the Journal of the American Statistical Association, for December, 1923, and September, 1925, and a large part of this chapter is based on these two articles.

ness activity and weight them as accurately as possible in accordance with their importance in the industrial scheme, we shall find that individual peculiarities will tend to iron out, and that we can get at least an approximation to the measurement of the business cycle.

Such has been the aim in the construction of an index of the physical volume of trade. Within recent years, there has been made available a large number of interesting business indicators—many series representing wholesale and retail trade—other series representing such varied activities as advertising, life insurance sales, communicative service, real estate transfers, Panama Canal traffic, etc. At the same time has come the development of reporting of actual debits to individual accounts in the banks of the leading cities, which has given us a more accurate account of check transactions than was afforded by bank clearings. There has also been a development of more accurate reporting of statistics in other lines for which earlier data are available; and new production series have recently been added. Furthermore, the railroads now report their car loadings from week to week, so that a very accurate picture of internal trade may be had. With all these data at our command, we can compute a comprehensive and representative index of business conditions from 1919 to date.

The work of evolving an index of the volume of trade in physical units was, however, complicated and made difficult because much of the new and important material—sales of retail stores, wholesale sales, bank debits, building permits, etc.—was in dollar values, and dollar values have been profoundly affected by the great price changes during and since the War. No direct comparison could be made between dollar figures and quantity figures without some adjustment for price changes. There were available, however, several very accurate and reliable price indexes measuring

CHART 16.

VOLUME OF TRADE, PRODUCTIVE ACTIVITY, DISTRIBUTION
TO CONSUMER.

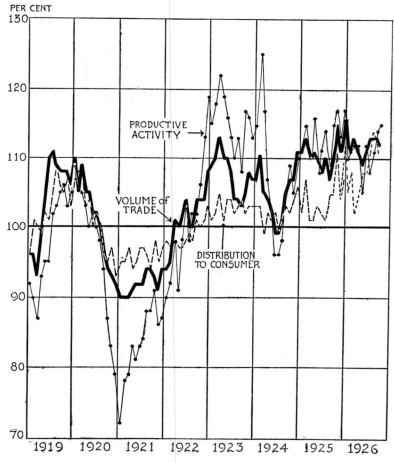

PRODUCTIVE ACTIVITY: See Chart 17, p. 74.

DISTRIBUTION TO CONSUMER: Consists of a weighted average of the following series, with weights as indicated:

Department Store Sales (8). See Chart 27, p. 110.
Chain Grocery Store Sales (6). See Chart 28, p. 112.
Chain Store Sales (excluding groceries) (3). See Chart 28, p. 112.
Mail Order House Sales (3). See Chart 29, p. 114.
Life Insurance Sales (2). See Chart 30, p. 116.
Real Estate Transfers (2). See Chart 31, p. 118.
Advertising (2). See Chart 26, p. 108.

CHART 17.

VOLUME OF TRADE, PRODUCTIVE ACTIVITY, PRIMARY
DISTRIBUTION.

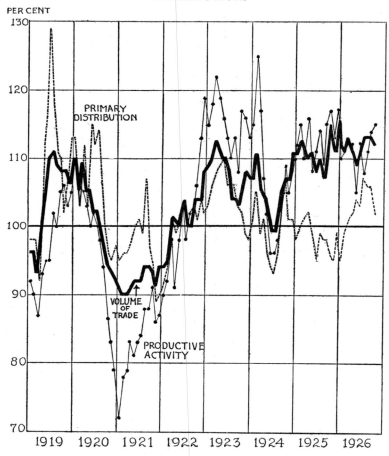

PRODUCTIVE ACTIVITY: Consists of a weighted average of the following series, with weights as indicated:

A. *Producers' Goods* (9). See Chart 19, p. 84.
B. *Consumers' Goods* (8). See Chart 19, p. 84.
C. *Employment* (6). Total number employed in 1648 representative factories in New York State.

> *Sources:* Annual and monthly, 1915-1924, N. Y. State Department of Labor.
> *Trend:* Difficult to determine. Index equals per cent of average, 1921-1924 (av. = 505,400).

Seasonal: 1914-1924,

J.	100.4	J.	98.0
F.	100.4	A.	98.0
M.	101.6	S.	99.2
A.	100.4	O.	100.4
M.	99.2	N.	101.6
J.	99.2	D.	101.6

D. *Automobile Production* (2). See Chart 20, p. 94.
E. *Building Permits* (4). See Chart 31, p. 118.

CHART 18.

VOLUME OF TRADE, FINANCIAL ACTIVITY, GENERAL
BUSINESS ACTIVITY.

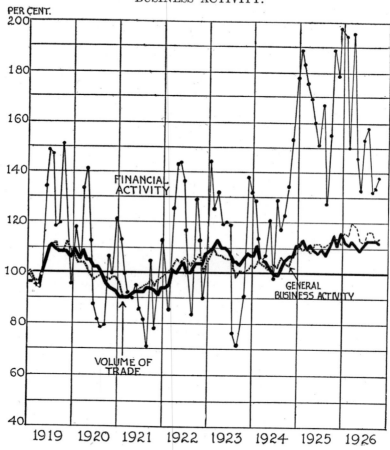

FINANCIAL ACTIVITY: Consists of a weighted average of the following series, with weights as indicated.

Number of Shares Sold on N. Y. Stock Exchange (2).   See Chart 34, p. 126.
New Corporate Financing (2).   See Chart 34, p. 126.
Future Sales of Grain (1).   See Chart 35, p. 128.
Future Sales of Cotton (1).   See Chart 36, p. 130.

GENERAL BUSINESS ACTIVITY: Consists of a weighted average of the following series, with weights as indicated:

Bank Debits, New York City (5).   See Chart 32, p. 122.
Bank Debits Outside New York City (8).   See Chart 32, p. 122.
Postal Receipts (1).   See Chart 33, p. 124.
Communication (1).   (Confidential.)
Electrical Power Production (2).   See Chart 33, p. 124.

the extent of certain of these price changes; as, for example, indexes of building costs, prices of chain groceries, etc. This made it possible to convert certain of these dollar series into series directly comparable with the series expressed in physical units, by dividing them through by their price indicators, and thus to get an estimate of volume from value at a constant price level. In other series, it was not so easy to eliminate the effect of price changes. Bank debits represent a very different problem, for the changes in wages, cost of living, wholesale prices, rent, stock prices, etc., in varying degree affect the total amount of debits, and a composite weighted price index had to be computed to eliminate the effect of price changes in this series. There were certain general tests as to the validity of the price indexes we used for other series. Thus, series representing wholesale trade, with the effect of price changes eliminated, ought to run fairly consistently with merchandise car loadings, and the movements of the production of consumers' goods ought likewise to correspond to these corrected wholesale trade figures. For almost all the series which needed correction, there were series in quantitative terms bearing such close relationships as to form a check upon the validity of the correcting factor. A further test was based on our observations of the persistence and stability of growth in economic series. (See Chapter II). In series expressed in dollar values, this stability is upset by great price changes, and, therefore, when price changes are eliminated, the deflated series should show a consistent trend, similar to that observed in quantitative series.

Altogether some fifty-six series were found available for combination into a composite index, representing the total volume of trade, by months back to the beginning of 1919. An important problem that had to be solved was how the several series should be combined into groups and what weights should be assigned to the groups. The series seemed to group themselves into those representing productive activity, primary or wholesale distribution, secondary or retail distribution, general business activity, and financial or speculative activity. As far as the materials were available, weights were assigned by the usual procedure; i.e., by comparing the value added in manufacture, or the value of the product, or the value of the commodities exchanged, and these data were checked by the figures for employment where possible.

There were, however, great difficulties in the way of a statistical determination of the relative value of these series. For instance, many of the series overlap. Merchandise car loadings, in the long run, correspond closely to the volume of merchandise sold, but they may vary widely from month to month, and hence both are included. Furthermore, certain of the groups are, taken separately, good indicators of the nation's trade. The total of production would be an excellent index, since there is no possibility of the storage of large quantities of goods at any time. But it is not safe to assume that the production of basic commodities alone is a true index of the country's trade, and since most indexes of production are overweighted with these basic commodities, we must attempt a far more inclusive picture of the total trade. Nor would it be safe to weight bank debits outside New York City, as the values reported would suggest, equally with the rest of the indexes combined; for there are many statistical complications, such as the accuracy of the determination of an index to eliminate the price distortion in this series which would make such a heavy weighting quite unjustifiable.

It seemed logical, after much experimentation, that if the data were adequate and really good samples, the three groups representing productive activity, wholesale distribution and retail distribution should have about equal weighting. The data for general business activity, representing bank debits, postal receipts, communication and similar series have been in this post-war period so complicated by extraneous factors, that their representative nature is probably less than that of the other three groups. This group ought accordingly to be weighted less heavily. Financial activity should have the lowest group weight because of its tendency to fluctuate from many and varied causes, and hence its unrepresentative nature as a measure of trade.

The weights tentatively assigned by statistical means were found to correspond quite closely to the logical expectation, and seemed to give consistent results. As finally determined, they were as follows:

Productive Activity	Weight	Distribution to Consumers	
1. Consumers' Goods	8%	13. Department Store Sales	8%
2. Producers' Goods	9	14. Chain Store Sales	3
3. Factory Employment...	6	15. Chain Grocery Sales ...	6
4. Motor Cars and Trucks	2	16. Mail Order Sales	3
5. Building Construction..	4	17. New Life Insurance....	2
	——	18. Real Estate Transfers ..	2
	29%	19. Advertising	2
Primary Distribution			——
6. Merchandise Car Load-			26%
ings	5%	General Business Activity	
7. Other Car Loadings....	2	20. Outside Debits	8%
8. Wholesale Trade	8	21. New York City Debits.	5
9. Exports	3	22. Postal Receipts	1
10. Imports	2	23. Communication	1
11. Panama Canal Traffic..	1	24. Electrical Power Produc-	
12. Grain Exports	1	tion	2
	——		——
	22%		17%

Financial Activity

25. Shares Sold on New York Stock Exchange	2%
26. New Corporate Financing	2
27. Grain Future Sales in Chicago	1
28. Cotton Future Sales in New York and New Orleans....	1
	——
	6%
Total of group weights................................	100%

Two of the components of the productive activity group were themselves weighted averages of a large number of series. These series, with their weights, are as follows:

Producers' Goods	Weight	Consumers' Goods	Weight
Cotton Consumption	17	Hogs Slaughtered	8
Woolen Mill Activity	9	Cattle Slaughtered	6
Pig Iron	10	Calves Slaughtered	1
Steel Ingots	21	Sheep Slaughtered	1
Lumber	12	Sugar, U. S. Meltings	11
Silk Consumption	2	Flour Milled	18
Cement	3	Cigars	4
Copper, U. S. Mine	4	Cigarettes	4
Zinc	1	Tobacco	3
Tin Deliveries	1	Gasoline	5
Petroleum	3	Tires	7
Gas and Fuel Oil	1	Newsprint	5
Sole Leather	3	Total Paper	8
Bituminous Coal	11	Boots and Shoes	9
Locomotives	2	Anthracite Coal	10
	100		100

When all these series are combined, with the weights
stated above, into a single series, they give the result shown
in Chart 16, representing an index of the total volume of
trade in the country. Before being included, each of the
series had, as described in Chapter III, been corrected for
secular trend, and, where necessary, for price changes,
seasonal variation, and calendar variation. These fluctuations in the Volume of Trade Index, then, represent a close
approximation to the real variations of trade which come
under the name of business cycles. From these measures
we see that trade was on the up grade in the first months
of 1919, and very rapidly assumed boom proportions by
June and July. A high level of activity was maintained
throughout all of 1919 and a secondary peak was reached
during the first three months of 1920. A recession, however, set in in the late spring and summer of 1920, and the
index fell below the "normal" line in September. The lowest point of the depression was reached in the first three
months of 1921, and business remained depressed for the
remainder of the year. A revival came about early in 1922,
and by March the index had again crossed the "normal" line

to prosperity. There was a slight hesitation in activity towards the middle of 1922, but the last months saw a rapid rise to a high level, and a peak was reached in March, 1923. A very high level was maintained through June with a recession, in the summer, of such slight proportions that the volume of trade did not decline below normal. By the end of the year, there was a brief upward swing towards the levels of early 1923, but by March, 1924, a genuine decline had set in and business was below normal during June and July of that year. There was a sharp recovery in September, with the movement continuously upward to a peak in the following February, and a high level has been maintained up to the present writing.

Let us consider next how far the general index of the volume of trade is an average which is representative of its component parts. Charts 16 to 18 show the Volume of Trade Index plotted against its more important factors. It should be noted that there is a general synchronism between the Volume of Trade Index and its component parts. Practically without exception, the series turn upward, reach their peaks, turn downward, and reach their troughs, simultaneously or within a few months' margin. The only notable exceptions are the financial or speculative series, which show a greater number of peaks and troughs than does the general volume of trade. As to the amplitude of the cycles, however, there is a wide variation between the series and the general average. The average range of variation of the Volume of Trade is between plus and minus 10% to 15%; that is, when business generally is at its worst, it is about 10% below the computed normal—when it is at the height of prosperity, it is 10% to 15% above. Its component parts, however, vary widely from this average range. Retail trade seldom shows a deviation of more than 5% above or below the line, and postal receipts lie well within the same zone. On the other hand, pig iron production runs 30-40% above normal in

prosperous times, and 40-60% below normal when business is greatly depressed. The curves of speculative activity show occasional extremes of 150% above normal. The
average Volume of Trade, then, is less representative in the
range of the fluctuations than it is in the synchronisms.
There is reason to believe, however, that it represents fairly
well the amplitude of general business—for the best single
barometers available (to be discussed in detail later) show
about the same amplitude.

Passing now to a detailed consideration of the series
included in the composite Volume of Trade Index, we find
that the most heavily weighted group is that representing
productive activity. This group includes a composite of
fifteen series representing producers' goods, a composite of
fifteen series representing consumers' goods, an index of factory employment, an index of the production of motor cars
and trucks, and an index of the volume of construction.
Chart 17 shows the relationship between the Index of
Volume of Trade and this index of productive activity. The
movements of the cycles in the composite and in the index
of productive activity synchronize almost perfectly, but it
is immediately evident from the chart how different is the
amplitude of the fluctuations. Productive activity ranges,
during this period, from about 30% below normal to more
than 20% above normal, an amplitude over twice as great
as that of the volume of trade. The index of productive
activity, then, is a very good indicator of the time movement of the business cycle, but tends to overestimate the
amplitude of the fluctuations.[2]

There are certain differences in the relative degree of the
fluctuations which should also be noted. Thus, in the prosperous months of 1919 and 1920 the Volume of Trade and

---

[2] Of course, this difficulty could be overcome by expressing all series in
terms of standard deviations, but that would defeat one of the major
purposes of this index; i.e., to measure directly the magnitude of the
fluctuations in different forms of activity, and to get a general average
of the sampling.

CHART 19.

PRODUCTIVE ACTIVITY, PRODUCERS' GOODS, CONSUMERS' GOODS.

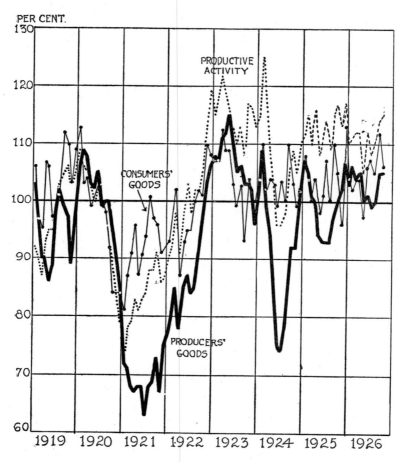

PRODUCTIVE ACTIVITY: See Chart 17, p. 74.

A. *Producers' Goods:* Represents a weighted average of 15 series, with weights as indicated.

COTTON CONSUMPTION (17). Total cotton, excluding linters.
Sources: Annual, 1870-1921, U. S. Census: "Cotton Production and Distribution, 1920-1921." Monthly, 1912 to date, releases from U. S. Census Bureau. "Cotton consumed, cotton on hand, active spindles and imports and exports of cotton."
Trend: Log parabola, 1870-1921, origin 1895. log y = 3.47128 + .016672x — .0001419x².

Seasonal: 1913-1920,

J.	106	J.	100
F.	94	A.	97
M.	104	S.	96
A.	102	O.	101
M.	103	N.	97
J.	101	D.	99

WOOL MILL ACTIVITY (9). Active hours (as percentages of capacity) of spindles and looms are weighted:

$$\frac{\text{worsted spindles} + \text{woolen spindles}}{2} + $$
$$\frac{6 \text{ (wide looms)} + 3 \text{ (narrow looms)} + 1 \text{ (carpet looms)}}{10}$$

Sources: Annual and monthly, 1917-1924, U. S. Department of Agriculture, and Census Bureau release: "Activity in Machinery in Wool Manufactures."
Trend: Trend difficult to determine. Index = per cent of average active hours, 1917-20 (80.5).
Seasonal: Period for which data are available too abnormal to measure seasonal satisfactorily.

PIG IRON PRODUCTION (10). Production of anthracite and bituminous pig iron, U. S. (excluding charcoal pig iron).
Sources: Annual, 1870-1923, American Iron and Steel Institute, 1923 annual report. Monthly, 1903-1924, "Iron Age."
Trend: Log parabola, 1870-1922, origin 1896. log y = 4.02298 + .028664x — .0003084x².

Seasonal: 1903-1921,

J.	102	J.	98
F.	93	A.	101
M.	104	S.	98
A.	101	O.	103
M.	101	N.	102
J.	97	D.	100

STEEL INGOTS (21). Production, excluding castings.
Sources: Annual, 1878-1898, production of ingots and castings, Annual Reports of American Iron and Steel Institute, 1899-1924, excluding castings, source as above. Monthly, 1917-1924—releases of American Iron and Steel Institute on "Monthly Production of Steel Ingots."
Trend: On data excluding castings (total from 1878 to 1898 are reduced by 3% to allow for castings). Period, 1878-1924, origin 1901.

Seasonal: 1917-1924,

J.	106	A.	102
F.	95	M.	100
M.	112	J.	97

J.	98	O.	106
A.	99	N.	100
S.	94	D.	91

LUMBER (12). Total cut by members of the National Lumber Manufacturers' Association, ranging from 30-50% of the total cut of the
United States.
Sources: Annual and monthly, Bulletins of the National Lumber Manufacturers' Association (1st week of each month).
Trend: Log straight line, 1913-1924, origin 1913. log y = 4.09858 +
.004471x.

Seasonal: 1914-1920,

J.	85	J.	103
F.	83	A.	114
M.	97	S.	108
A.	99	O.	111
M.	118	N.	95
J.	108	D.	79

SILK CONSUMPTION (2). Estimated deliveries to mills, i.e., stock in New
York warehouses at end of month plus imports of month, minus stock
at end of month.
Sources: Annual and monthly, 1920-1924, Silk Association of America,
annual reports, and U. S. Census, Survey of Current Business.
Trend: On silk imports, 1881-1919, origin 1900. log y = 4.01731 +
.029454x was adjusted to the consumption data.
Seasonal: No marked seasonal.

CEMENT PRODUCTION (3). Total of natural, Puzzolan, and Portland cement,
from 1880 to 1911; thereafter, of Portland cement only.
Sources: 1880-1911, U. S. Geological Survey "Mineral Resources," 1915.
Monthly, 1912-1924, Portland Cement Association and Department of
Commerce releases: "Portland Cement Output."
Trend: Log straight line, 1911-1924, origin 1911. log y = 4.86949 +
.016412x.

Seasonal: 1912-1924,

J.	60	J.	113
F.	67	A.	119
M.	83	S.	115
A.	103	O.	120
M.	119	N.	105
J.	115	D.	81

COPPER PRODUCTION (4). Smelter production, 1880-1906, thereafter total
mine production.
Sources: Annual, 1845-1917, U. S. Geological Survey, "Mineral Resources," 1918, 1921. Monthly, 1918-1920, Engineering and Mining
Journal; 1921-1924, American Bureau of Metal Statistics, and Survey
of Current Business.
Trend: Parabola, 1900-1912, and 1924, origin 1900. y = 558.3 +61.5683x
— .77224x².

Seasonal: 1911-1924,

J.	102	J.	97
F.	93	A.	101
M.	105	S.	97
A.	101	O.	101
M.	105	N.	96
J.	102	D.	100

ZINC PRODUCTION (1). Production of primary zinc from both foreign and
domestic ores (including, at present, a small amount of secondary zinc
in monthly tabulations).

Sources: Annual, 1882-1919, U. S. Geological Survey: "Mineral Resources," 1918, 1921. Monthly, 1920-1924, American Zinc Institute report on "Zinc—All Companies."

Trend: Log parabola, 1882-1924, origin 1903. log y = 5.24397 + .029911x — .0002907x^2.

Seasonal: 1917-1918 and 1920-1924,

J.	110	J.	97
F.	102	A.	93
M.	113	S.	89
A.	107	O.	92
M.	108	N.	94
J.	98	D.	97

TIN DELIVERIES (1). Deliveries to mills, exclusive of Bolivian ore.

Sources: 1900-1924 (annual and monthly), New York Metal Exchange: "Official Daily Market Report."

Trend: Log straight line, 1900-1918, origin 1909. log y = 4.63319 + .013443x.

Seasonal: 1909-1920,

J.	94	J.	115
F.	103	A.	101
M.	109	S.	103
A.	93	O.	102
M.	96	N.	82
J.	106	D.	96

PETROLEUM PRODUCTION (3). Crude petroleum marketed or transported from producing properties (averaging 99% of total production).

Sources: Annual, 1876-1924, U. S. Geological Survey, "Mineral Resources," 1921, and "Summaries of Statistics of Crude Petroleum." Monthly, 1913-1924, J. E. Pogue: "Economics of Petroleum," p. 254, and U. S. Department of Interior, Bureau of Mines, "Petroleum Statistics."

Trend: Log straight line, 1906-1920, origin 1913. log y = 4.39316 + .033074x.

Seasonal: 1913-1921,

J.	98	J.	104
F.	90	A.	102
M.	103	S.	100
A.	100	O.	103
M.	102	N.	98
J.	101	D.	99

GAS AND FUEL OIL PRODUCTION (1). Output of refineries.

Sources: Annual, 1909, 1914, U. S. Census, Abstract of Manufactures, 1914. Monthly, 1917-1924, U. S. Bureau of Mines, "Output of Refineries in U. S."

Trend: Log parabola, 1910-1922, origin 1916. log y = 6.72587 + .059947x — .001379x^2.

Seasonal: 1917-1921,

J.	93	J.	104
F.	88	A.	109
M.	95	S.	107
A.	95	O.	106
M.	102	N.	101
J.	101	D.	99

SOLE LEATHER PRODUCTION (3). Total production.

Sources: Annual and monthly, 1918-1924, Tanners' Council, "Leather Statistics—Sole Leather."

Trend: Trend difficult to determine. Index = per cent of average monthly production, 1918-1922 (= 1,610,010 sides).

Seasonal: 1918-1922,

J.	102	J.	98
F.	90	A.	101
M.	100	S.	97
A.	103	O.	103
M.	108	N.	92
J.	109	D.	97

BITUMINOUS COAL PRODUCTION (11). Total production.
Sources: Annual, 1822-1921, U. S. Geological Survey, "Mineral Resources," 1921. Monthly, 1913-1924, same as annual and Dept. of Commerce, Bureau of Mines, "Weekly Report on the Production of Anthracite and Bituminous Coal."
Trend: Log parabola, 1888-1922, origin 1905. log y = 4.47888 + .023539x — .000559x^2.

Seasonal: 1913-1921,

J.	107	J.	97
F.	92	A.	106
M.	102	S.	106
A.	83	O.	113
M.	92	N.	104
J.	95	D.	103

LOCOMOTIVES (2). Railway locomotives shipped by three large companies.
Sources: Annual, 1900-1924, and monthly, 1918-1924, Federal Reserve Board and U. S. Dept. of Commerce, Survey of Current Business.
Trend: Log straight line, 1900-1918, origin 1909. log y = 5.11507 + .004063x.
Seasonal: No seasonal.

B. *Consumers' Goods:* Represents a weighted average of 15 series, with weights as indicated.

CATTLE SLAUGHTERED (6) under Federal inspection, including about three-quarters of total slaughterings.
Sources: Annual, 1907-1923, U. S. Department of Agriculture, Year Book, 1923. Monthly, 1913-1924, *ibid,* 1924, and U. S. Bureau of Animal Industry, "Service and Regulatory Announcements."
Trend: Log straight line, 1900-1922, origin 1911. log y = 3.90035 + .004639x.

Seasonal: 1913-1922,

J.	101	J.	92
F.	84	A.	100
M.	87	S.	110
A.	85	O.	127
M.	86	N.	120
J.	96	D.	112

CALVES SLAUGHTERED (1) under Federal inspection, including about three-quarters of total slaughterings.
Sources: Same as for Cattle Slaughtered (see above).
Trend: Log straight line, 1907-1924, origin 1907. log y = 3.22492 + .025327x.

Seasonal: 1913-1925,

J.	86	J.	104
F.	79	A.	96
M.	102	S.	98
A.	119	O.	102
M.	125	N.	94
J.	113	D.	82

SHEEP SLAUGHTERED (1) under Federal inspection, including about three-quarters of total slaughterings.
Sources: Same as for Cattle Slaughtered (see above).

Trend: Log straight line, 1906-1924, origin 1915. log y = 4.07206 + .000588x.

Seasonal: The seasonal index for sheep slaughtered shows a marked change during the period 1913-1924, due to the progressive shortening of the modal age at slaughtering. From about 1919 to date there seems to be a more stable movement, but the nature of the data makes this index subject to frequent revision. Index, 1919-1924:

J.	101	J.	104
F.	87	A.	111
M.	92	S.	116
A.	88	O.	114
M.	94	N.	99
J.	99	D.	95

HOGS SLAUGHTERED (8) under Federal inspection, including about three-quarters of total slaughterings.

Sources: Same as for Cattle Slaughtered (see above).

Trend: Log straight line, 1901-1919, origin 1910. log y = 4.51585 + .009276x.

Seasonal: 1913-1919,

J.	142	J.	82
F.	115	A.	66
M.	100	S.	61
A.	88	O.	86
M.	98	N.	114
J.	98	D.	150

SUGAR MELTINGS (11). From 1915 to date, meltings at all United States ports—before 1915, meltings at Atlantic ports only, comprising 73% of the total meltings (1916-1924), were raised by 37% to be equivalent to "all ports" data.

Sources: Annual and monthly, 1894-1915, Weekly Statistical Sugar Trade Journal. 1916-1921, American Sugar Bulletin. 1922-date, U. S. Department of Commerce, Survey of Current Business.

Trend: Log parabola, 1894-1924, origin 1909. log y = 3.45171 + .011156x + .0001208x^2.

Seasonal: 1916-1924,

J.	68	J.	123
F.	98	A.	116
M.	127	S.	85
A.	127	O.	82
M.	128	N.	69
J.	128	D.	49

FLOUR PRODUCTION (18). Total output estimated from weekly reports of 50-60% of all mills in the United States.

Sources: Annual and monthly, 1914-1924, Miller's Almanac. Currently from Russell's Commercial News.

Trend: Straight line, 1914-1924, origin 1919. y = 1211.45 + 15.01x.

Seasonal: 1914-1924,

J.	104	J.	89
F.	90	A.	109
M.	96	S.	115
A.	83	O.	127
M.	85	N.	120
J.	80	D.	102

CIGAR CONSUMPTION (4). Number of large cigars manufactured in U. S. A., Porto Rico and the Philippines, and small cigars in U. S. and Porto Rico, for U. S. domestic consumption.

Sources: Annual, 1870-1924, monthly, 1913-1924, U. S. Bureau of Internal Revenue report on tax-paid products.

Trend: Log parabola, 1900-1924, origin 1912. log y $= 3.93224 + .00325x - .000655x^2$.

Seasonal: 1911-1924,

J.	92	J.	101
F.	88	A.	105
M.	98	S.	104
A.	95	O.	115
M.	100	N.	107
J.	103	D.	92

CIGARETTE CONSUMPTION (4).   Total number manufactured for domestic consumption.

Sources: Same as for Cigar Consumption (see above).

Trend: Log straight line, 1900-1920, origin 1910. log y $= 3.93825 + .068885x$.

Seasonal: 1911-1920,

J.	94	J.	114
F.	91	A.	110
M.	97	S.	103
A.	90	O.	111
M.	99	N.	102
J.	105	D.	84

TOBACCO CONSUMPTION (3).   Total manufactured for domestic consumption.

Sources: Same as for Cigar Consumption (see above).

Trend: Log parabola, 1900-1920, origin 1910. log y $= 4.59339 + .008343x - .0007052x^2$.

Seasonal: 1911-1920,

J.	97	J.	99
F.	96	A.	108
M.	106	S.	102
A.	99	O.	110
M.	102	N.	96
J.	99	D.	86

GASOLINE PRODUCTION (5).   Total output of refineries.

Sources: Annual, 1914-1917, J. E. Pogue: "The Economics of Petroleum" (1921). Annual and monthly, 1918-1924, U. S. Bureau of Mines "Refineries Statistics in U. S."

Trend: Log parabola, 1914-1922, origin 1918. log y $= 3.52625 + .079427x - .0034164x^2$.

Seasonal: 1917-1924,

J.	98	J.	103
F.	89	A.	103
M.	99	S.	101
A.	99	O.	103
M.	105	N.	99
J.	103	D.	98

TIRE PRODUCTION (7).   Production of casings of pneumatic cord and fabric, and balloon casings of about 75% of the industry.

Sources: Annual, 1914-1924, U. S. Census, and Rubber Association of America. Monthly, 1920-1924, Rubber Association of America "Statistical Service Bulletin."

Trend: Gompertz curve on logs, 1914-1924, origin 1914. The six points to which the Gompertz formula was applied were points on a parabolic log trend, 1914-1924 (log y $= 3.29494 + .054125x - .0046995x^2$). The Gompertz trend is log y $= 3.564319 - .667177 (.696008)^x$.

Seasonal: (link relative method) 1920-1925,

J.	91	M.	115
F.	93	J.	107
M.	115	J.	97
A.	106	A.	113

S. 94   N. 88
O. 97   D. 84

NEWSPRINT PRODUCTION (5). Total production, U. S. A.
Sources: Annual and monthly, 1913-1922, Paper Trade Journal and Federal Trade Commission. 1923-1924, Monthly Bulletin of the Newsprint Service Bureau.
Trend: Difficult to determine. Index = per cent of average (= 1,336,000 tons), 1913-1922.

Seasonal: 1913-1921,

J.	106	J.	98
F.	92	A.	101
M.	101	S.	95
A.	101	O.	103
M.	101	N.	98
J.	102	D.	102

PAPER PRODUCTION (8). Total production, U. S. A., of all kinds.
Sources: Annual, 1899-1919, U. S. Census. Monthly, 1917-1924, U. S. Federal Trade Commission and American Paper and Pulp Association: "Summary of the Paper Industry."
Trend: Straight line, 1899-1922, origin 1910. $y = 4,400 + 203.7x$.

Seasonal: 1918-1922,

J.	98	J.	104
F.	89	A.	108
M.	100	S.	104
A.	95	O.	110
M.	99	N.	98
J.	101	D.	94

BOOTS AND SHOES PRODUCED (9). Total, U. S. A.
Sources: Annual, 1900-1921, U. S. Census. Monthly, 1922-1924, U. S. Census Bureau: "Report on the Production of Boots and Shoes."
Trend: Log straight line on data for 1900, 1904, 1909, 1914, 1919, 1921-1924, origin 1900. $\log y = 2.35431 + .006781x$.

Seasonal: 1922-1924,

J.	100	J.	84
F.	99	A.	101
M.	113	S.	102
A.	105	O.	112
M.	100	N.	100
J.	92	D.	92

ANTHRACITE COAL PRODUCTION (10). Total, U. S. A.

Sources: Annual, 1821-1921, U. S. Geological Survey, "Mineral Resources," 1921. Monthly, 1913-1924, same as annual and Dept. of Commerce, Bureau of Mines, "Weekly Report on the Production of Anthracite and Bituminous Coal."
Trend: Log parabola, 1870-1924 (omitting strike years of 1902 and 1922), origin 1870. $\log y = .259413 + .024729x - .0002089x^2$.
Seasonal: 1913-1925 (omitting April-August, 1922).

J.	97	J.	101
F.	85	A.	102
M.	103	S.	98
A.	94	O.	109
M.	104	N.	102
J.	104	D.	101

productive activity showed about the same percentage increases above normal. The depression of 1921 was, however, greatly exaggerated in the production series, and, likewise, the sharp expansion of 1922-'23 reached greater proportions than the total trade of the country indicated. From 1924 onward, the two series have shown pretty much the same degree of fluctuations. It is evident that business cycles affect productive activity to a greater extent than they do the general run of business, and to a differential degree in times of prosperity and depression. Chart 19 shows the chief components of the productive activity series. Here again the time movement of the components is the same, but the amplitude of the fluctuations varies considerably. The series representing producers' goods (heavily weighted with iron and steel, cotton, lumber and bituminous coal) show depressions as deep as 40% below normal, whereas the series representing consumers' goods (heavily weighted with sugar, flour, anthracite coal, boots and shoes, paper, and hogs) does not fall more than 20% below normal. The principal deviation in factory employment from the index of productive activity was in the boom of 1920, when it reached over 20% above normal. At other times, the amplitude of its fluctuations has corresponded fairly well with the general index of productive activity. The index of motor cars and trucks (Chart 20) has corresponded more closely to the index of producers' goods and in turn to that of productive activity and to the general Index of the Volume of Trade than has the series representing building permits. The building boom from 1922 has achieved tremendous proportions, the index of building construction often rising 60 to 80% above the estimated normal.

Weighted almost as heavily as productive activity in the total Volume of Trade are the groups representing primary and secondary distribution.

Primary distribution includes indexes of car loadings, wholesale trade, exports, imports, grain exports, and Pan-

ama Canal traffic. Chart 17 shows the relation of primary
distribution to the total Volume of Trade and to productive activity. The synchronism between the Volume of
Trade and primary distribution is high but is not so great
as between the Volume of Trade and productive activity.
The amplitude of the fluctuations, on the other hand, corresponds much more closely to the Volume of Trade than
does that of productive activity. Primary distribution
reached a high peak in 1919, almost 30% above normal,
and showed much less of a relative depression in 1921 than
any of the series we have yet considered. The most heavily
weighted component of primary distribution is the series
representing wholesale trade. This series, the sales of
wholesale concerns in the second Federal Reserve district,
has been found to be an excellent sample of wholesale
trade in the country as a whole. It corresponds very closely
indeed to the general movement of primary distribution,
both as regards time movement and the amplitude of the
cycles (Chart 21). Exceptions are the greater depression
in 1920, where the wholesale trade index dropped to 20%
below normal, whereas primary distribution as a whole
reached only 5% below normal, and in the boom of 1923,
where wholesale trade reached a maximum several months
earlier than the index of primary distribution. The car
loadings series has been subdivided because of its complicated nature, into two series, one representing merchandise
(less than carload lots) and miscellaneous, and the other
representing the widely divergent items of coal, coke, forest
products, grain, grain products, and livestock. The former
series is, naturally, a much more satisfactory indicator of
business and is weighted accordingly. Merchandise and
miscellaneous car loadings show about the same amplitude
as the total Volume of Trade and correspond quite closely
to the average index. Other car loadings fluctuate much
more widely than do the merchandise and miscellaneous
(their range being from about 25% below to 25% above

CHART 20.

PRODUCERS' GOODS, AUTOMOBILE PRODUCTION, BUILDING PERMITS.

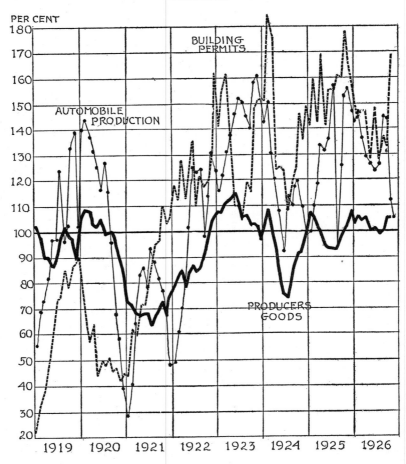

PRODUCERS' GOODS. See Chart 19, p. 84.

AUTOMOBILE PRODUCTION. The index is a weighted average of passenger and truck production indexes, passenger cars weighted (4), trucks (1).

PASSENGER AUTOMOBILES. Total number of cars produced, U. S. A.

Sources: Annual, 1900-1924, "Facts and Figures of the Automobile Industry," 1925. Monthly, 1921-1924, U. S. Department of Commerce, Survey of Current Business, Nov., 1924, and current releases from Commerce Department: "Automobile Production."

Trend: Gompertz curve on logs, 1910, 1915, 1920, origin 1900. log y =

$$\frac{.9027}{e^{-.1929x} + .2545}$$

Seasonal: 1914-1920, computed on shipments,, adjusted to be comparable with production.

J.	95	J.	90
F.	100	A.	98
M.	116	S.	98
A.	119	O.	96
M.	114	N.	82
J.	104	D.	88

MOTOR TRUCKS. Total number produced in U. S. A.

Sources: Same as for passenger automobiles.

Trend: Log straight line, 1916-1922, origin 1915. log y = 3.98088 + .055481x.

Seasonal: 1921-1923,	J.	67	J.	105
	F.	79	A.	116
	M.	116	S.	101
	A.	121	O.	97
	M.	127	N.	81
	J.	122	D.	68

BUILDING PERMITS. See Chart 31, p. 118.

CHART 21.

PRIMARY DISTRIBUTION, DEPARTMENT STORE SALES,
WHOLESALE TRADE.

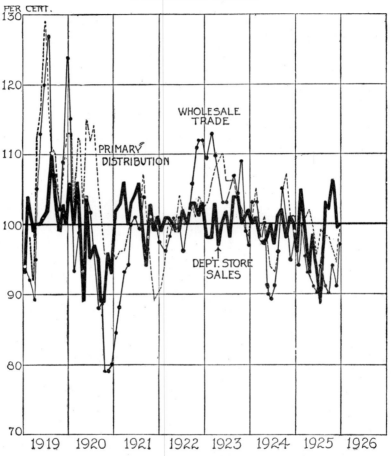

PRIMARY DISTRIBUTION. See Chart 22, p. 98.

DEPARTMENT STORE SALES. See Chart 27, p. 110.

WHOLESALE TRADE. Total sales, reduced to 1913 dollars, of about 200 firms in the 2nd Federal Reserve District. The lines of business with their weights according to relative importance in this district are: Shoes (7), drugs (3), stationery (2), men's clothing (10), women's dresses (7), women's cloaks and suits (8), groceries (37), cotton jobbers (10), silk (10), hardware (3), jewelry (1), diamonds (1), machine tools (1). Price changes are allowed for by dividing through by the U. S. Dept. of Labor wholesale price index, reweighted and combined with earnings in N. Y. State. The components of the wholesale price index are reweighted as follows (in rough approximation to their importance in the N. Y. trade): Food (37), cloths and clothing (45), metal and metal products (4), chemicals and drugs (3), housefurnishings (3), miscellaneous (8). This index is combined with an index of New York State average factory earnings (N. Y. State, Dept. of Labor) in the proportion 5 to 1, and the current months' wholesale trade index is divided by an average of the component for the current month and the third month previous.

Sources: 1919 to date. Reports Dept. of the Federal Reserve Bank of N. Y.

Trend: On sales divided by prices—computed on quarterly averages reduced to daily basis. Log straight line, 1919-1924, origin 1st quarter 1922. The monthly totals, after allowance for price changes, are reduced to a daily basis. The number of working days per month is estimated by subtracting from the calendar days the number of Sundays and the following holidays: 1 Jan., 22 Feb., 30 May, 4 July, Labor Day, Thanksgiving and 25 Dec.

Seasonal: On daily basis, 1919-1924.

J.	92	J.	88
F.	108	A.	110
M.	114	S.	121
A.	96	O.	116
M.	86	N.	102
J.	84	D.	83

CHART 22.

PRIMARY DISTRIBUTION, MERCHANDISE AND MISCELLANE-
OUS CAR LOADINGS, OTHER CAR LOADINGS.

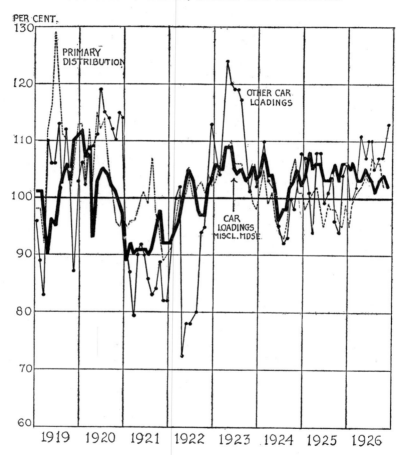

PRIMARY DISTRIBUTION. Consists of a weighted average of the following series, with weights as indicated:

Merchandise and Miscellaneous Car Loadings (5). See Chart 22, p. 98.
"Other" Car Loadings (2). See Chart 23, p. 102.
Wholesale Trade (8). See Chart 21, p. 96.
Exports (3). See Chart 24, p. 104.
Imports (2). See Chart 24, p. 104.
Grain Exports (1). See Chart 35, p. 128.
Panama Canal Traffic (1). See Chart 25, p. 106.

MERCHANDISE AND MISCELLANEOUS CAR LOADINGS. Number of revenue cars loaded and received from connections of merchandise (less-than-carload-lots) and miscellaneous freight. Total monthly data are pro-rated from weekly returns.

Sources: Annual and monthly, 1919-1924, American Railway Association, Car Service Dept, "Revenue Freight Loaded and Received from Connections."

Trend: The trend is computed on quarterly averages of the monthly data, reduced to an average daily basis—to allow for the influence of holidays. Monthly totals are divided by the number of working days in the month, estimated by subtracting from the calendar days the number of Sundays and the following holidays: Jan. 1, Feb. 22, May 30, July 4, Election Day (½), Thanksgiving, Dec. 25, Labor Day (½). Log straight line, 1919-1925 (quarterly averages of daily items); origin, 1st quarter 1922. $\log y = 2.94856 + .004497x$.

Seasonal: On daily basis, 1919-1924.

J.	87	J.	102
F.	91	A.	105
M.	97	S.	111
A.	98	O.	111
M.	100	N.	105
J.	102	D.	91

normal). Chart 22 shows the relation of the two car loading series to the index of primary distribution. Merchandise and miscellaneous car loadings are closely related to the index of primary distribution, exceptions being the very high point reached in 1919 by primary distribution when merchandise-miscellaneous car loadings were below normal, and the relatively severe depression in car loadings in 1921 when primary distribution showed only a very slight decline. "Other car loadings," representing, as it does, the movement of basic products, might be expected to show a close correspondence to our index of the production of producers' goods. Chart 23 shows this relationship to be close, both as regards time movement and amplitude of fluctuations. Chart 24 shows the relationship of exports and imports to the index of primary distribution. It will be noticed that this relationship is less close than others which have been considered up to this point. Imports follow the general movement more closely than do exports, due largely to the prolonged depression in exports throughout 1922-1923 and most of 1924. Grain exports (Chart 25) fluctuate widely. Their movement depends on a wide variety of circumstances, such as the conditions of the crops at home and abroad, business conditions, etc. Panama Canal traffic shows wide fluctuations (from about 30% below to 60% above normal), and tends to show the same cyclical movement observed in the indexes of Volume of Trade and primary distribution, with a lag of some months.

Secondary, or retail distribution, fluctuates within narrow limits as compared with wholesale or primary distribution. The former keeps well within the limits of ten per cent above and below normal, whereas the latter rose, at one period, to thirty per cent above normal. The fluctuations in secondary distribution tend to be smaller in amplitude than the volume-of-trade cycles, except in the years 1919 and 1920 when they were about equal. The time movement corresponds very closely to that of the Volume of Trade. Included in this group are series representing department store sales, chain store sales, chain grocery store sales, mail order house sales, life insurance sales, real estate transfers, and advertising. Department store sales refer only to those in the second Federal Reserve district, but, as in the case of wholesale trade, they have been found to be a highly representative sample. Department store sales fluctuate very narrowly, scarcely ever deviating more than 7% from normal. The cyclical fluctuations synchronize fairly well with those of the Volume of Trade Index, but there is an irregular, see-saw movement from month to month which somewhat obscures the real cyclical movement. These sales show a correspondence, by no means invariable, with the production of consumers' goods. (Chart 27). Chain store sales (Chart 28), show even less cyclical movement than do department store sales. This index represents predominantly the sale of five and ten cent stores, but includes also the sales of shoe, apparel, drug, candy, and cigar stores. The fluctuations around the secular trend are slight, and they represent one of the more stable aspects of retail trade. The same thing is true of chain grocery stores, for which we have computed a separate index. Both these series are subject to many fluctuations from month to month, but these are relatively unimportant, and tend to iron themselves out. The cyclical movement is almost negligible. The sales of mail order houses, on the other hand, have showed wide fluctuations, varying from about 30% above and below normal. The volume of mail order sales depends in large part on the condition of the agricultural population. The agricultural depression of 1921 had a tremendous effect on mail order sales, and these sales did not reach "normal" until December, 1922. The fluctuations in this series represent business cycles less than they do crop cycles. (Chart 29). Life insurance sales are another index of the purchasing power of the consumer. These sales follow fairly well the cyclical movement in the

CHART 23.

PRODUCERS' GOODS, CAR LOADINGS OTHER THAN MERCHAN-
DISE AND MISCELLANEOUS.

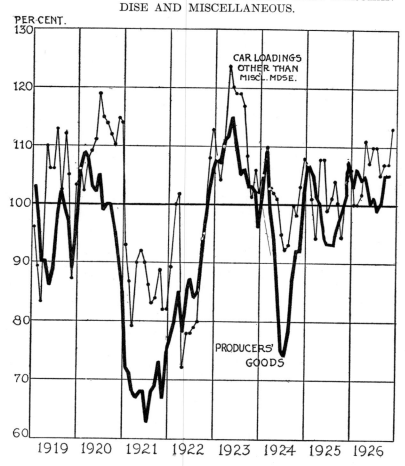

PRODUCERS' GOODS. See Chart 19, p. 84.

"OTHER" CAR LOADINGS. All car loadings of freight, exclusive of merchandise (less-than-carload lots), and miscellaneous, i.e., number of cars loaded and received from connections for the following classes of revenue freight: grain and grain products, coal, coke, forest products, ore, and livestock.

Sources: Same as for Merchandise and Miscellaneous. See Chart 22, p. 98.

Trend: Computed on monthly data prorated from weekly data reduced to daily basis. (For holiday allowance see page 99.) Log straight line, computed on quarterly averages of daily items, 1919-1924, origin 1st quarter 1922. log y = 2.77192 + .001516x.

Seasonal: On daily basis, 1919-1924.

J.	98	J.	103
F.	97	A.	110
M.	91	S.	115
A.	80	O.	117
M.	94	N.	105
J.	99	D.	91

CHART 24.

PRIMARY DISTRIBUTION, EXPORTS, IMPORTS.

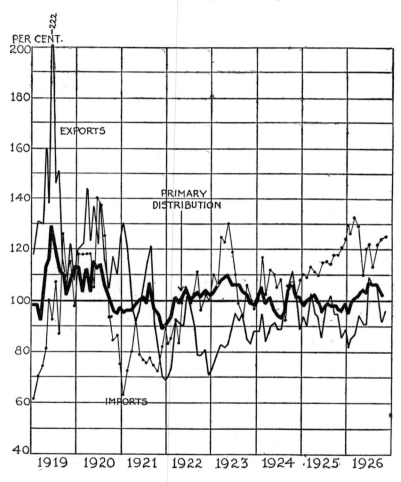

PRIMARY DISTRIBUTION. See Chart 22, p. 98.

EXPORTS. Total value of exports of merchandise from the United States, with allowance made for price changes by dividing dollar figures by the Department of Labor index of wholesale prices. The current figure for exports is divided by an average of the price index for that month and the two months previous.

Sources: Annual, 1870-1922, Statistical Abstract of the United States, 1923. Annual and monthly, 1913 to date, U. S. Department of Commerce, "Monthly Summary of Foreign Commerce of the United States" and releases on "Total Value of Exports and Imports of the United States."

Trend: On value divided by prices. Log parabola, 1880-1922, origin 1901. log y = 4.21853 + .015634x — .0001281x².

Seasonal: 1903-1922,

J.	111	J.	79
F.	95	A.	85
M.	100	S.	100
A.	96	O.	117
M.	92	N.	118
J.	87	D.	120

IMPORTS. Total value of imports of merchandise into the United States, with allowance for price changes, as in exports.

Sources: Same as for Exports.

Trend: Trend on value divided by prices. Log parabola, 1876-1922, origin 1899. log y = 4.06262 + .014374x — .0001007x².

Seasonal: 1903-1913,

J.	104	J.	92
F.	100	A.	99
M.	110	S.	95
A.	102	O.	102
M.	98	N.	101
J.	93	D.	104

CHART 25.

EXPORTS, GRAIN EXPORTS, PANAMA CANAL TRAFFIC.

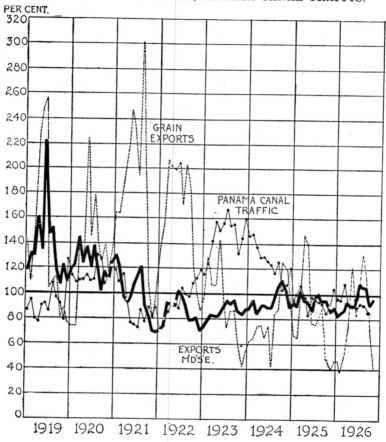

EXPORTS. See Chart 24, p. 104.

GRAIN EXPORTS. See Chart 35, p. 128.

PANAMA CANAL TRAFFIC. Total tons of commercial cargo passing through the canal in both directions, in American and foreign vessels.
Sources: Annual and monthly, 1915-to date, The Panama Canal Record.
Trend: Log straight line, 1918-1923, origin 1918. $\log y = 0.7515 + .0812x$.

Seasonal: 1916-1922,

J.	105	J.	98
F.	95	A.	96
M.	101	S.	94
A.	101	O.	107
M.	108	N.	100
J.	95	D.	100

CHART 26.

VOLUME OF TRADE, ADVERTISING, DISTRIBUTION TO CON-
SUMER.

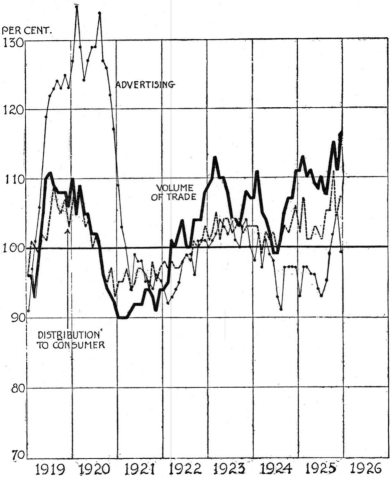

ADVERTISING. The index of advertising is composed of a weighted average of newspaper and magazine advertising indexes, newspaper weighted (2), magazine (1).

NEWSPAPER ADVERTISING. Lineage in 107 leading newspapers in following 23 cities: New York, Chicago, Philadelphia, Detroit, Cleveland, St. Louis, Boston, Baltimore, Los Angeles, Buffalo, San Francisco, Milwaukee, Washington, Cincinnati, New Orleans, Minneapolis, Indianapolis, Providence, Columbus, St. Paul, Oakland, Birmingham, Houston.

Sources: Annual and monthly, 1914-1923, Editor and Publisher, International Year Book number, 1924. 1924-to date, New York Evening Post Statistical Department, "Total Newspaper Advertising of Principal Cities of U. S."

Trend: Log straight line, 1910-1924, origin 1910. log y $= 2.75754 + .023585x$.

Seasonal: 1914-1924,

J.	96	J.	85
F.	87	A.	85
M.	106	S.	98
A.	109	O.	112
M.	110	N.	106
J.	101	D.	105

MAGAZINE ADVERTISING. Lineage of general, women's, class, and weekly magazines.

Sources: Annual and monthly, 1908-1925, Printers' Ink. The data from Jan., 1924, are not exactly comparable with previous data—hence link relatives are formed of comparative data of year previous and applied from Jan., 1924, to date.

Trend: Log straight line, 1909-1923, origin 1916. log y $= .17331 + .016654x$.

Seasonal: 1914-1923,

J.	75	J.	84
F.	94	A.	76
M.	108	S.	90
A.	119	O.	109
M.	119	N.	110
J.	109	D.	107

DISTRIBUTION TO CONSUMER. See Chart 16, p. 72.

CHART 27.

PRODUCTIVE ACTIVITY, CONSUMERS' GOODS, DEPARTMENT
STORE SALES.

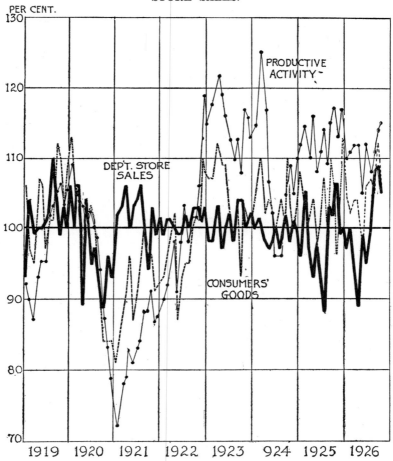

PRODUCTIVE ACTIVITY. See Chart 17, p. 74.

CONSUMERS' GOODS. See Chart 19, p. 84.

DEPARTMENT STORE SALES. Total sales of 45 department stores reporting in the 2nd Federal Reserve District (excluding purely apparel stores). Twelve stores are in New York City. Price changes are allowed for by dividing the index of sales on 1919 base by the U. S. Department of Labor cost of living index (interpolated between quarters from the Massachusetts cost of living index compiled by the Massachusetts Commission on the Necessaries of Life).

Sources: Annual and monthly, 1919-1925, Reports Department, Federal Reserve Bank of New York.

Trend: On sales (on 1919 base) divided by cost of living, log parabola, 1919-1925, origin 1st quarter 1922. $\log y = 2.43011 + .008207x - .0001826x^2$. Trend is computed on quarterly averages of daily items. The monthly totals, after allowance has been made for changes in the cost of living, are reduced to a daily basis. The number of working days in a month is estimated by subtracting from the total calendar days the number of Sundays, the number of Saturdays from July 1 to Labor Day, and the following holidays: 1st Jan., 22nd Feb., 30th May, 4th July, Labor Day, Thanksgiving, 25th December. These holidays are weighted (1.5) if they occur on Saturday from Labor Day to July 1st.

Seasonal: Special allowance must be made because of the Easter trade. Easter, being a movable holiday, the trade is thrown, in varying amounts, into March or April each year. Assuming the influence of Easter on the sales to be confined to the two weeks before and one week after Easter, weights are arbitrarily assigned as follows: If Easter occurs before April 7—first week (.5), 2nd week (2), 3rd week (1.5). If after April 7—1st week (1), 2nd week (2), and 3rd week (1). These weights are applied to the percentage of Easter selling days in each month for each year—equations are formed, inserting the seasonals found in the usual way, and are solved for the unknown "Easter influence." The varying Easter seasonals found in this way are:

	1919	1920	1921	1922	1923	1924	1925	1926	1927
March	88	89	91	88	90	88	88	89	88
April	103	102	100	103	101	103	103	102	103

The seasonal index for the other months, based on data, 1919-1924, are, on a daily basis:

J.	88	J.	83
F.	82	A.	75
M.	—	S.	92
A.	—	O.	114
M.	99	N.	117
J.	97	D.	162

CHART 28.

CHAIN GROCERY STORE SALES, CHAIN STORE SALES.

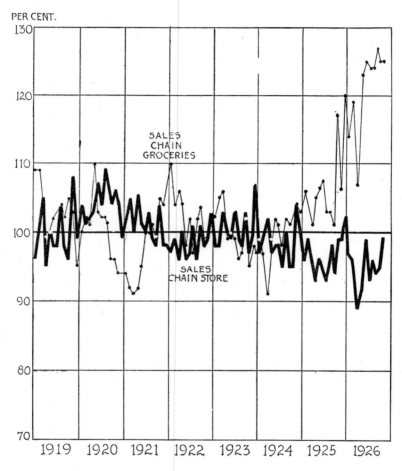

CHAIN GROCERY STORE SALES. Total sales of 27 chains throughout the
United States. Price changes are allowed for by dividing the dollar
totals by an index of the cost of groceries.
Sources: Federal Reserve Board. (Price index confidential.)
Trend: On sales divided by price-of-groceries index. Trend computed
on quarterly averages, reduced to daily basis. Log parabola, 1919-1924,
origin 1st quarter, 1922. $\log y = 4.00232 + .02133x - .0004527x^2$. The
monthly totals, after allowance has been made for price changes, are
reduced to a daily basis. The number of working days in each month
is the same as for Mail Order Sales (see Chart 29, p. 114).
Seasonal: On daily basis, 1919-1924.

J.	99	J.	98
F.	106	A.	90
M.	104	S.	96
A.	102	O.	99
M.	101	N.	104
J.	96	D.	105

CHAIN STORE SALES. Total sales, throughout the United States, of twenty
chains having their main offices in the New York Federal Reserve
District, including 5- and 10-cent, candy, apparel, drug, cigar, and
shoe stores. Price changes are allowed for by dividing the total sales
(exclusive of 5- and 10-cent store sales) by the U. S. Department of
Labor cost of living index (interpolated from the index of the Massachusetts Commission on the Necessaries of Life), and combining with
the 5- and 10-cent store sales divided by 100.
Sources: Reports Department, Federal Reserve Bank of N. Y.
Trend: On sales, allowing for price changes. Trend computed on
quarterly averages, reduced to daily basis. Log straight line, 1919-1924,
origin 1st quarter 1922. $\log y = 3.11868 + .013478x$. The monthly
totals, after allowance has been made for price changes, are reduced to
a daily basis. The practice with regard to holiday closing varies from
one type of chain to another. After the price change has been allowed
for, 86% of the stores are estimated to close generally on Sundays and
holidays, 14% to stay open all the time. Therefore, in allowing for the
number of working days per month, deductions of .86 of a day were
made for the following: all Sundays, 1st Jan., 22nd Feb., 30th May,
4th July, Labor Day, Thanksgiving, 25th December.
Seasonal: Special allowance was made for Easter, using the method
employed in regard to Department Stores. See Chart 27, p. 110.
Assuming the 3 weeks' influence of sales, the first week is weighted (1).
2nd week (2), and Easter week (1). This gives the following special
values for March and April:

	1919	1920	1921	1922	1923	1924	1925	1926	1927
March	88	94	98	88	96	88	89	94	88
April	102	96	92	102	94	102	101	96	102

The seasonal indexes for the other months, based on data 1919-1924,
are on a daily basis:

J.	77	J.	90
F.	85	A.	89
M.	—	S.	97
A.	—	O.	106
M.	98	N.	106
J.	94	D.	168

CHART 29.

DEPARTMENT STORE SALES, MAIL ORDER SALES.

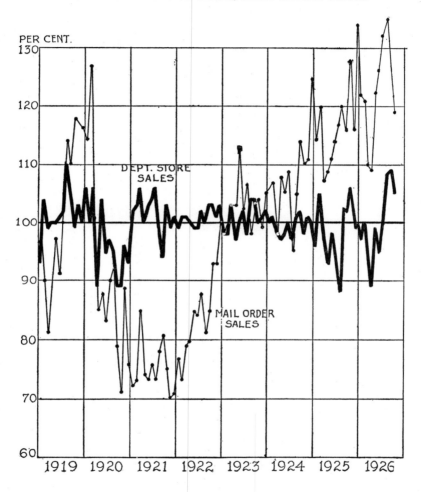

DEPARTMENT STORE SALES. See Chart 27, p. 110.

MAIL ORDER SALES. Total sales of 3 large companies. Price changes are allowed for by dividing the dollar totals by the U. S. Dept. of Labor cost of living index (interpolated from Massachusetts Commission on Necessaries of Life index of cost of living in Massachusetts).

Sources: Annual and monthly, Reports Department of the Federal Reserve Bank of N. Y. (partly confidential).

Trend: On sales divided by cost of living. Data for two companies only are known from 1911 to 1919. These figures are raised for this period by multiplying by the average ratio of the three companies to the two companies, 1919-1924. Parabola, 1913-1924 (omitting 1921, when the mail order business fell to a very low degree), origin 1913. $y = 1642.5 + 101.48x - 3.1925x^2$. The ordinates of the trend are divided by 306, the average working days per year, and the monthly totals, after allowance has been made for changes in the cost of living, are reduced to a daily basis. The number of working days in a month is estimated by subtracting from the total calendar days the number of Sundays and the following holidays: 1st January, 22nd February, 30th May, 4th July, Labor Day, Thanksgiving, 25th December.

Seasonal: On daily basis, 1919-1924.

J.	95	J.	73
F.	99	A.	72
M.	110	S.	98
A.	107	O.	125
M.	87	N.	130
J.	87	D.	117

CHART 30.

VOLUME OF TRADE, LIFE INSURANCE SALES.

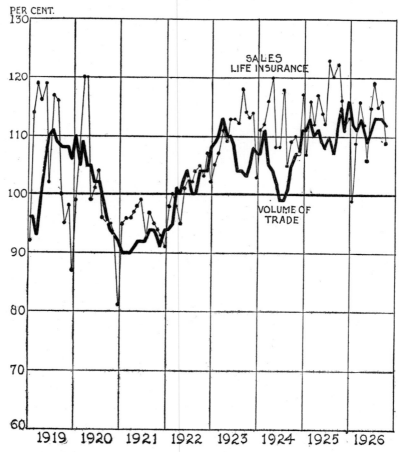

LIFE INSURANCE SALES. New ordinary paid for business (excluding group insurance) of companies having 88% of legal reserve ordinary business in force in the United States on January 1, 1923.

Sources: Annual, 1907-1912, Life Insurance Year Book, 1922. Monthly, 1913-1924, Life Insurance Sales Research Bureau: "Monthly Survey of Life Insurance Sales."

Trend: The trend is computed on the dollar sales divided by U. S. Dept. of Labor cost of living index (interpolated between quarters from the Massachusetts Commission index of the cost of living in Massachusetts). Log straight line, 1907-1924, origin 1907. log y = 2.07756 + .029064x.

Seasonal: 1921-1924,

J.	91	J.	96
F.	92	A.	92
M.	109	S.	84
A.	106	O.	98
M.	112	N.	96
J.	106	D.	118

CHART 31.

VOLUME OF TRADE, BUILDING PERMITS, REAL ESTATE
TRANSFERS.

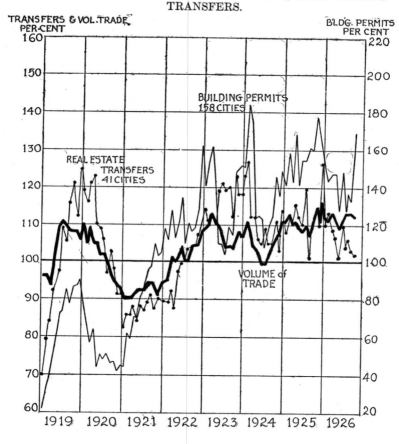

BUILDING PERMITS. Volume of building construction estimated from value of permits by dividing value by an index of building costs. The index is computed on the data for several series combined and adjusted to be equivalent to a series for 158 cities in the United States. From 1917-1925 actual annual data for 158 cities are totalled. From 1906 to 1916 link relatives, formed from Bradstreet's tabulations of 39-162 cities are applied to the data for the 158 cities (i.e., Bradstreet's 1916 data divided by their 1917 data gives a relative which is applied to the figure for the 158 cities in 1917 and so on). From 1900-1905, data from Leonard P. Ayres' tabulation for 50 cities, are multiplied by 1.281, which is the average ratio, 1906-1910, of the 158 cities (estimated as above) to the 50 cities. From 1894 to 1899, data from J. S. Meiklejohn's tabulation for 12-24 cities are multiplied by 5.401, which is the average ratio, 1900-1903 of the 158 cities (estimated from Ayres' tabulation) to the 12-24 cities. The monthly data from 1906-1925 are treated similarly to the annual data. From 1903-1905, however, the Harvard tabulation of 20 cities is multiplied by 1.687, which is the average ratio, 1906-1910 of the 158 cities (estimated from Bradstreet's tabulation) to the 20 cities. From 1900-1902, Meiklejohn's data for 12-24 cities are multiplied by .4413, which is the ratio for 1903 of the 158 cities (estimated from Harvard tabulation) to the 12-24 cities. These adjustments are made primarily for the purpose of getting a comparable series on which a trend can be computed. They are admittedly empirical, and the results can be considered as being approximations only. Comparison of this index, obtained by piecing together these several series with certain other indexes of building construction (one compiled by the Federal Reserve Bank for 3-7 cities extending from 1882 to date, one compiled by the F. W. Dodge Corporation, and others) shows sufficiently strong similarities to lend confidence to this series. Allowance for price changes, 1913 to date, is made by dividing the actual dollar value of permits for each month by an index of the cost of building weighted as follows: Index of the cost of building material (3), index of building wages (2). Before 1913, Leonard P. Ayres' index of the cost of building.

Sources: 158 cities: Research Section of the Federal Reserve Bank of New York, 1917 to date, monthly. 39-162 cities: Bradstreet's. 50 cities: Leonard P. Ayres' "The Prospects of Building Construction in American Cities" (1922. Cleveland Trust Co.). 20 cities: Harvard Review of Economic Statistics, Pre. vol. I, Jan., 1919, p. 74, and later issues. 12-24 cities: Research Section, Federal Reserve Bank of N. Y. Index of cost of building material: U. S. Department of Labor. Rates of building wages, 1913-1921: U. S. Department of Labor. 1921 to date: National Association of Builders' Exchanges. (Indexes compiled by Research Section of the Federal Reserve Bank of N. Y.)

Trend: On volume estimated from value. Straight line, 1895-1925, origin 1910. $y = 85.54 + 2.542x$.

Seasonal: The seasonal index shows a tendency towards a regular change from year to year. This tendency is marked in the months of February, April, June and December. Trends were, therefore, fit to the relatives of the actuals (price change allowed for) to a 12 months moving average for these months, as follows:

February, 1905-1923, origin 1914; $\log y = 1.85724 + .002377x$.
April, 1905-1923, origin 1914; $\log y = .10651 - .00287x$.
June, 1905-1923, origin 1914; $\log y = 2.07533 - .003743x$.
December, 1904-1922, origin 1913; $\log y = .89026 + .003249x$.

The trend ordinates were taken as the seasonals for these four months, and the other months were adjusted to them. The resulting indexes, 1919-1926, are as follows:

	1919	1920	1921	1922	1923	1924	1925	1926
January	74	74	74	74	75	75	75	76
February	74	75	75	75	76	76	77	77
March	120	120	120	120	120	120	120	120
April	124	123	122	121	120	120	119	118
May	121	120	120	120	119	119	119	119
June	114	113	112	112	111	110	109	108
July	110	110	110	110	110	110	110	110
August	104	104	104	105	105	105	105	105
September	96	97	97	97	97	97	97	97
October	95	95	96	96	96	97	97	97
November	86	87	87	87	87	87	87	87
December	82	82	83	83	84	84	85	86

REAL ESTATE TRANSFERS. Number of transfers for deeds, mortgages, and mortgage releases, etc., for 41 cities throughout the United States.

Sources: Annual, 1900-1924, National Association of Real Estate Boards. Monthly, 1916 to date, "News Service" of National Association of Real Estate Boards.

Trend: Log straight line, 1900-1924, origin 1912. log y = 1.17625 + .028379x on Atlanta, Ga., data, adjusted to 41 cities.

Seasonal: 1916-1924,

J.	95		J.	99
F.	84		A	98
M.	107		S.	97
A.	109		O.	105
M.	111		N.	97
J.	105		D.	93

Volume of Trade, (Chart 30) although the maxima and minima of the two series do not always synchronize. Life insurance sales show a variability about twice as great as the Volume of Trade Index and their own general group (secondary distribution). A combined index of the lineage of magazine and newspaper advertising gives interesting results. The movement is quite regularly cyclical, corresponding in all its important aspects to the Volume of Trade. (Chart 26.) Advertising reached tremendous heights in 1919-1920, because of the attempts partially to absorb war profits in advertising. This index has tended to deviate somewhat from the Volume of Trade in the prosperous period of 1924-1925, and has tended to stay below the "normal" line. The index of urban real estate transfers bears a fairly close cyclical resemblance to the Volume of Trade (Chart 31), although its range of fluctuations is considerably greater. It bears a general resemblance, as might be expected, to the volume of building, but this relationship is by no means invariable.

Those series grouped under the heading "General Business Activity" are, naturally, less specific indicators than the others which we have had under consideration. The group index corresponds more closely to the total Volume of Trade than has any group yet considered. The most important of these series are the ones representing debits to individual accounts. Since most of the business of the country is done by checks,[3] debits to individual accounts give a very accurate picture of the total business done at any time. The series representing total bank debits was divided into two separate series, one representing debits to accounts in New York City, and the other debits to accounts in 140 of the larger cities. This was necessary because, whereas debits in the country at large represent all phases of business activity, automatically weighted accord-

[3] Kemmerer has estimated the checks drawn as representing 80-85% of the total business of the country.

CHART 32.

VOLUME OF TRADE, DEBITS OUTSIDE N. Y. CITY, N. Y. CITY
DEBITS.

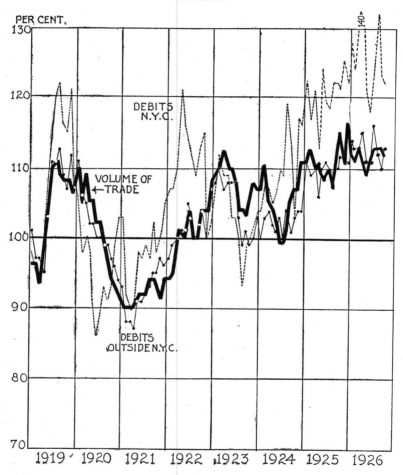

DEBITS OUTSIDE NEW YORK CITY. Total debits to individual accounts in 140 centers, outside New York City. Prior to 1919, debits are estimated from total outside bank clearings by multiplying clearings by 1.1395 (average ratio, 1919-1922 of debits to clearings).

Sources: Bank clearings outside New York City, 1881-1922, Financial Review, 1895, 1907, 1919, and Commercial and Financial Chronicle. Monthly debits in 140 centers, Federal Reserve Bulletin.

Trend: Trend is computed on dollar figures, divided by the General Price Level. For composition of General Price Level, see p. 138. Trend is a log parabola, 1881-1921, origin 1901. log y = 3.64833 + .019692x — .000172x². The monthly ordinates of the secular trend are adjusted to a daily basis by dividing by 25.25 (average number of working days for month). The monthly totals after allowance has been made for changes in the general price level are reduced to an average daily basis. The number of working days in a month is estimated by subtracting from the total calendar days the number of Sundays, and the following holidays, weighted as indicated: New Years (1), Washington's Birthday (1), 4th July (1), Labor Day (1), Thanksgiving (1), Christmas (1), Memorial Day (.95), Lincoln's Birthday (.7), Columbus Day (.9), Election Day (.8), Armistice Day (.6), Good Friday (.3). The weights were determined by the universality of the holiday. Holidays observed in all centers have weight of 1.

Seasonal: Daily basis, 1919-1925.

J.	102	J.	98
F.	100	A.	90
M.	97	S.	98
A.	99	O.	105
M.	97	N.	108
J.	98	D.	108

NEW YORK CITY DEBITS. Total debits to individual accounts in N. Y. City. Prior to 1919, debits are estimated by multiplying N. Y. City clearings by 1.05 (average ratio, 1919-22 of debits to clearings).

Sources: Same as for Debits Outside New York City.

Trend: Trend is computed on dollar figures, divided by the price level of New York City. Log straight line, 1898-1922, origin 1910. log y = 3.93634 + .010578x. The monthly ordinates of secular trend are adjusted to a daily basis by dividing by 25.3 (average number of working days per month). The monthly totals, after allowance has been made for price changes, are reduced to an average daily basis. The number of working days in a month is estimated by subtracting from the total calendar days the number of Sundays and the following holidays: 1st January, 12th and 22nd February, 30th May, 4th July, Labor Day, 12th October, Election Day, Thanksgiving Day, 25th December.

Seasonal: Daily basis, 1919-1924.

J.	104	J.	97
F.	102	A.	85
M.	99	S.	92
A.	98	O.	105
M.	100	N.	106
J.	103	D.	109

CHART 33.

VOLUME OF TRADE, ELECTRIC POWER PRODUCTION, POSTAL
RECEIPTS.

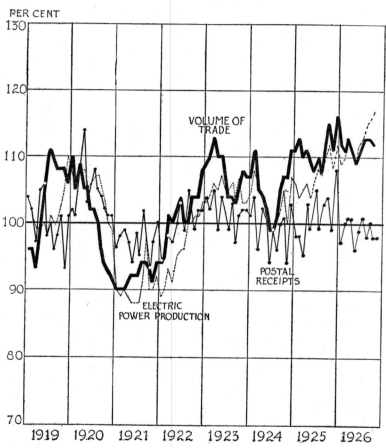

ELECTRIC POWER PRODUCTION. Total production of electric power in public utility plants in U. S. A.

Sources: Annual, 1907-1917, U. S. Census of Central Electric Light Power Stations, 1917. Monthly, 1919-1924, U. S. Geological Survey releases: "Production of Electric Power and Consumption of Fuel by Public Utility Plants in U. S." Feb. 4, 1925, and later issues.

Trend: Log parabola, 1912-1924 (estimated), origin 1912. log y = 4.24641 + .056157x — .0011205x^2.

Seasonal: 1919-1924,

J.	107	J.	97
F.	96	A.	98
M.	102	S.	97
A.	97	O.	102
M.	99	N.	103
J.	97	D.	105

POSTAL RECEIPTS. Receipts at 50 selected cities from sales of stamped paper, postage on second class matter mailed at pound rate, postage paid on matter mailed without stamps, and box rent.

Sources: Annual and monthly, U. S. Post Office Department, Information Service "Statement of Postal Receipts at 50 Selected Offices."

Trend: Log straight line monthly data, 1918-1921, origin Jan., 1920. log y = 4.28169 + .002646x.

Seasonal: 1914-1921,

J.	101	J.	86
F.	94	A.	88
M.	110	S.	96
A.	101	O.	107
M.	98	N.	103
J.	95	D.	121

CHART 34.

VOLUME OF TRADE, NEW CORPORATE FINANCING, SHARES
SOLD ON N. Y. STOCK EXCHANGE.

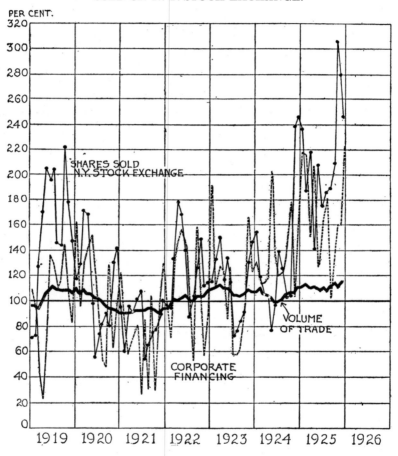

NEW CORPORATE FINANCING. Total domestic and foreign, including refunding.
    Sources: Annual, 1919-1925, January issues of Commercial and Finan-
    cial Chronicle. Monthly, Last issue each month of Commercial
    and Financial Chronicle.
    Trend: Trend difficult to determine. Index is per cent of monthly
    average, 1919-1922 (= 233.2 mill. dollars).
    Seasonal: No marked regular seasonal variation.

SHARES SOLD ON THE N. Y. STOCK EXCHANGE. Total number of shares sold.
    Sources: Annual, 1899-1920, Financial Review. Annual 1921 to date, and
    monthly 1900 to date, Commercial and Financial Chronicle, Bank and
    Quotation Section.
    Trend: 1900-1924, omitting 1914, origin 1900. log y = 5.24767 +
    .003095x.
    Seasonal: No marked regular seasonal variation.

CHART 35.

VOLUME OF TRADE, GRAIN EXPORTS, GRAIN FUTURE SALES.

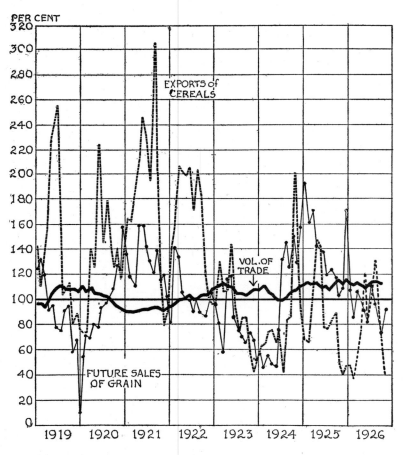

GRAIN EXPORTS. Total number of bushels of wheat, wheat flour, corn, oats, rye, and barley exported each month from the United States.

Sources: Annual, 1889-1924, Chicago Board of Trade Annual Reports, 1920 and 1924. Monthly, 1900-1924, U. S. Department of Commerce's "Monthly Summary of Foreign Commerce" and "Domestic Exports of Principal Grains and Grain Products."

Trend: Trend difficult to determine. Index = per cent of average, 1899-1922 (= 310.7 million bu.).

Seasonal: 1900-1914. Obtained from link relatives given in Harvard Review of Economic Statistics, 1919.

J.	97	J.	97
F.	86	A.	113
M.	77	S.	128
A.	68	O.	139
M.	67	N.	132
J.	80	D.	116

GRAIN FUTURE SALES. 1918-1920. Bushels estimated from dollar tax receipts on sales for future delivery, Chicago, by dividing total sales by average cash prices of grain (weights: wheat 53, corn 27, oats 20). 1921 to date, actual bushels of futures sold.

Sources: Annual, 1910-1918, Federal Trade Commission "Grain Trade," vol. V, p. 35, 1920. Monthly, 1918 to date, Reports from Illinois Customs District to Federal Reserve Bank of Chicago and U. S. Dept. of Agric., Report of Grain Futures Administration.

Trend: Straight line trend, 1910-1918, adjusted.

Seasonal: 1921-1925,			
J.	93	J.	97
F.	103	A.	96
M.	118	S.	95
A.	99	O.	104
M.	90	N.	96
J.	110	D.	99

CHART 36.

VOLUME OF TRADE, COTTON FUTURE SALES.

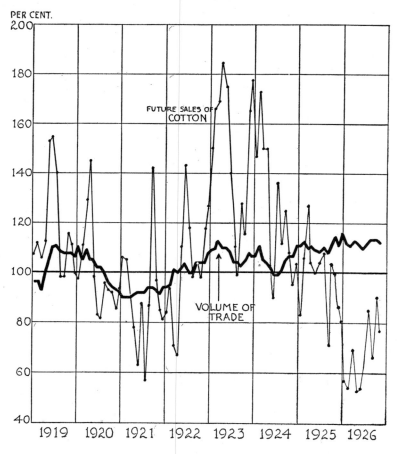

COTTON FUTURE SALES. Total bales estimated from tax receipts on sales for future delivery in New York and New Orleans, by dividing total sales by the average monthly cash price of cotton.

Sources: Annual and monthly tax receipts reported to Federal Reserve Bank of N. Y. by the New York Custom House, Cotton Futures Broker for the New York district, and obtained from the Federal Reserve Bank of Atlanta for the Louisiana Customs district.

Trend: Log straight line, 1918-1922, origin 1920. log y = 4.93665 + .027377x.

Seasonal: 1918-1922,

J.	97		J.	84
F.	81		A.	106
M.	80		S.	120
A.	80		O.	140
M.	83		N.	135
J.	84		D.	110

ing to the pecuniary importance of the different lines, debits in New York City represent, in large part, financial and speculative activity. It is evident that this would exaggerate and distort the picture of general business, since New York City debits include about 45% of all debits. Hence the separation of the two series and the greater weight given debits outside New York City. Chart 32 shows the relation of the two debits series to the Volume of Trade. Outside debits are almost perfectly correlated with the total Volume of Trade Index, both as regards the time movement and the amplitude of the fluctuations. The significance of this remarkable correlation will be discussed in the following chapter. New York City debits fluctuate more widely than the Volume of Trade, their range being from about 20% above to 15% below normal. They tend to synchronize with the Volume of Trade, the chief exceptions being the trough which was reached in New York City debits in 1920, ten months earlier than in the Volume of Trade, and the peak in May 1922 as against he Volume of Trade peak in March 1923. Postal receipts show a slight cyclical movement, with, however, a general correspondence to the cycles in the Volume of Trade (Chart 33). Since 1920, the receipts have varied scarcely more than 6% from normal. Electric power production shows a very smooth cyclical movement, corresponding both as to time of change and amplitude of fluctuations to the Volume of Trade. Electric power production is a very sensitive indicator of the activity in many different forms of business.

The most erratic group is, as might be expected, that representing financial or speculative activity. The whole group is, therefore, given a. weight of only six per cent in the total Volume of Trade. It includes series showing shares sold on the New York stock exchange, new corporate financing, the volume of future sales of grain, and the volume of future sales of cotton. The group index shows he same cyclical movement as that of the Volume of Trade (Chart 18), and does not, as has been claimed, forecast the Volume of Trade, but tends more often to synchronize with it. There are many peaks and troughs superimposed on the larger waves which have no counterpart in the Volume of Trade. The amplitude of the fluctuations is very much greater than in the Volume of Trade, varying between 30% below to 90% above normal. What is true of the financial group as to general agreement with the Volume of Trade, magnitude of fluctuations, and irregularity of month to month movement is true also of shares sold on the New York stock exchange, and corporate financing as is shown in Chart 34. Shares sold have varied from 50% below to 150% above normal, and corporate financing from 75% below to 120% above normal, a truly amazing range of variation. Grain futures have also shown an erratic movement, and have little connection with the Volume of Trade, but a somewhat general synchronism with the movement of grain exports (Chart 35). Cotton future sales likewise fluctuate wildly, and show relatively little connection with the Volume of Trade (Chart 36).

This detailed discussion of the similarities and differences existing in the components of the Volume of Trade leads to the conclusion that there is a great similarity in the time movement of the cycles in practically all of the series, so that the composite Index of Volume of Trade, to a high degree, reflects broad, general tendencies. It is not merely a weighted average, but strongly a mode as might reasonably be anticipated.

CHAPTER VI

BANK CLEARINGS AS A MEASURE OF BUSINESS CYCLES [1]

THE composite index of the Volume of Trade, discussed in the preceding chapter, is evolved by sampling and weighting the various elements of the industrial process. It seems probable that the sampling has been wide enough and the weighting reasonable enough to give us an accurate picture of the total volume of trade of the country. Unfortunately, this index cannot be computed for years earlier than 1919; for, prior to that date, the series available would not give a sampling sufficiently representative to form a satisfactory composite indicator of the total volume of trade. There is, however, one process in the industrial system which is peculiarly sensitive to changes in every phase of business, and which reflects the whole trade of the country and weights it automatically according to the pecuniary importance of the factors involved. That process is the payments made by bank checks; for, in this country, 80 per cent or more of payments of all kinds, in the exchange of goods, property, and services are made by means of bank checks. We have, since 1919, a very accurate index of payments by bank checks, through the compilation of debits to individual accounts. Before 1919, we have a comparable series in the compilation of checks going through the clearing houses. Debits are, of course, a fuller record, and their totals are larger than are clearings, but they follow the same general trend, and correspond almost

[1] A large part of this chapter is based on two articles by the author appearing in the Quarterly Journal of the American Statistical Association for June, 1924, and September, 1924.

exactly, even in the minor fluctuations, to the clearings
figures for the five years for which we have the data of
both series. It is possible, therefore, to construct a long,
comparable series by raising clearings prior to 1919 to
the level of estimated debits by multiplying clearings by
the average ratio they bear to debits from 1919-1922:

$$\frac{\text{Debits}}{\text{Clearings}} = 1.14.$$

This gives a monthly series running from 1875 to date.

There is such a close relationship between our Volume
of Trade Index and the index of bank debits outside New
York [2] that, if we likewise reduce bank clearings to a volu-
metric basis, it will be possible to consider it a very satisfactory extrapolation of our Index of the Volume of Trade.

There are many problems involved in eliminating the
distortion caused by price changes from the bank debits
series. It is obvious from Chart 37 how great this distortion was during the War. The various estimates of physical production which have been made all show that the
increases during the War were no greater than in some
previous periods in the boom phase of the business
cycle. It is, therefore, probable that the trend of clearings
corrected for prices would, during the War and post-war
period, be a continuation of the pre-war tendencies, i.e., it
is improbable that there has been any sudden break or
change of direction in the general growth. This gives us
an *a priori* basis for estimating the amount of distortion
that was caused by war-time inflation. The problem then
becomes one of forming an index of prices which, when
debits are expressed on its base, will reduce them to a continuation of the pre-war trend. Debits will be affected by
changes in the general level of all prices, and it is, there-

[2] Bank debits outside New York City represent about 55 per cent of the
total. N. Y. C. debits, representing 45% of the total, are so largely influenced by financial and speculative transactions that they are invalidated
as a business indicator.

CHART 37.

INDEX OF THE GENERAL PRICE LEVEL, COMPARED WITH WHOLESALE PRICES AND WAGES.

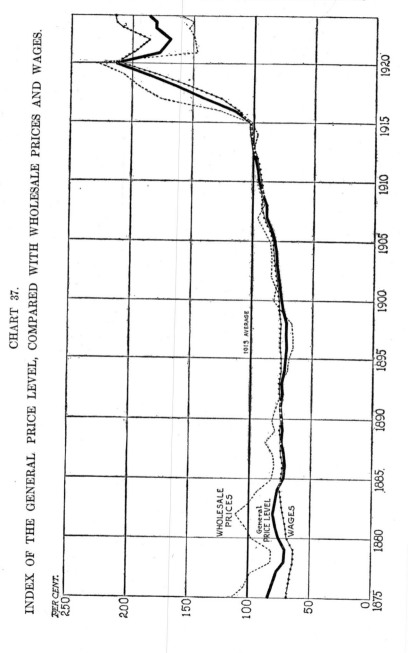

The General Price Level is a weighted index (1913 = 100), weights assigned as described on p. 138.

The sources for the components of this index are as follows:

Commodity Prices at Wholesale: 1875-1889, Monthly Index of Basic Commodities compiled by Federal Reserve Bank of New York; 1890-1899, monthly figures interpolated from quarterly series of the United States Department of Labor; 1900 to date, Department of Labor monthly index.

Wages: 1875-1913, Department of Labor annual index of unskilled labor; 1914 to date, earnings in New York State factories and Federal Reserve Bank index of Average Weekly Hiring Rate for Unskilled Labor. Wages of teachers and clerks, 1875-1913, Burgess' "Trend of School Costs"; 1914 to date, average wages for teachers in the United States, Research Bulletin, Journal of the National Education Association, March, 1923. Wages of clerical workers in New York State factories, 1914 to date, New York State Department of Labor.

Cost of Living: 1875-1889, estimates of family budgets compiled by Russell Sage Foundation; 1890-1909, Cost of Living index estimated from retail food index of United States Department of Labor; 1910 to date, United States Department of Labor index for 32 cities; monthly figures interpolated from data published by Massachusetts Commission on the Necessaries of Life.

Rents: 1875-1913, special study on rents by Russell Sage Foundation, unpublished; 1913 to date, Shelter Index compiled by United States Department of Labor; monthly figures interpolated between annual and quarterly figures.

See Appendix, Table 23, A, B, C, D, pp. 286-291.

fore, necessary to construct a very representative price index, and to weight its components as nearly as possible in accordance with their importance. We have available indexes of wholesale prices, the cost of living, wages, rent, security prices, etc., but we have no specific knowledge as to how much each one contributes to the total of bank clearings. We can, however, form rough estimates for the purpose of weighting, and these weights can be shifted to approximate the index that has seemed *a priori* probable. An empirical index was computed, giving something like equal weights to commodity prices, wages, and the cost of living, and one-third as much for stock prices. When bank debits were corrected by the index the pre-war trend was continued in such a way as to fulfill satisfactorily our *a priori* conditions.

There is a more precise test of the validity of this index of the general price level. For reasons stated in the preceding chapter, our index of the Volume of Trade is thought to be quite representative of the total trade of the country, and ought, therefore, to correspond closely to corrected bank debits. If, then, we divide the bank debits (deviations from the normal, uncorrected for price changes) by the Volume of Trade Index, the resultant should conform closely to the price index which we have computed empirically. This result did conform closely, and the empirical weights for the price index were shifted slightly to make the conformity even closer. These weights, as finally used, were:

Commodity prices at wholesale 2
Composite of wage payments 3½
Cost of living 3½
Rents 1

It is, then, quite probable that this index will remove the greater part of the influence of a changing price level from the bank debits series, and we are in a position to form a measure of business cycles over a long period of time which

CHART 38.

BANK CLEARINGS OUTSIDE N. Y. CITY, AN INDEX OF THE
GENERAL PRICE LEVEL, BANK CLEARINGS DIVIDED
BY THE GENERAL PRICE LEVEL.

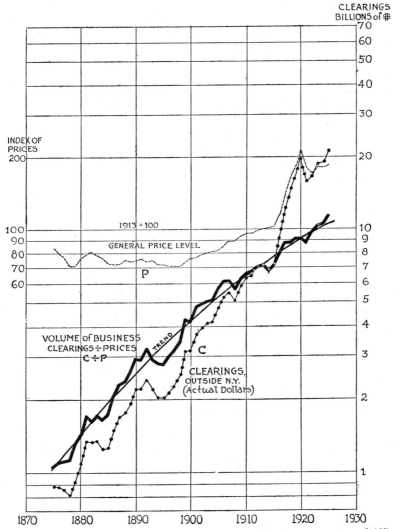

See Appendix, Tables 18, p. 277, and 23, p. 286, for data; pp. 123 and 137,
for sources. (Annual data on clearings have been reduced to monthly
averages here.)

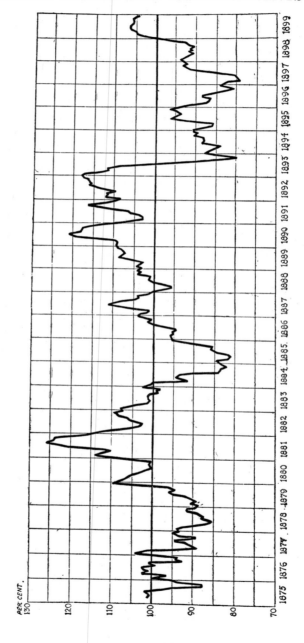

CHART 39.

A CLEARINGS INDEX OF BUSINESS.

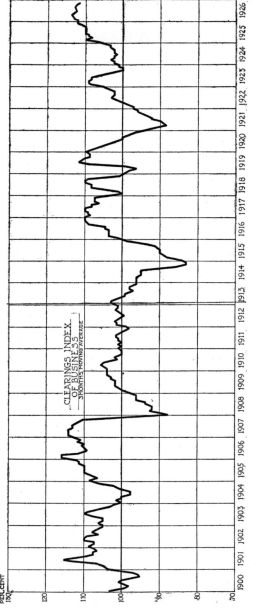

See Appendix, Table 24, p. 292.

conforms closely to our Volume of Trade Index, and which we may therefore consider an extrapolation of our Volume of Trade.

Chart 38 shows the series for outside bank clearings raised to the debits level, and also the estimated general price level. It can readily be seen how the clearings have followed the price movements, and how this price movement has obscured the secular and cyclical elements in clearings. The distortion was relatively slight in the earlier years, when there was a very gradual deflation or inflation of the currency, but the violence of price changes from 1916 to 1922 largely obscured every other factor. The result of eliminating the price distortion is also shown in this chart in the series entitled "Volume of Business," which represents clearings divided by the general price level. To this series a secular trend has been fitted and it takes the form characteristic of the growth in so many of the series discussed in Chapter II, i.e., a parabolic curve with a decrescent rate of growth. Up till about 1900 the high rate of growth represents less a real increase in the volume of business than it does in the establishment of new clearing houses, but from 1900 there has been a stable and consistent line of growth, with practically no interfering factors. The rate of growth has been about 3½ per cent per year, approximating the rates of growth which we found to be characteristic of general production.

After correcting these bank debits and clearings for price change, seasonal variation, and secular trend, we get the result shown in Chart 39, "A Clearings Index of Business." This shows quite clearly the large wave-like movements in business for the last half century. There was a depression in the seventies, with a recovery in 1878, culminating in the boom of 1881, and followed by a sharp recession in that same year. In 1884 and 1885 came the trough of this depression, but towards the end of 1885 business was rapidly approaching normal. From 1887 until 1893 business was generally at a very high level, but was followed by a crisis and recession in 1893, and a depression as prolonged as the preceding prosperity, extending from 1893 to the end of 1898. The recovery of 1898-1899 was but slightly checked in 1900, and a high degree of prosperity was held from 1901 to 1904, when, after the "Rich Man's Panic," business receded for a few months, to reach an even higher level of prosperity in 1905-6-7. After the panic of 1907 came a deep depression in 1908, but business had recovered to normal by the spring of 1909. It remained dull, but usually above normal, through 1912, with a gradual recession in 1913 and a depression in 1914. In 1915 there was a recovery, and 1916 saw the beginning of the war boom, which held quite well, with a slight recession in 1918, through most of 1920. From 1919 through 1922 the Clearings Index corresponds almost exactly to the Volume of Trade Index, and in subsequent years this congruence has continued, with occasional deviations.

We have, then, through our Composite Index of the Volume of Trade, and our Clearings Index of Business, an adequate indicator of the cycles of business for fifty years or more. An interesting tendency suggested by this long-time index is that depressions are lessening in severity. The depth of the troughs is not quite so much below normal in the 1914 and 1908 depressions as in those of 1884 and 1894, and the depressions in the latter half of the period have been matters of months whereas previously they extended over years.

CHAPTER VII

VELOCITY OF BANK DEPOSITS AS A MEASURE OF BUSINESS CYCLES [1]

IT HAS long been familiar to bankers that in times of prosperity the rate at which deposits are checked out has been notably greater than in times of depression. With little relative variation in the amount of deposits, the amount of checks drawn against these deposits will tend to vary widely with successive phases of the business cycle. It was interesting to discover that actually in the variations in the velocity of bank deposits was found a very sensitive barometer of business. Chart 40 shows the Volume of Trade Index and two samplings of the velocity of bank deposits in the United States, one representing the 141 reporting centres used in debits, and the other representing nine cities, viz., Boston, New York, Albany, Syracuse, Rochester, Buffalo, Binghamton, Chicago, and San Francisco. The larger swings of the velocity series show a very close relationship to the larger swings in the Volume of Trade Index, both as regards the time element and the amplitude of the fluctuations. The only notable differences in the movement are the slowness of velocity to fall in the depression of 1920-'21, and again its lag in rising in the prosperity of 1922-'23.

The exact statistical meaning of the "velocity of bank

[1] Several papers published by the author form the basis of this chapter. These are "A New Index of Business Activity," Quarterly Publication of the American Statistical Association, March, 1924, "Deposits Activity as a Measure of Business Activity," The Review of Economic Statistics, Oct., 1924; "New Measures of the Business Cycle," Harvard Business Review, Oct., 1924; and "Turnover of Deposits a Measure of Business Activity," Journal of the American Bankers Association, Feb., 1924.

deposits" is the ratio of the amount of checks drawn each month in any particular centre to the average of demand deposits for that month in that centre. It represents the number of times, on the average, that a dollar of demand deposits is paid out in a particular centre for a specific unit of time. The accurate compilation of velocity was made possible only after the Federal Reserve Board had inaugurated the system of reporting debits to individual accounts in the larger cities of the country. Deposits are also reported very fully by the reporting banks of the Federal Reserve System. It happens that the series representing net demand deposits (from about 700 banks in 100 cities) and those representing debits (from clearing-house groups in 141 centres) are not exactly comparable; so, precise computations were first made for the nine cities named above, which were highly representative of all sections of the country, and for which exactly comparable data are obtainable.

For the statistical problems which arose in computing the ratios, a formula was worked out, through the cooperation of Professor Irving Fisher, Professor E. W. Kemmerer, and Mr. J. H. Riddle, then of the Reports Department of the Federal Reserve Bank of New York. This formula brought about adjustments which enabled a direct comparison of demand deposits and checks drawn.[2]

[2] For a full account, see W. R. Burgess, "Velocity of Bank Deposits," Journal of the American Statistical Association, June, 1923, pp. 727-740. Burgess describes the steps in the computation as follows: "Certain adjustments were necessary before a direct comparison could be made of demand deposits of individuals and checks drawn against such deposits. From the figures for checks drawn, or debits, certain deductions had to be made for withdrawals of time and Government deposits. Withdrawals of time deposits were estimated by computations made for six New York City banks for a number of different periods, which showed an average rate of turnover of time deposits at a rate of two times a year. Exact figures were available for Government withdrawals. Net demand deposit reports were amended by subtracting from them the net amounts due to banks, which were shown in New York City by the records but for other cities were estimated from the relative proportion of net amounts due to banks to net demand deposits shown by the total figures reported for all reporting banks in the different cities. A sample computation, which indicates the various adjustments necessary before arriving at a ratio between checks

CHART 40.

VOLUME OF TRADE, VELOCITY OF BANK DEPOSITS, 141 CITIES,
VELOCITY OF BANK DEPOSITS, 9 CITIES.

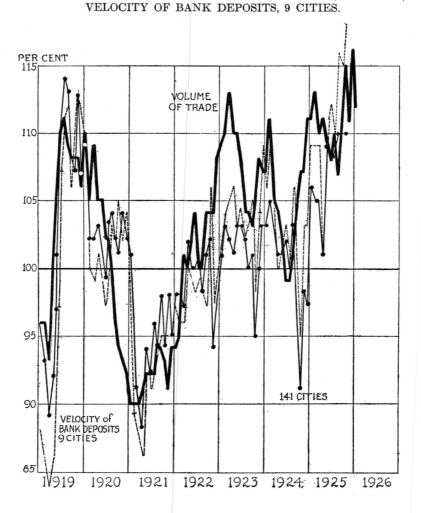

See Appendix, Table 25, p. 294 ff., for the original data, 141 cities, and each of the nine cities separately; Table 26, p. 299, for index of 141 cities.

Source: Reports to Federal Reserve Bank of N. Y.

Base of Indexes: Average turnover rates, 1919-1925.

141 cities	41.4
Chicago	45.0
N. Y. City	77.1
Boston	34.9
San Francisco	39.6
Albany	28.8
Binghamton	22.2
Buffalo	22.2
Rochester	22.4
Syracuse	9.5

SEASONAL INDEXES

	New York City	141 Cities	Chicago	Boston	San Francisco	Albany	Binghamton	Buffalo	Rochester	Syracuse
Jan.	104	102	101	103	98	98	101	105	102	97
Feb.	104	102	105	99	98	100	101	98	97	95
Mar.	104	100	104	104	106	93	95	94	96	96
Apr.	104	99	103	106	103	99	106	97	99	102
May	102	99	98	99	99	100	104	98	96	99
June	100	100	100	102	99	106	104	100	106	102
July	96	95	97	96	95	100	105	103	98	102
Aug.	84	87	91	81	91	93	86	92	91	89
Sept.	91	95	98	92	105	96	91	96	102	98
Oct.	101	105	99	104	101	99	100	105	104	106
Nov.	104	106	99	104	101	101	100	105	103	109
Dec.	106	110	105	110	104	115	107	107	106	107

The actual rates of turnover vary widely as between cities. Thus, as shown clearly in Chart 41, the annual rate of turnover in New York City is between 60 and 90, in Chicago between 40 and 50, in San Francisco between 35 and 45, in Boston between 25 and 45, and the five New York State cities show a turnover ranging between 7 and 50 (the average of the five cities ranges between 18 and 25). This variation seems to be in fairly close proportion to the population of the cities, but is even closer to the

drawn and demand deposits of individuals, is shown in Table I. As the table indicates, the figures were converted to an annual rate of turnover." (p. 729.)

TABLE I

METHOD OF COMPUTING VELOCITY OF BANK DEPOSITS

42 NEW YORK CITY REPORTING BANKS

000 omitted except columns 6, and 12

	1	2	3	4	5	6
Week ended	Debits to individual accounts total for each week	Time deposits ÷ 26 (to be subtracted)	Government withdrawals each week (to be subtracted)	Revised debits for each week	Total debits each month	Number of working days in each month
1922						
Jan. 4.....	$4,529,355	$7,120	......	$4,522,235	....	..
11.....	4,592,367	7,370	$5,884	4,579,113	....	..
18.....	4,766,247	7,196	16,884	4,742,167	....	..
25.....	3,933,296	7,367	6,233	3,919,696	$18,571,486	25
Feb. 1.....	4,233,272	7,333	......	4,225,939	....	..

	7	8		9	10	11	12
Week ended 1922	Average daily debits	Annual rate of debits col. 7 × 302 (working days in year)	Date	Net demand deposits	Net due to banks (to be subtracted)	Revised demand deposits (average)	Annual rate of turnover of deposits (col. 8 ÷ col. 11)
Jan. 4.....	....	....	1922 Jan. 4..	$3,866,822	$804,960	....	...
11.....	....	....	11..	3,850,902	799,187	....	...
18.....	....	....	18..	3,788,338	781,546	....	...
25.....	$742,859	$224,343,418	25..	3,754,903	782,753	$3,023,130	74.2
Feb. 1.....	....	....	....	....	....	....	...

Comments:

Column 2: An investigation in New York City showed that time deposits turned over on the average about twice a year. Checks drawn against time deposits each week therefore amount to about 2/52, or 1/26, of the amount of time deposits.

Column 5: In arriving at the monthly figures, the debits for weeks at the beginning and end of the month are included in proportion to the number of working days falling within the month. For example, 2/5 of the debits of the week ended January 4 and 5/6 of the debits of the week ended February 1, are included in January.

Column 10: This column is the excess of "Due to Banks" over "Due from Banks." If there is no excess, no correction is made.

CHART 41.

VELOCITY OF BANK DEPOSITS (ACTUAL RATES OF TURNOVER)

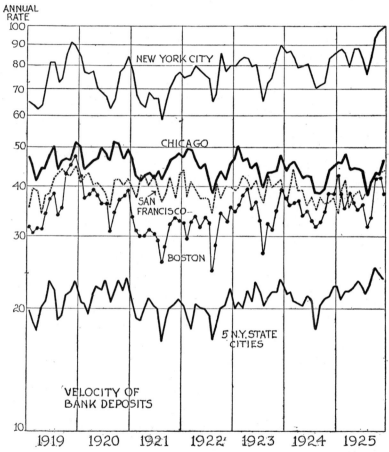

Sources, data etc. See note to Chart 40, p. 146, and Appendix, Table 25, pp. 294 ff.

amount of bank deposits in the cities. The greater the extent of the financial operations in any city, the more rapid is the turnover of the bank deposits. The rate of turnover for the country as a whole is estimated as between 25 and 35.

In the combined weighted index of the nine cities, New York was given a weight of 1 as against a weight of 2 for the average of the other eight cities. Theoretically, the weighting for New York should be somewhat higher, since the best estimates place New York debits as 45 per cent of those of the whole country, but the New York weighting was damped down because of the supposed undue influence of speculation on New York City debits, and because the other eight cities were thought to be geographically and commercially representative of a wide range of activities.

There was no observable secular trend in the velocity series, but a rather marked seasonal variation. The index was, therefore, computed by taking the percentage deviations of the actual turnover, corrected for seasonal variation, from the average turnover 1919-1924.

Then having made an accurate computation of the velocity in a sample of nine cities, it was thought worth while to extend the sample to a larger number of cities, even though the same degree of accuracy could not hold. As noted above, net demand deposits are reported weekly to the Federal Reserve Board by 700 banks from 100 cities, and these deposits are not from exactly the same cities as are the debits reported from 141 centres. A careful comparison of the totals of the debits of the 100 cities with the 141 centres showed, however, that there was little difference even in the crude totals, and that the fluctuations in the two series were exactly comparable. It was interesting, therefore, to compute the rate of turnover of demand deposits for the 100 cities against the debits for the 141 centres, even though the resulting ratios would tend to be too high. The result obtained by this method, which was less detailed but contained far wider sampling than in the case of the nine cities, was a high degree of congruence with the smaller and more accurate sampling.

Because of the close connection between the cycles in the velocity of bank deposits and the cycles in the Volume of Trade Index, it was highly desirable to know how far back this connection has existed; that is, to obtain, if possible, some measure of velocity over a long period and test its congruence with the Clearings Index of Business.

There were many difficulties in the way of obtaining any reasonable sort of a computation of velocity over a long period. An attempt to extract a comparable set of velocity figures from the demand deposits in National Banks (available back to 1909) was not satisfactory. The sampling of demand deposits, as shown alike by those of the National Banks for the whole country and for the reserve cities alone proved useless. An attempt was finally made to use the global figures of individual deposits which included time and demand deposits. There was also some further difficulty with these figures due to the fact that the individual deposits in the National Banks grew for a time more rapidly than the amount of clearings reported for the country, resulting in a slow but irregular secular decline in the rates of turnover. Due to the irregularity of this secular movement, the only logical trend seemed to be a moving average, and, after much experimentation, a seven-year moving average seemed to give the most satisfactory results. The series finally used, then, was based on the total individual deposits in National Banks and the total clearings for the country, with corrections for secular trend and seasonal variation.

This result is shown in Chart 42, plotted against the Clearings Index of Business. Here again a very remarkable degree of congruence is found to exist, both with regard to the time movement, and the amplitude of the fluctuations. There are, of course, exceptions to this gen-

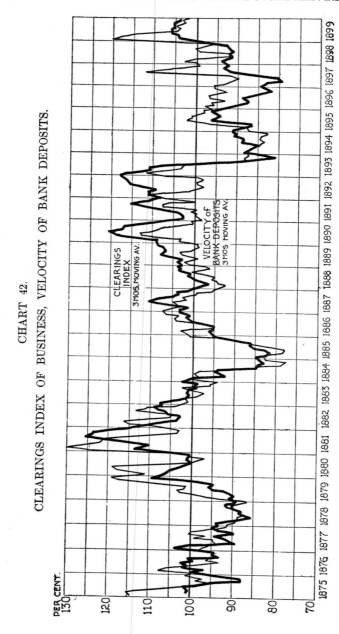

CHART 42.

CLEARINGS INDEX OF BUSINESS, VELOCITY OF BANK DEPOSITS.

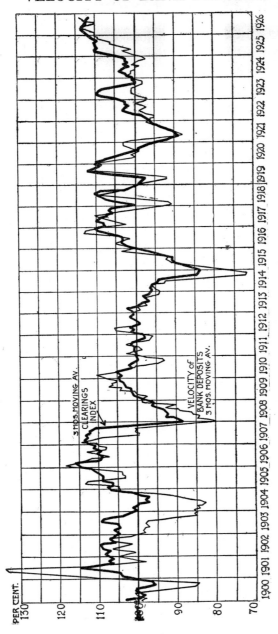

See Appendix, Table 26, p. 299, and Table 24, p. 292.

eral rule of congruence, as, for example, in the upward lead of velocity in 1878-'9, the downward lead of velocity in 1886-'7, 1895, and again in 1903, and the greater amplitude of the fluctuations in velocity in the periods 1879-1881 and 1900-1904. Bearing in mind, however, the nature of the material used, it is remarkable indeed that so great a congruence is found to exist.

The conclusion arises that the activity of bank deposits is actually a feasible measure of business activity, and, with due reservations as to the limitations of the methods of computation, may usefully be employed as such. This long-time series representing velocity is of a much lower order of accuracy than the long-time Clearings Index of Business, but it affords an interesting corroboration of our use of the Clearings Index as an index of business activity.

CHAPTER VIII

OTHER MEASURES OF BUSINESS CYCLES

IT is interesting to compare these results with some previous measures of the fluctuations of trade over an extended period.

One of the best-known and most widely used of the composite curves is that which was computed by the Comptroller's Department of the American Telephone and Telegraph Company. This index has been described by M. C. Rorty in the Harvard Business Review.[1] In 1923, it was composed of the following series [2] weighted as indicated:

Rorty says of this index [3] that it "is a composite of several of the best long-term statistical series, which have been specially selected because of the conformity of their movements with what seem to be the basic changes in production and distribution. However, it includes no measures of agricultural activity or retail trade, except as such items are indirectly reflected in freight movements and bank clearings, and it includes only a very limited list of non-agricultural raw materials. It is, therefore, primarily a measure of manufacturing activity and the physical movement of commodities. Nevertheless, with all these limitations, it represents, perhaps, as serviceable an approach as

---

[1] M. C. Rorty: "The Statistical Control of Business Activities," Harvard Business Review, Jan., 1923, pp. 154-166.

[2] Loc. cit., p. 160.

Pig Iron Production	20	Cotton Consumption	10
Unfilled orders, U. S. Steel		Activity wool machinery	10
Corporation	10	Paper Production	10
Freight Car Demand	10	Lumber Production	5
Car Loadings	5	Leather Production	5
Net freight ton miles	5	Power Production	5
Coal Production	5		

[3] Loc. cit., p. 159.

CHART 43.

CLEARINGS INDEX OF BUSINESS, HARVARD INDEX OF TRADE, A. T. & T. GENERAL BUSINESS INDEX.

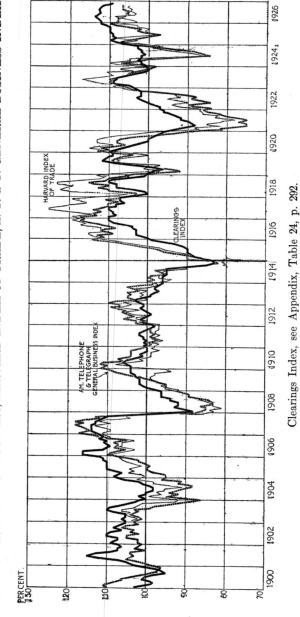

Clearings Index, see Appendix, Table 24, p. 292.

Harvard & A. T. & T. Index, see preceding page and p. 160, for sources and descriptions of the construction of these indexes.

can be made to a single 'all purpose' business index." The index was constructed on principles similar to the indexes of trade already described; i.e., allowance has been made for seasonal and secular change, and the index expressed as a percentage of a computed normal. Chart 43 shows this index, which extends from 1877,[4] plotted against the Clearings Index of Business from 1900 to 1924. The same cycles appear in the two indexes but there is not entire synchronism between them. The Clearings Index preceded the A. T. and T. index by about six months on the up-grade in 1907-'8, and lagged by about the same amount in the slight depression of 1911. It lagged also in the up-grade of 1915-'16, preceded in the high point of 1919-'20 and in the down-grade of 1920-'21, and lagged again in the upward movement of 1924. At other times, the two curves have shown synchronous movements. The amplitude of

---

[4] The index does not contain the same series over the whole period, for "there have been successive additions of new series, accompanied by an elimination of a smaller number of the older and less satisfactory series. The reliability of the curve is, therefore, somewhat greater in recent than in earlier years" (Rorty, op. cit., p. 160).

We are indebted to the American Telephone and Telegraph Company for a statement in regard to these eliminations and additions: from 1877 to 1884 the curve is based upon the cycles of active blast-furnace capacity, from 1885 to 1891 an average of cycles of blast-furnace capacity and bank clearings outside New York City, and from 1892 to 1903 an average of the cycles of blast-furnace capacity, bank clearings outside New York, and Bradstreet's wholesale commodity price index. In 1903, the U. S. Bureau of Labor Statistics wholesale commodity price index was substituted for Bradstreet's index and pig iron production for blast-furnace capacity and two new series were added: Bradstreet's index of failures, and railroad gross revenues. A series on the production of copper was added in January, 1909. At this point also, a series on freight car demand was substituted for railroad gross earnings. Beginning with 1913, coal production and cotton consumption were added to the curve. In June, 1920, a change was made in the series on freight car demand. In 1921, a series on debits to individual accounts in banks outside New York was substituted for the series on bank clearings. At this time, also, the series on prices and failures were eliminated from the composite curve. Series on unfilled orders of the U. S. Steel Corporation, wool consumption, and the production of paper, lumber, and leather were added in January, 1921. In April, 1922, debits to individual accounts and figures on copper production were eliminated, and figures on the activity of wool machinery were substituted for the series on wool consumption. A further change at this time consisted in the addition of data on freight car loadings, net ton miles of revenue and non-revenue freight, and power production.

CHART 44.

CLEARINGS INDEX OF BUSINESS COMPARED WITH PRODUCTION INDEXES

Normal = 100

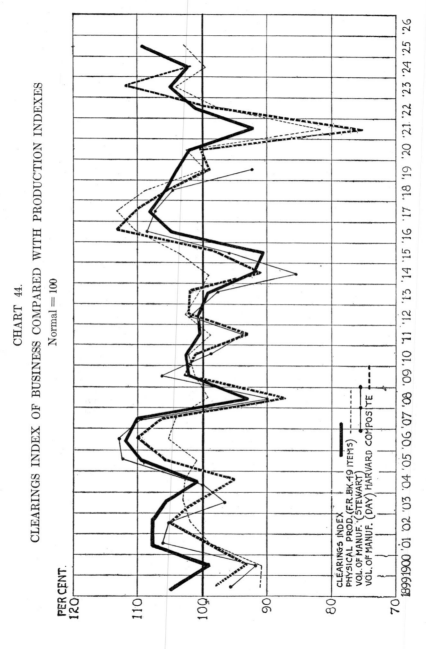

Sources: Clearings Index and Physical Production (49 items) in per cent of normal, Reports Department, Federal Reserve Bank of New York.— Volume of Manufacturing (Stewart), original on 1911-1913 base, American Economic Review, March, 1921, p. 68. (Per cent of normal computed by Federal Reserve Bank of New York.)—Volume of Manufacturing (Day), Harvard Review of Economic Statistics, July, 1925, p. 208.

fluctuations in the A. T. and T. curve is somewhat greater than in the Clearings Index, particularly in the post-war period. These differences can largely be accounted for by the heavy weighting of basic production in the A. T. and T. curve, and the absence in this curve of the stabilizing factors of retail trade. The amplitude of fluctuation corresponds more nearly to the index of productive activity (Chapter V, Chart 17), than to the Volume of Trade or Clearings Index.

A similar composite index is the Harvard Index of Trade, (Chart 43) constructed by Warren M. Persons.[5] This index is "designed to give a view of the combined fluctuations of trade, transportation, manufacturing activity, and industrial employment in the United States, month by month, since 1903." [6] From 1903-1915, the index was an unweighted average of the following series, (the average multiplied by the standard deviation of bank clearings):

Bank clearings outside New York.
Imports of merchandise.
Gross earnings of 10 leading railroads.
Production of pig iron.
Industrial employment.

For the war and post-war periods, weighted averages of the following series were used, with weights as indicated:

1915-1919		1919-1923	
Net ton miles of freight	2	Total railroad car loadings	6
Production of pig iron	1	Production of pig iron	1
Raw cotton consumed	1	Production of steel ingots	1
Industrial employment	2	Raw cotton consumed	1
		Industrial employment	3

Very much the same may be said of the relationship of the Harvard index to the Clearings Index as was said about the American Telephone and Telegraph index and the Clearings Index. The same cycles are shown, but there are

[5] Warren M. Persons: "An Index of Trade for the United States," Harvard Review of Economic Statistics, April, 1923, pp. 71-78.
[6] Loc. cit., p. 71.

marked differences both in the time movement and the amplitude of the fluctuations. The same reason for the differences appears to obtain; i.e., that the Harvard index is heavily weighted for the production and movement of basic commodities, and is, therefore, more nearly a representation of productive activity than of the volume of general trade.

It is of interest also to compare the annual averages of the Clearings Index with various measures of annual production in basic industries. Chart 44 shows the Clearings Index of Business plotted with the indexes of production discussed in Chapter II. The production indexes move together fairly well, but not always in exact synchronism. Stewart's index reached a low point in 1903, Day's in 1904, and the Federal Reserve Bank's in 1905. Day's and Stewart's both reached their high point in 1916, and the Bank's in 1917. Otherwise, the movements in the three series synchronize quite well.

In addition to these composites, there have been frequent attempts to use a single series as a barometer of business. The Clearings Index of Business is, of course, a single series, but is representative of all phases of business in which payment by checks enters as a factor, and, therefore, should be considered in the category of composites. But most other single barometers receive their justification on quite another ground; i.e., because the very close interrelations existing in capitalistic enterprise cause reverberations and repercussions from the fluctuations in certain basic series all through the industrial system. There is little doubt that this is true with regard to the major swings, but, for several reasons, it may be unwise to consider these basic series as truly representative of the cyclical movement in the volume of trade. They may be over-sensitive, and respond more quickly or more violently than general business; and, more important still, they are each of them subject to fluctuations due to the inherent nature of particular industries,

CHART 45.

CLEARINGS INDEX OF BUSINESS FOR HALF A CENTURY

Compared with Pig Iron Production

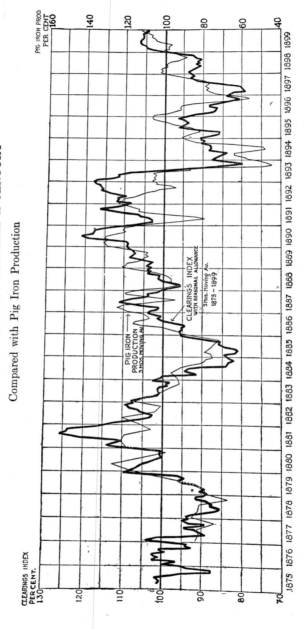

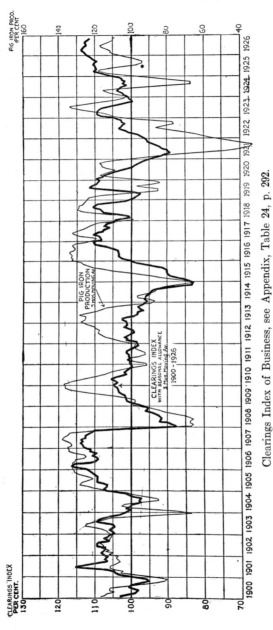

Clearings Index of Business, see Appendix, Table 24, p. 292.

Index of Pig Iron Production. Sources, see notes Chart 19, p. 85, and Appendix, Tables 5, p. 242, and 27, p. 300.

CHART 46.

CLEARINGS INDEX OF BUSINESS AND INDEX OF RAILWAY FREIGHT TRAFFIC.

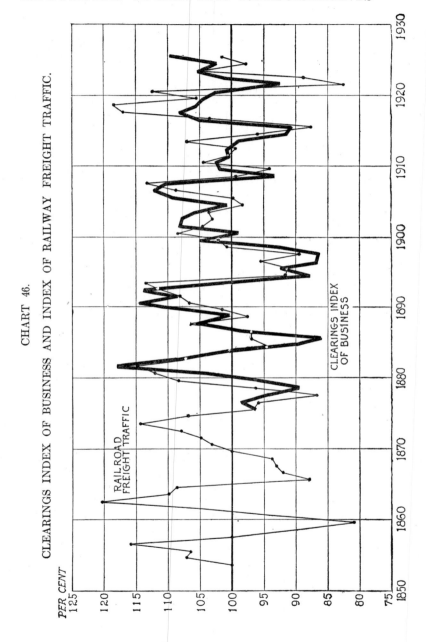

Clearings Index of Business, see Appendix, Table 24, p. 292.
Index of Railway Freight Traffic.
Sources, see Chart 8, p. 38; data, Appendix, Tables 2, p. 238, and 28, p. 304.

CHART 47.

VOLUME OF TRADE, ELECTRIC POWER PRODUCTION AND
MERCHANDISE AND MISCELLANEOUS CAR LOADINGS.

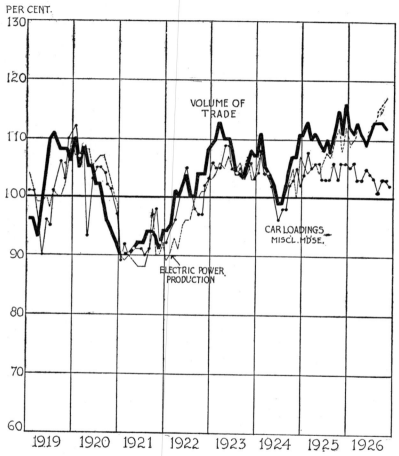

Volume of Trade Index, see Chapter V.

Index of Electric Power Production, see Chart 33, p. 124, and Appendix, Table 19, p. 279.

Index of Car Loadings, Merchandise (L. C. L.) and Miscellaneous, see Chart 22, p. 98, and Appendix, Table 8, p. 264.

which will have no counterpart in the movements of general trade.

In the absence of better indicators, however, certain series representing important industries may be taken as indicative of general trade. Probably the most frequently used of such barometers is the series representing pig iron production. It is reasonable to suppose that this series would indicate the cycles in industry, for our industrial development over the past fifty or one hundred years has been closely bound up with the development of the iron trade. Chart 45 shows the relation of pig iron cycles to the Clearings Index of Business. The time relationship was very close until the last fifteen or twenty years. The relative fluctuations were also quite comparable in the two series (the absolute amplitude of fluctuations in pig iron being twice that of clearings). A careful examination, even of these earlier years, shows, however, that there were erratic movements in pig iron, as, for example, the sharp drop in 1887, which have no counterparts in general trade. The synchronism is not perfect, pig iron showing a considerable lead over clearings on the rise in 1886, the fall in 1892, and the rise in 1896-'7, etc., and a lag in the fall in 1883-'4, the fall in 1887-'8, and the fall in 1896. From about 1908 onward, the movements are so divergent as to suggest that pig iron has lost its value as a barometer of business. There is relatively little synchronism, nor are the amplitudes comparable. Pig iron may regain its value as a barometer, but it certainly cannot be considered as a satisfactory index of general trade during the last two decades. Much the same may be said of the use of the volume of freight traffic as a business index, as shown in Chart 46.

There are, however, at least two components of the Volume of Trade Index which are themselves excellent barometers of the cycles of general trade. These are the series representing merchandise and miscellaneous car loadings, and electric power production.   Chart 47 shows these two series plotted with the Volume of Trade.   Merchandise and miscellaneous car loadings comprise the loadings of all sorts of raw materials and manufactured products, and hence tend to be really representative, a physical composite almost as representative as bank clearings.   The movement corresponds very closely indeed to the Volume of Trade, both in amplitude and synchronism.   An exception is the slowness of car loadings to rise above normal in 1919, at a time when the volume of trade gave indications of well-established prosperity.

Electric power production responds closely to the needs of the industry, and hence is a good barometer.   This shows a very smooth cyclical movement synchronizing well with the volume of trade, except for a lag through 1919 and part of 1920.

The various measures of business cycles discussed in this chapter are all interesting as indicators. Their value, in every case, depends largely upon the needs of the investigator.   In general, the composites give a more representative picture of general trade than do the single barometers.

CHAPTER IX

THE USE OF "DEFLATED" DOLLAR VALUE SERIES AS MEASURES OF BUSINESS [1]

In two preceding chapters, mention has been made of the method of reducing certain of our dollar series to a basis of comparability with quantity series by making allowance for fluctuations in the value of money. No problem in our investigations has aroused more perplexities than the use of such series as bank clearings, the value of building permits, exports, imports, retail store sales, etc., as measures of business. So violent, for example, were the fluctuations in the broad levels of prices during the ten years from 1915 that such series lost all close comparability. And yet it has been shown how important some of these series are as measures of trade. Bank clearings, wholesale and retail trade, exports and imports, building and the like are almost indispensable in any real measure of business.

Furthermore, many of the quantity series—particularly those representing the production of basic commodities—have been subject to wide and often unrepresentative fluctuations (as caused by prolonged strikes, severe crop failures, etc.).

We have ton miles of railway traffic; but a large part of this series is made up of the movement of coal and ores and lumber and grains and similar things, again basic commodities. It was interesting to find that railway traffic, expressed in ton miles, and also that iron production ex-

[1] Based on article by the author on "Deflated Dollar-Value Series as Measures of Business." Harvard Review of Economic Statistics, April, 1926, pp. 85-100.

perienced in 1921 the most violent slump, measured either in percentages or in actual quantities, of any year in the three-quarters of a century for which we have actual figures of ton mileage and iron production. Railway traffic in 1921 fell 25 per cent below 1920, and iron production 55 per cent. Obviously, had there been any such corresponding fall in general trade, or even in general production and employment, a considerable part of the nation would have starved.

For the last eight years we have car loadings, but, at least taken as a whole, these are subject to the same sources of error or distortion. As we have seen by taking out the wider variables, the movement of basic commodities, we have in merchandise and small-lot loadings an excellent measure of general trade. But we had no means of knowing this until we had some *a priori* trustworthy measure of general trade itself.

We have employment figures, and recent studies [2] have given these a new interest; but the present current series have little value as measures of business growth and give us no satisfactory idea of what is the normal expectancy at any given time. The number of factory operatives reported as employed in New York State, for example, was as large in 1914 as at the present time, although we now know that the factory product in general has considerably increased. The number employed rose enormously in and after the War and has since shown a generally declining tendency, quite unrepresentative of the general state of industry. As for average daily or weekly earnings, or wage rates, these are, of course, related to the general price level, and these, too, are in dollar values.

We have in electric power production, measured in kilowatts, a new and interesting quantity series; and as electricity now enters so widely into domestic use, in the broadest sense, it might well be expected that this would be

[2] e.g., W. A. Berridge.

a valuable index of general trade. But how closely its fluctuations from a rather steep trend of growth would measure general trade, both in extent and in time, we could not know until, again, we had some objective test.

We have motor car production. But this amazing industry has grown at the same fabulous rate as did railway traffic for the fifteen or twenty years following 1845, and precisely as was true of the latter, seemed for a time almost impervious to the reverses or slumps in other lines of trade and hence a poor barometer. And much the same seems to have been true of oil production in recent years.

And this about ends the available list of quantity series of business data. Consider what remains:

Undoubtedly one of the most potent influences in the prosperity of the last four years has been the tremendous building boom which began in 1921. Leonard Ayres has recently referred to it as "the greatest building boom ever known anywhere." But how do we know this? Hearsay and ocular testimony, and building wages, and the price of building materials, and the scarcity of building workers, and the real estate booms, and newspaper advertisements of them, and the flush times usually characteristic of periods of great construction all may tell us much, and tell it vividly. But these things are no definite measure.

The only numerical measures are the elaborate compilations of building contracts awarded, or building permits issued, made by several different organizations and embracing the whole country, or at least its urban population. But these are in dollar figures (with the exception of square feet measures, which are still experimental,) and while such figures may tell us much of the growth, say, since 1921, even since then a considerable part of the increase shown has been due to the rise of builders' wages and the price of building materials. They can tell us little as to the status of building in 1921, or the extent of the shortage in several years previous, due to the War's restrictions, or whether this deficit has been made up, or how much would be the excess of this year's building over normal needs, as estimated from the growth of population or the computed trend of building in past years.

But building construction is one of the important factors in our business cycles, and at the present time this is perhaps the most important matter about which we should like to know in attempting to estimate what is to come. The only way, so far as the writer knows, that these questions may be answered, or these figures become comparable over an extended period, is by the method which has been so widely employed; viz., to devise careful measures of the cost of building, in wages and in materials, and by this means eliminate from the dollar data the average effect of price changes and wage changes. Reducing the whole series, then, to the common basis of 1913 building dollars, as we may so term them, we have been able to carry back computations for a number of cities, by years, for more than half a century. Making due allowance for the normal growth of building and population, and measuring the excess of previous years over this computed trend, it would appear that, at least so far as the last fifty years' experience of this country shows, Leonard Ayres' statement as to the present building boom is justified.

Now consider the internal evidence of comparability. We know how even, and at what an evenly decrescent rate, has been the growth of urban population over ten-year periods, within the past half century. Population growth is in quantity values and provides as trustworthy statistical information as anything available. Reducing permit values to a common base of 1913 building dollars, we have found much the same even rate of growth as in population and in a wide variety of economic series, such as was shown in Chapter II in the case of iron production, coal production, railway traffic, imports of silk, and many others, all of which are in quantity values. If we find the same sort of growth, and, it might be added, something of the same sort of fluctuations from this computed line of growth, in this reconstructed building series, does it not seem that we have here nearly as trustworthy information as in our best quantitative series?

So also with our information as to the amount or volume of exports and imports and the so-called merchandise balance of trade which was once regarded so vital a factor in our national prosperity. This information extends back now for more than a century. The figures portray in a broad way the colossal growth of the nation's trade. But for the most part they are expressed in dollars, and these dollar aggregates show wide variations in growth and decline. In no period has this uncertainty been more acute than in the last ten years. In the War and after, the dollar values of our exports rose to fabulous sums. Many studies have been made in the endeavor to reduce these erratic values to some common base. It seems a highly difficult problem, but perhaps not insurmountable. We were able to compute a series reduced to a common-value basis which indicated that the war growth, however large, was not far above the normal or computed trend of previous years. It was interesting to find that these computations checked closely with others made by Prof. W. A. Berridge, based upon and controlled by definite tonnage figures prepared for the U. S. Shipping Board in two representative years.

But of far greater significance and value, as shown in Chapter VI, are bank clearings or total bank debits. These are of a much more heterogeneous character than our imports or exports, and are perhaps more representative of the vast and complex volume of exchanges which make up the total trade of the nation than any other single series we possess. If, indeed, they were not expressed in dollars, and therefore subject to the fluctuations of monetary value or purchasing power, they would perhaps provide as near to complete or astronomical knowledge of all kinds of trade and transactions as it would ever be possible to obtain. But reported bank clearings, and the later debits, have likewise shown the same erratic changes, especially in the last ten years, as our dollar figures for foreign trade, for building construction, and almost everything else; therefore, they have lost the high value as measures of business which they possessed before the War. But even before the War their growth was influenced both by the previous long periods of deflation and inflation, and unless we could devise some kind of common denominator of monetary value, valid through a long period, any close comparability of these most valuable data was out of the question.

In constructing an index of the Total Volume of Trade —as described in Chapter V, it was necessary to use many series expressed in dollar values, and hence to find price indexes with which to "deflate" these series to comparable quantity bases. Our earlier experiments with the use of even such a broadly inclusive index as the Bureau of Labor Statistics' index of wholesale prices showed the crudity of the results obtained when this price index was applied to debits. We therefore made an attempt to compute an index of the general price level, in which we combined indexes of wholesale prices, the average cost of living in workers' families, a composite of wage payments, and one of rents. These were weighted empirically, following as far as possible all clues to be obtained from the available census data as to the total payments in the country for wages, the total value of all manufactured products, the estimates of the national income prepared by the National Bureau of Economic Research, the estimated aggregate of stock market transactions in dollars, and the like. Because of the effect of the large transactions on the New York Stock Exchange, separate price levels were computed for New York City and for the entire country excluding New York City, and two indexes of debits were similarly computed. As explained in Chapter VI, these empirical weights in the general price level of the country were shifted slightly to make the greatest possible conformity between "deflated" debits and the Volume of Trade Index. Further confidence was felt in this deflating index when it was found that the rate of growth over a long period of deflated debits corresponded closely to the growth in production found by King, Day, Stewart, and Snyder to approximate 3½ per cent per year (see p. 51).

We have, then, for the index of the variations of trade derived from bank clearings, so adjusted or "deflated," three comparisons or tests. First, the broad consistency of growth and the same constantly decrescent rate of growth as shown in so many other quantity series; second, there is, from about 1900, a close comparability with the rate of growth of a composite of production of basic commodities; and the third, from 1919, a close comparability in its monthly fluctuations with those of a broad composite of samplings from almost every field of industrial and business activity.

In Chapter V we discussed in detail the agreement of the component series in our Index of the Volume of Trade, from 1919. One of the surprising findings in the 28 major series (the 30 indexes from the production series being grouped in two major series) was the general concordance between them, especially as to their time relations. The composite of the whole proved to be not a mere average or median but highly representative of the mode.

But amid these general correspondences of the different series there were, of course, notable exceptions, and precisely those which perhaps might reasonably be expected. The most conspicuous of these were building activity, automobile production, the composite of 15 series of production of the so-called "producer type" of goods, and especially and most notably pig iron production, car loadings of basic commodities, coal, iron, etc., (i.e., other than L. C. L. and miscellaneous merchandise), grain exports, Panama Canal traffic, new securities issued, sales of stock on the New York Exchange, future sales of grain and cotton, mail order sales, and general exports. The differences here were both of time relations and the percentages of deviation from the computed base, but chiefly in the latter.

On the other hand, and again, perhaps, as might reasonably be expected, we found very close resemblances between each other and the composite of the entire set of series, in production of consumers' goods (15 series); merchandise and miscellaneous car loadings; department store sales adjusted; toll line telephone traffic; electric power production, and, of course, the index of outside bank debits. Of these six series four are in quantity data, and only two derived from "deflated" dollar values.

Finally, as I have described in detail in Chapter VII we found a fair degree of congruence between our composite of the Volume of Trade and an index derived from the varying velocity of demand deposits in banks. On the basis of this similarity, we carried these computations back fifty years, with data that were clearly much less comparable than those available in the last seven years, but still obtaining a fair degree of concurrence with our Clearings Index of Business. This index of velocity is the ratio between total debits in selected cities, by months, and the average demand deposits of the banks of these cities for the same month. Though not strictly quantitative in a physical sense, the evidence seems to be that they are not sensibly affected by variations in price levels. They may, therefore, be reasonably included as a part of the available evidence.

We have also made other attempts to gain comparable relative values from dollar series. For example, from the amount of tax paid on contracts on grain futures in Chicago, and, taking a weighted monthly average of grain prices, we devised estimates of grain speculation that in a general way correspond very well with the actual figures in bushels, month by month, which have been published subsequent to the construction of this index.

Again, we constructed an index of cotton trading in New York and New Orleans, for which we have no objective test [3] save that it seems characteristic that the volume of trading in futures should fall rapidly with the marked fall in the price of cotton, and that this is closely analogous to what we know definitely is the case in stock transactions on the New York Stock Exchange.

Upon another line we found that the annual figures for total bank loans and investments in all the banks of the country, since 1900, when reduced to a comparable basis of 1913 dollars by dividing with our Index of the General Price Level, show a remarkably steady trend of growth, closely comparable to the trend of growth in physical production and likewise of bank clearings deflated in the same manner. This seems to the writer an important finding for a rational theory of banking and credit, apparently showing that the demand for credit represents simply the growth of the volume of production and trade multiplied by the general price level.

It is noteworthy that, especially since 1913, savings bank deposits, so measured, have shown no such growth, while, for example, assets of building and loan associations, and new life insurance written, have, on the contrary, shown a much steeper rate of growth. This seems to show that unless we can approximately measure the variations in monetary value of such figures as bank loans and deposits, life insurance written, and the like, they have, in the last ten years, little clear meaning and, further, may be highly misleading.

Again, in the last seven years we have had for the first time, in the reports to the Federal Reserve Board, definite figures as to wholesale and retail trade, business in depart-

[3] That is, for current months. The United States Federal Trade Commission, in its reports on "Cotton Trade," publish fiscal year totals.

ment stores, chain stores, mail order stores and the like; but all in dollar values. For the most part each of these showed a huge rise in 1919-'20 and a violent fall in 1921, while since the beginning of 1923 they have shown a fairly constant rate of growth. In this latter period wholesale and, presumably, retail prices have been relatively stable, and as in this period we have had marked variations in physical production and distribution, the presumption would be that a considerable part of the rise and fall of 1919-'21 was due to price changes; and we find that by "deflation" by means of the cost of living index for retail trade, and a weighted index of wholesale prices for wholesale trade, we obtain adjusted measures fairly consistent with, for example, the rise and fall of merchandise car loadings.

In the same way, running back fifty years, we find that the rate of growth in the relative volume of bank clearings is consistently of the same character whether the movement of prices has been violent or slight; in other words, whether the price correction be large or near to zero. It is surprising how small were the changes in the general price level, according to our measures, in the thirty years from 1875 to about 1905. In this period the extreme variations of the index were within a range of 15 points and the widest deviation from the 30-year average scarcely 10 per cent.

If, now, as we found, the fluctuations of our Clearings Index of Business were much wider in these thirty years than in the subsequent twenty years, and especially than in the last three and a half years when the price level has changed so little, this must be due to the clearings themselves and not to the correcting index.

I do not know whether all these comparisons or suggested tests are conclusive or objective evidence of the validity and value of adjusted or deflated dollar data. To me, in its cumulation, this evidence seems strong. Further, there seems to me a certain reasonableness and consistency in the results that could scarcely be due to chance or obtainable if the fundamentals of the method were not sound. Those series agree which good theory suggests should agree, and others vary widely which should vary widely; and this is true whether the series are derived from a quantity basis or from deflated dollar values.

To sum up, the total trade of this nation now mounts up to unimaginable sums. According to our computation the aggregate value of all checks drawn exceeds 700 billions of dollars a year. This means a total volume of transactions in checks and money exceeding 800 billions. And by far the larger part of this vast trade relates to the production and distribution of food, clothing, and the astonishing variety of common needs and luxuries of everyday life, and to the command of human service which all this involves. Relatively but a minor part goes for new construction; and it seems, therefore, difficult to believe that those quantity series which relate chiefly to basic production can furnish us with an adequate measure of the trade or exchanges of a hundred and more millions of people.

On the other hand, in bank clearings and other dollar series we have precisely such a wide sampling of this heterogeneous mass as comprehensiveness would demand; and with this new measures of changes in average monetary value by which these dollar data may be restored to their former comparability and prestige.

By these alone, it seems to the writer, may we gain any just idea or true measure of the growth or fluctuations of trade which we have come to call the business cycle. And building upon the solid foundations which the last seven years have provided, we may carry back these computations over a long period and obtain trustworthy ideas of business changes in the last half century such as no other method will afford.

It may be freely admitted that the method is not without its dangers, especially in inexperienced hands. But if the findings are checked, step by step, with every kind of quantity data available, as our knowledge widens we grow to confidence in the results. For the rest it seems to the writer that much of the distrust which many feel toward deflated series arises from two misconceptions. The first is that a meticulous accuracy is attainable even with our most cherished quantity data. It is not. And the other is that the "deflating" indexes, to be of value, must themselves be of meticulous accuracy. For the most part price changes, and therefore these deflating indexes, are *slow moving* and do not often affect the cyclical swings. The huge upheaval of 1919-'21 was quite extraordinary, and, like that of our Civil War, may not recur in half a century. In periods of slowly changing prices, price changes in any series, to a large extent, will be taken care of in the computation of a long-time secular trend.

Moreover, for aught we know, we may have entered upon a period of relatively stable monetary value wherein the dollar data may come to be used without adjustment or "deflation." The main objection to the use of these data relates to a period that may soon have only an historical interest; but if we are to preserve any kind of continuity or obtain any kind of comprehensive measure of business over wide periods, the use of the dollar data, "deflated" if needs be, is ineluctable.

CHAPTER X

BUSINESS FAILURES AND BUSINESS CYCLES [1]

INTERESTING light is thrown on the problems connected with business cycles by statistics of business failures. We have Bradstreet's and Dun's compilations of failures for a period running back to the close of the Civil War. These compilations include data both as regards the number of failures, the number of firms in business, and the amount of liabilities involved in the failures.

The number of failures has grown at an even pace with population, and also with the number of firms in business, as is shown in Chart 48. Over a period of time, one firm in every hundred in business and one firm for each 6,000 of the population fails regularly. With all the changes that have occurred in the world of business, the percentage of failures has remained a constant. It appears as though, of the number of persons starting in business, a fixed proportion is predestined to fail—that there is some psychological determinism involved. The whole character of industry has been revolutionized during these sixty years, vast corporations have grown up, huge trusts have been formed, and yet the individual business adventurer continues to function—and to fail—with an amazing regularity.

It was stated that the percentages of failures to firms in business are constant only if viewed over a long period. The percentages will fall in years when prices are rising and trade is brisk, when even the badly equipped and in-

[1] See earlier study on the same subject by the author in "The Nation's Business," November, 1924, page 42-44.

efficient firms can achieve a certain success, and they will rise in years when business turns downward, and depression sets in. An index of business failures becomes an inverse measure of business cycles. This is shown in Chart 49, where the percentage of firms failing to the total number in business each year is plotted against the annual averages of the Clearings Index of Business. There is a high degree of negative correlation between the two series. The Clearings Index registers prosperity by a high level, the business failures index registers prosperity by a low level. The two series usually cross the "normal" line at the same time, and the one reaches its maximum simultaneously as the other reaches its minimum.

This series does not, however, tell the whole story of business failures, for the liabilities involved in the failures are of far greater importance economically than are the crude numbers or percentages of firms failing. These liabilities are expressed in dollars, and are, therefore affected by price changes. They are, then, comparable with the dollar totals of bank clearings, which are affected by price changes in much the same way. Chart 50 shows the total liabilities of firms failing each year from 1880 to date, compared with bank clearings outside New York City. Liabilities show a very slight secular growth. Charting the ratio of liabilities to bank clearings, however, gives quite a different picture. Here we find that the trend of the total liabilities, expressed in proportion to the amount of business done (bank clearings) has been steadily declining over a period of half a century. This decline has been from an average of about $4000 liabilities to a million dollars of bank clearings to an average of about $1000 liabilities to a million dollars of bank clearings. That is to say, the relative liabilities are today about one-fourth the relative liabilities half a century ago.

The implication of this decline in liabilities is, obviously, that the risk in business has declined to the same degree.

CHART 48.

POPULATION, U. S. A., NUMBER OF FIRMS IN BUSINESS, AND
NUMBER OF FIRMS FAILING.

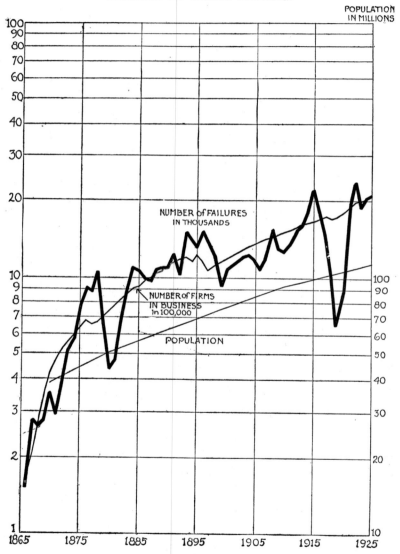

Population, U. S. A., see Chart 1, p. 24.

Number of Firms in Business, Number of Failures. *Source:* R. G. Dun & Co.'s "Record of Insolvencies covering a period of 60 years for the United States and 50 years for Canada." Reprint from Dun's Review, Jan. 9, 1926.

CHART 49.

CLEARINGS INDEX OF BUSINESS AND RATIO OF FAILURES TO
TOTAL FIRMS IN BUSINESS.

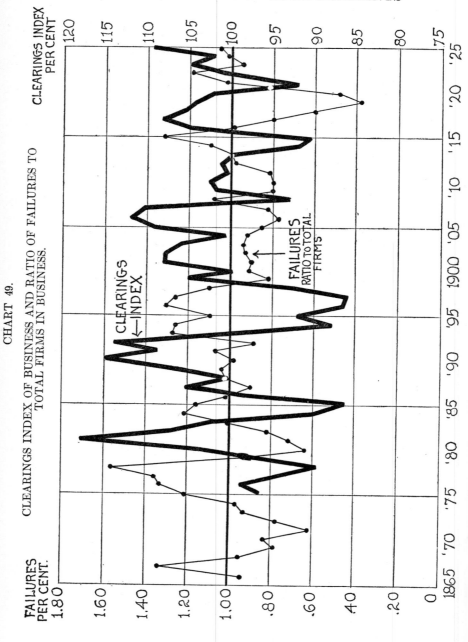

Source of Failures Ratio: R. G. Dun & Co.'s "Record of Insolvencies
Covering a Period of 60 Years for United States and 50 Years for
Canada." Reprint from Dun's Review, Jan. 9, 1926.

CHART 50.

BANK CLEARINGS OUTSIDE NEW YORK CITY AND TOTAL
ANNUAL COMMERCIAL FAILURE LIABILITIES, U. S. A.

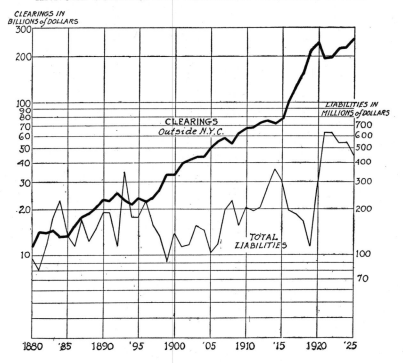

Bank Clearings Outside New York City, see Appendix, Table 18, p. 277, and Chart 32, p. 122. ("Clearings" are actually debits 1919-1925, and have been raised to correspond to debits prior to 1919.)

Total Annual Liabilities. *Source:* R. G. Dun & Co.'s "Record of Insolvencies Covering a Period of 60 Years for the United States and 50 Years for Canada." Reprint from Dun's Review, Jan. 9, 1926.

CHART 51.

NUMBER OF COMMERCIAL FAILURES OF LIABILITIES UNDER AND OVER $100,000.

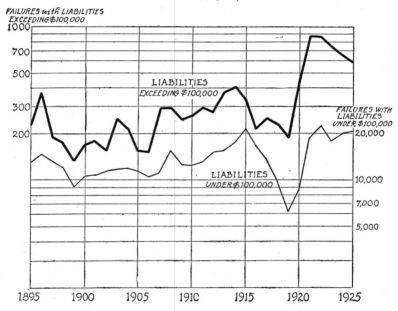

Source: R. G. Dun & Co.'s "The Record of Insolvencies Covering a Period of Sixty Years for the United States and Fifty Years for Canada." Reprint from Dun's Review, Jan. 9, 1926.

This implication, together with the fact that the proportion of firms in business failing has shown no decline, suggests two interesting possibilities. The one is that it is, as a rule, small business ventures which fail. as contrasted with "big business"; the other is that all business is better managed, and more safely conducted now than fifty years ago.

Some evidence on these points is obtained by comparing the failures exceeding $100,000 liabilities with those of less than $100,000 liabilities. Chart 51 makes it evident that the rate of growth in the failure of firms with larger liabilities has been greater than that of those failing with lesser liabilities. This does not necessarily contradict the possibility that more failures occur in small business. The rise in the price level has necessitated a steadily larger average amount of capital investment, and this has brought about a steady transfer of firms from the less than $100,000 class to the more than $100,000 class, and hence has considerably raised the upper limit of what we would consider "small business." It seems, however, that there is no real evidence that the advance in business stability has been due to the development of large corporations, although this has undoubtedly been a contributing factor. A more important factor has probably been the integration of business. There is no longer the same degree of experimenting in business, which led to the wild booms characteristic of the seventies, eighties, and earlier periods.

On the basis of this progressive stabilization of industry, as observed in the chart of relative liabilities, it becomes of interest to inquire just how great is the actual risk on the amount of credit extended. This risk can be roughly measured by the relation of the amount of savings for capital investment to the real losses involved in failures.

Cassel [2] estimates a savings of about 20% of the annual

[2] Gustav Cassel: "The Theory of Social Economy," 1924, p. 63.

income in the countries of Western Europe. King[3] has made a very careful estimate of the volume of savings in the United States, and finds that the average ratio of total savings to income for the years 1909-1918 was about 16%. Friday[4] estimates the savings for 1923 as 17% of the total income, and for 1924 as 20% of the total income.

The annual income during the last two or three years has probably been about 70 billion dollars.[5] Assuming 16% of this income to be saved, this gives some $10,000,000,000 annually for new ventures.

How, then, does this compare with the reported liabilities of firms failing in the United States? For the last three years, liabilities have averaged less than $600,000,000 per year, or about 6% of the savings. These reported failures tend to be swollen totals. There are many cases of resumption, and it is probably safe to estimate that not over two-thirds of the reported liabilities represent real failures. This reduces the real liabilities to $400,000,000, and, of that amount, only a part represents actual losses to the creditors, so that the real annual losses to creditors through business failures in the past three years can safely

---

[3] W. I. King: "The Net Volume of Saving in the United States," Journal of the American Statistical Association, December 1922, p. 467. His estimates of the percentages of the income saved, year by year from 1909 to 1918 are as follows:

1909	17.09%
1910	17.12%
1911	13.66%
1912	15.99%
1913	13.77%
1914	12.52%
1915	21.00%
1916	27.36%
1917	16.90%
1918	— 3.08%

[4] David Friday, "Increasing the National Wealth," The New Republic, Feb. 13, 1924; "A Year's Savings," The New Republic, March 11, 1925.

[5] "Income in the United States during 1919, 1920 and 1921," by National Bureau of Economic Research. It estimates total income as follows for these years:

1919	67.3	billions
1920	74.2	"
1921	62.7	"

be estimated as between $250,000,000 and $400,000,000. It is clear, then, that the losses by failures are from 2½% to 4% of the annual savings, and, viewed from the larger economic aspects, are not very important. It is, indeed, conceivable that the nation's losses from inadequate or antiquated mechanical equipment, inefficient organization, strikes, and lockouts, and other economic maladjustments, might exceed in a single month the entire losses for a year from business failures.

CHAPTER XI

PRICES AND THE BUSINESS CYCLE

THE business cycle is regarded by many as essentially a "price cycle," or "credit cycle," with a presumption that prices are its fundamental basis. Whatever the relationship of prices to the business cycle, it should be obvious that this relationship cannot be analyzed in price series in the same way as in other economic series.

There is, in the first place, the question of secular trend. Can there, strictly speaking, be a "secular trend" in the price level? The concept of secular trend depends on the hypothesis that there is a persistence and stability of growth (although this "growth" may be negative or decrescent) in an economic phenomenon. Although a secular trend can be determined accurately only as regards past data, the computed trend should give at least some basis for short-period or proximate prediction.

Chart 15 shows the movement of wholesale prices in the United States from 1790 to date. There was an upward movement or "inflation," culminating in the War of 1812, then a downward movement, or "deflation," until the early fifties, a tremendous inflation during the Civil War period, a long period of deflation until the middle nineties, and an equally long period of inflation to 1914, and finally the violent inflation during the World War and the drastic decline following its conclusion.

But these processes of inflation and deflation cannot be considered secular trends in the sense that they were used regarding other economic series, for there is no possible basis of predictability of the future movement of prices from the movement of the immediate past. There may be a gradual depreciation or appreciation of the currency over a period of time, but there is no fundamental continuity in the nature of these movements.

Similarly, the concept of a "normal" price level is difficult to interpret. The only sense in which the concept of "normality" in regard to average prices is valid is in their relationship to the world's gold supply. Cassel has developed this concept in a very ingenious way.[1] He estimates (after Lexis) the total supply of gold in the world in 1850 as ten billion gold marks. The annual loss is assumed to be 2/10 of 1 per cent per year, and the supply is cumulated by adding the production each year (or period) from 1850 to 1910, allowing for this loss, and is progressively decreased from 1850 to 1800 by subtracting production and allowing for the loss. The actual gold supply from 1850 to 1910 was found to have increased 5.2 times, representing an annual rate of 2.8 per cent. This uniform rate of increase, applied to the 1850 base, gives the "normal gold supply," and the deviations of the actual supply from this normal may be assumed to bear a close relationship to the trends in the price level, for an even rate of increase would have perfectly maintained the balance between the volume of trade and prices. Cassel's chart of the price level in England and the relative gold supply from 1800 to 1910 bears out this relationship in a remarkable way, and leads to his conclusion that "the main cause of the secular variations of the general price level lies in the changes of the relative gold supply." [2]

The cyclical movement in prices varies decidedly with the type of price index considered. The General Price Level, which is representative of a wide variety of price indexes, shows a very slight cyclical movement (Chart 37). One of the most sensitive general indexes of prices is the Depart-

[1] Gustav Cassel, "The Theory of Social Economy," 1924, pp. 441-455.
[2] Loc. cit., p. 447.

ment of Labor wholesale price index. This index shows a decided cyclical movement, corresponding to business cycles observed in other economic series, but the variation from crest to trough tends to be slight, as compared with the long-term movement. The difficulty of measuring this cyclical variation has been indicated above, i.e., because of the logical difficulties in the way of applying the concept of secular trend to price series.

Persons analyzed a very large number of price series to test them for a correspondence with the business cycle.[3] He found that the prices of only a few commodities reflect the business cycle. Of ninety-one series he tested, only ten met his requirements of flexibility, sensitivity and conformity to the cycles of business series. These ten were, however, representative of a wide variety of commodities.[4] This ten-commodity index is very sensitive indeed to business conditions, and, for the period 1900-1914, showed an amplitude of fluctuations, from peak to trough and trough to peak, ranging from 28 to 51 points and averaging 36 points, compared with a range of 4 to 19 points, and an average of 9 points for the Bureau of Labor index.[5]

Chart 52 sets forth the relationship between several price indexes and the Volume of Trade Index. A striking difference is found in the movement of the Volume of Trade Index, at its peak in the third quarter of 1919 and the "all commodities" index of wholesale prices which reached its peak nine or ten months later. This represented a general lag in all prices at wholesale—as is evidenced by the similar lag in the index of non-agricultural prices. This latter index, however, corresponds at times more closely to trade fluctuations than does the general commodity in-

[3] Warren M. Persons and Eunice S. Coyle: "A Commodity Price Index of Business Cycles," Harvard Review of Economic Statistics, Nov., 1921, pp. 353-369.
[4] The commodities included were cottonseed oil, coke, pig zinc, pig iron, bar iron, mess pork, hides, print cloths, sheetings, and worsted yarns. Loc. cit., p. 353.
[5] Loc. cit., p. 356.

CHART 52.

VOLUME OF TRADE AND PRICE INDEXES.

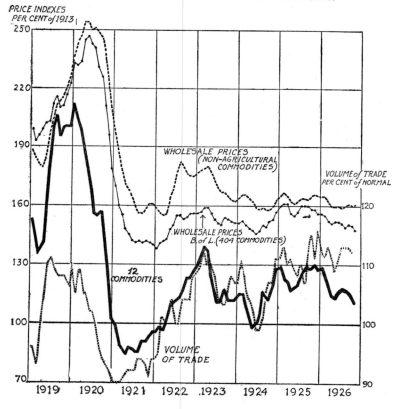

Index of Volume of Trade, see Chapter V.

Wholesale Prices, Department of Labor, 404 commodities. Wholesale Prices (Non-Agricultural Commodities). *Source:* U. S. Department of Labor "Monthly Labor Review."

Wholesale Prices, 12 commodities. These commodities were chosen because of their early movement and tendency to conform to the general movement of the volume of trade. They are weighted by reciprocals of their average arithmetic deviation from the 1919-1925 average price. The commodities included, with their weights, are as follows:

Scrap steel ...... .040	Silk .... .024	Cottonseed oil .. .023
Copper .... .077	Burlap .... .030	Lard .... .022
Zinc .... .056	Woolen rags.... .012	Linseed oil ..... .015
Scrap rubber .... .050	Hides .... .023	Turpentine ..... .013

Data: See Appendix, Table 30, p. 306.
Source: Federal Reserve Bank of N. Y.

dex, due to the fact that the latter is heavily weighted with farm and food prices. This is evidenced by the discrepancy between the Volume of Trade Index and the wholesale price index from about the middle of 1923 to the present—a discrepancy largely accounted for by the marked rise in farm prices up to August 1925, and then their equally marked decline.

The construction of the twelve-commodity price index represented an attempt to segregate certain of the early moving commodities, and to form a price index which was sensitive to the movement in our trade index. The criteria determining the selection of these commodities were that they should precede markedly the general commodity index and that they should be commodities for which weekly quotations were readily available. The result of a wide scrutiny was the choice of twelve early-moving commodities of a rather curious character.

Thus, iron and steel prices are among the pronounced laggards, and therefore excluded. But scrap steel seems very sensitive to trade conditions and moves much earlier.

Among the textiles, all cotton goods were excluded because they are too deeply influenced by the price of cotton itself, which is, of course, a *crop* price. Woolen goods are likewise all influenced by the world-price of wool; therefore, are not a good business indicator. But this was not true of woolen rags, prices for which move early and for which there is a curiously wide market. So, too, the prices of burlap and also of silk.

Other scrap prices were sought, such as for scrap brass and copper, but here the markets seem not very active and the prices sluggish. There is a large market for scrap rubber, in fact, two markets, one for scrap tires and the other for boots and shoes and the like. Prices of the latter proved the more serviceable.

On the other hand, hides proved an excellent barometer. So, at times, were lard and cottonseed oil. Both are influenced, by the price of hogs on the one hand and of cotton on the other, but taken together, they serve very well.

Other sensitive indicators were linseed oil and turpentine, copper and zinc, which completed the list of twelve.

Next, as to the weighting. In the best of our all-commodity indexes, like the Bureau of Labor, each commodity is weighted as nearly as possible according to total value-in-exchange. Such things as iron and coal and corn and cotton and hay, being of enormous annual value, have a correspondingly heavy weight, and these big basic products largely dominate the whole index, often giving it a slow-moving or even capricious character (especially from the crop side).

In the new index the aim was the reverse of this, and that was to obtain a series of price movements very sensitive to trade changes, i.e., business indicators; and as each was chosen for its value *for this purpose,* it was determined to give to each an equal weighting. This was achieved by a very simple means. Some of the commodities chosen have very wide price movements and others have not. They were, therefore, weighted inversely to their average fluctuations in the last seven years.

The general congruence of the new index of prices and our Index of Trade is striking. There is a slight difference in the peak reached in the 1919-'20 period; but both make their low at the beginning of 1921, undergo a very sharp rise into the first quarter of 1923, dip down sharply in 1924, and then rise again.

The conclusion arises that the General Price Level shows little relationship to the cyclical movement in business, that wholesale prices show a closer relationship, and that wholesale prices of certain individual commodities may be a very sensitive index of business conditions.

But the rather shallow waves in general prices show a still closer relationship to the cycles in interest rates. Chart 53 shows the yield of forty-five high-grade bonds plotted

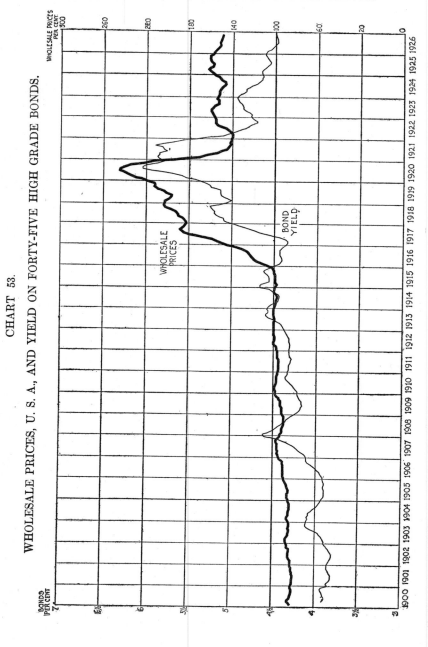

CHART 53.

WHOLESALE PRICES, U. S. A., AND YIELD ON FORTY-FIVE HIGH GRADE BONDS.

Wholesale Prices, U. S. A., see Chart 15, p. 58.

Yield of 45 High Grade Bonds: Average of yield on 15 railroad bonds, 15 municipal bonds, and 15 public utility bonds.
Source: Standard Daily Trade Service, Annual Statistical Bulletin, 1926, p. 10.
Data: See Appendix, Table 29, p. 305.

against the Department of Labor wholesale price index. The similarity in the cyclical movement is evident.

It seems probable also that the trend of prices has a real influence on the amplitude and duration of business cycles. In the period of falling general prices through the '70's and '90's depressions were more severe, and of longer duration, than in the following period of rising prices.

CHAPTER XII

THE INTEREST RATE AND THE BUSINESS CYCLE[1]

So MUCH has been written on the theory of interest rates and their influence; yet so indecisive have been the available facts. As usual, theories are more abundant as the facts are few. It has been widely assumed, for example, that the 60 or 90 day rate on commercial paper is the typical interest rate and that its gyrations are characteristic of interest rates generally. As a matter of fact, this rate applies probably to scarcely 1 or 2 per cent of the total amount of money loaned in one form or another in the United States.

The questions here to be considered are: what are the typical and dominant interest rates of the country; how much do they vary; and how much influence has this variation on the changes in the trade cycle? We may distinguish for this study six or seven chief types of interest which, in decrescent order of variability, run as follows:

1. The call money rate in New York, applying at the present time to from 1 billion to nearly $2\frac{1}{2}$ billions of loans, and varying in recent years from as low as 1 per cent to 12 per cent and more.

2. The commercial paper rate, applying to a considerably less amount of loans, and varying in recent years between about 3 and 9 per cent or more, according to the quality (the real rate to borrowers, of course, is $\frac{3}{4}$ to 1 per cent above the quoted rate).

3. The discount rate of the Federal Reserve banks, ap-

[1] This chapter is based on an article by the author in the American Economic Review, vol. XV, no. 4, December, 1925.

plying to a sum which in recent years has varied as widely as from nearly 3 billions to less than 200 millions; range of rate within this period, 3 to 7 per cent.

4. The so-called "open-market" rate, bankers' acceptance bills, applying at times to something like a billion or more of acceptances and sometimes to less than half this amount; the rate usually about 1 per cent less than the lowest prime customers' rate.

5. Line of credit or customers' rate, the characteristic and typical "bank rate" of the country, applying to a total of from 15 to 20 billions of bank loans; rate varying according to locality and wealth of the community and ranging in the Eastern money centers in recent years between about 3½ and 7 per cent; somewhat more for less desirable loans.

6. The interest rate on bonds, applying to 30 to 40 billions of corporation bonds and mortgages and more than 30 billions of federal, state and municipal government bonds; the average rate on corporation bonds varying within recent years between 4½ and 7 per cent, with, of course, higher rates on many issues.

7. Real estate and farm mortgages, applying to something like 8 to 10 billions of farm mortgages and some 15 billions or more of urban mortgages; the prevailing rate ranging, according to localities, from 5½ to 9 or 10 per cent, but varying in each locality from year to year only within narrow limits.

8. In addition to all this there is the large volume of current and casual credit extended by manufacturers, jobbers, retailers and dealers of all sorts to their customers. From the point of view of the business cycle this is probably the most important and influential form of credit. The amount of such credit is quite incalculable, but its volume is very large; and it is known to vary pretty closely with the swings of the business. This is mainly for the sale of goods to customers on short or long terms; and the ac-

tual rate of interest paid varies extraordinarily. It may be nominal, or even zero; i.e., the cash and on-credit price may be the same. But in general this rate is high. Thus, for example, a customary bill of sale of goods at 60 days, with 5 per cent off for cash, would run at an interest rate of 35 per cent per annum. Such a rate, naturally, is not paid, save in small amounts, by any one who is able to borrow or obtain the money in any other way. It is the highest known form of commercial interest rate, outside of the pawnbrokers.

This computation, then, of known or estimable amounts, would bring the gross total of money loaned from one class of people to another in the United States at the present time to something like 120 or 130 billions of dollars; and the actual total, including, of course, much that is in a sense duplication, i.e., borrowing simply to reloan, would be many billions more. How does this total amount of loaned capital compare with the total amount of capital employed in the commerce and trade of the United States? The answer is not easy.

The total of taxable possessions in the United States, the so-called "wealth" of the nation, as it is quite irrelevantly termed, is estimated by the census at something like 320 billions for 1922. It is a loose and rather meaningless figure save for barometric purposes; and it includes, of course, all residences and so-called luxuries.

The total amount of stocks and shares in corporations of all kinds is computed from the corporation tax returns at about seventy-five billions for 1922. At the present time there are about two million firms reported by the commercial rating agencies as doing business in the United States. If, outside of incorporated companies, their average capital was even as high as $10,000, this would amount to only about 20 billions.

If then the amount of invested capital of owners and shareholders does not much exceed a hundred billions, possibly a third or more of the total business capital of the United States in all forms of industry and trade, excluding agriculture, is derived from loaned funds; which in itself, if verified, would be an interesting result. And this might be true even if we deduct all governmental borrowings, although a considerable part of these borrowings is actually invested in going business enterprises, as waterworks, good roads, municipal plants, and the like.

A *priori*, then, the variability of the interest rate might be regarded as a profound influence in our business affairs. But, as we have seen, for the great bulk of these loaned funds, the short period or "cyclical" variability is extremely low. As to the total loaned on real estate, constructions and farms, say 25 billions, this short period variability is for the most part near zero. The scarcity or plentifulness of funds is the dominant influence here.

Of equally slight influence upon business as a rule is the rate on governmental borrowings, amounting, now, federal, state and other, to another 30 billions or more. Only in war times and after war times, as a rule, does the federal government come into the market for heavy sums; and such times are almost invariably periods of inflation when money rates are always kept at an artificially low level. All the precepts of wisdom and the counsels of history to the contrary, finance ministers will almost inevitably endeavor to make a record of borrowing money at low rates, heedless of the invariable consequences of their policies.

We come now to the quantitatively most important of all interest rates, in so far as business and trade are concerned, the line of credit or customers' rate charged by the commercial banks. These are the rates which apply to the great bulk of bank loans, probably two-thirds and more, or at the present time around 20 billions. It may be said at once that here we can only ascertain something like the median; it is not possible to attain even a fairly representative average. This is because even in a given bank, at a given time, there is no fixed customers' rate; but the rate varies according to the financial position of the borrower, his standing at that particular bank, and other factors. This, at least, is true of the larger banks.

But, on the other hand, there are literally thousands of banks in the United States whose nominal rate to the customers, year in and year out, is practically unchanged at 6 per cent, or 7 per cent, depending upon the locality and sometimes the state laws. The variability is not in the normal rate but in arrangements that may be made, such as the amount of balance which the bank requires a customer to keep. And it may be added that, of course, the nominal rate charged is not usually the real rate or cost to the borrower. Probably the average requirement for a customer's balances for all the banks of the country would be not far from 20 per cent. If, therefore, this balance is derived from the customer's loan, and he pays a nominal 6 per cent and must keep $\frac{1}{5}$ of the sum in the bank as a balance, then the actual rate or cost to the borrower is $\frac{1}{4}$ more, or $7\frac{1}{2}$ per cent, since the bank itself has the use of $\frac{1}{5}$ of the loan.

In a very rough way this may be said to be about the standard bank rate in the more settled and wealthy portions of the United States, year in and year out, without regard to trade cycles or anything else.

This is not true, especially, of the larger banks in the larger cities. Here there is a considerably greater variability. For information on this point we are indebted to the Federal Reserve Board for the collection of monthly reports from 34 cities in the United States since 1919. These are highly representative years; for they reveal probably the extreme of variations within the last half century. We know definitely that the averages for commercial paper rates in 1920 were the highest for any year since 1873; so we may infer that the bank customers' rate underwent a similar range. The range from this point to the extreme

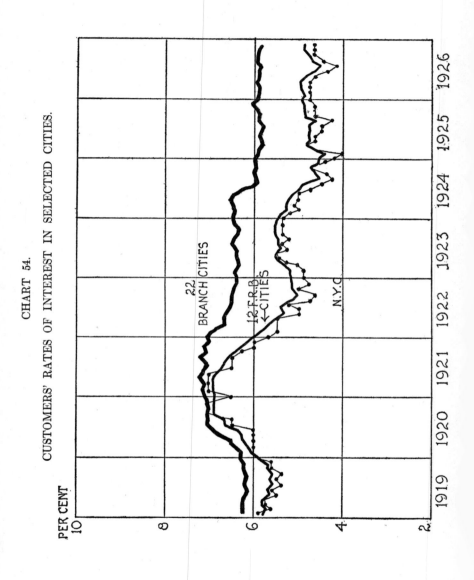

CHART 54.

CUSTOMERS' RATES OF INTEREST IN SELECTED CITIES.

Sources: Federal Reserve Bank of New York, Reports Department.
Data: See Appendix, Table 31, pp. 306-307.

CHART 55.

COMMERCIAL PAPER AND CUSTOMERS' RATES IN NEW YORK CITY, AND AVER-
AGE CUSTOMERS' RATES IN 34 CITIES.

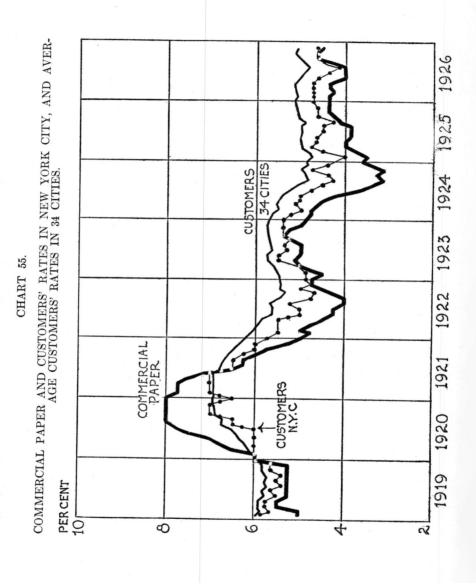

Sources: Federal Reserve Bank of New York, Reports Department.
Data: See Appendix, Tables 31 and 32, pp. 306 and 308.

ease of 1924 probably represents nearly the outside limits of variability for the last two generations.

The accompanying chart (54) shows the averages of prevailing customers' rates in New York City from 1919, with those of twelve Federal Reserve cities, and of 22 other cities having Federal Reserve bank branches. It was found that the prevailing customers' rates in New York City have not varied within this period very widely from the average in the twelve Federal Reserve bank cities, save that in general customers' rates in New York City have been slightly lower, and at one time considerably lower, than the average for twelve cities, in which New York is, of course, included. For New York City the prevailing customers' rates varied from below 5½ per cent in 1919 to 7 per cent through 1920 and part of 1921, falling in 1922 to nearly 4½ per cent and, after a brief rise, falling to a still lower level in 1924. Chart 55 shows the averages of prevailing customers' rates in New York City from 1919, with the familiar commercial paper rates, 4 to 6 months, and also with a computed average for 34 cities. The latter represents an approximation to the national average.

In general it was found that the customers' rates in other Reserve cities, and likewise the weighted average for the 22 branch bank cities reporting, corresponded in their movements pretty closely to the New York rates, but with a somewhat lessened amplitude of variation. Still less was the variability of a computed weighted average for the 34 reporting cities and, correspondingly, less yet for the estimated national average. The range for these two latter averages, which are approximations, was from slightly above 7 per cent to below 5 per cent.

To what percentage of the total of bank loans in the country would this range of variability apply? We have rather little information. The total of bank loans in the 34 cities here grouped is nearly one-half of the total commercial loans in the United States. If these rates apply to two-thirds of their loans on the average, then it might be estimated that these rates affected 10 billions or more of bank loans. It seems quite certain that the remaining 5 to 10 billions or more of commercial loans would be affected much less.

Still less would these wide variations affect another large group of standard bank loans, viz., those on real estate and other mortgages. Very roughly it may be estimated that these amount to perhaps a quarter of the total bank loans of the country, or, at the present time, to something like 6 or 7 billion dollars. The rates on this type of loan vary slowly and within relatively narrow limits.

We come now to the wider variables, the loans on commercial paper, acceptances, the loans on stocks and bonds, and especially "street loans." The commercial paper and acceptance markets, broadly the "bill markets," have had nothing like the development in the United States that they have had, for example, in Great Britain; and their present importance is of rather recent growth. How the commercial paper rate varies as compared with the average of customers' rates is set forth in the preceding diagram. Very roughly the variation is nearly twice that of standard customers' rates in leading cities. Very roughly speaking, this extreme variability of the commercial paper rate applies to considerably less than 10 per cent of the total of commercial loans.

As already stated, bankers' acceptance bills vary closely with the most favorable rate on prime customers' loans; and the total amounts involved are of something the same order as the volume of commercial paper outstanding.

Total loans on stocks and bonds in the banks of the United States represent a constantly large part of bank loans, and now amount to around 25 per cent of the total in all commercial banks. The amount can only be estimated but at the end of 1925 it exceeded 9 billions of dollars. These loans, in the weekly Reporting Banks from

100 selected cities of the country, amounted to about 40 per cent of the total loans of these banks; but nearly half of these loans are in the banks of New York City. A further large proportion lies in other financial centers, like Boston, Philadelphia and Chicago; and the proportion grades off rapidly from these.

More than one-third of these loans are the so-called street loans, or brokers' loans in New York City which, it is now disclosed, reached, at the beginning of 1926, 3½ billions. For the larger part, the rates on these loans are the familiar "call money" rates in New York City; and these rates were formerly subject to violent fluctuations. Even as late as the stock boom of 1906-'07, they ran up at times to 100 per cent and more. Since the founding of the Federal Reserve system and the development of the acceptance market, these extreme rates, which were a severe indictment of our banking methods, have tended to disappear; and in the period since the close of the war the highest renewal rates have rarely exceeded 10 per cent.

These spectacularly high rates have greatly agitated many minds in the supposition that they much affect other bank rates and hence the business of the country. But their importance has been absurdly exaggerated. The total amount of funds, which in recent years has been attracted to New York City by these high rates, has possibly at no time exceeded more than 3 or 4 per cent of the total loanable bank funds of the country. Surplus bank funds flow to New York and other money centers rather in times of slack business demands for credit than in times of intense stock speculation. If in recent years the minimum of call loans has been under a billion dollars and the maximum something more than twice this, call money rates can scarcely affect the interest rates paid by commerce and industry to anything like the extent that many have supposed.

The remainder of the loans on stocks and bonds are made

at varying rates, from that on the so-called "time money," in New York, chiefly brokers' and other speculative loans, to the ordinary bank loans on this type of collateral, which is at about the best customers' rate on prime commercial paper. The larger part of speculative loans is of the "call money" type, since that is ordinarily the lowest available rate.

What proportion of the estimated total of 9 billions or so of stock and bond loans is speculative, and how much for commercial purposes, is quite impossible to say. A very large number of business men will invest in securities at favorable times and carry these at the bank, paying for them more or less from the profits of business; and at other times making use of securities owned to obtain money for ordinary business ventures, at the lowest prevailing rates. This practice has had a notable development since the war.

To sum up, then, we see that the great bulk of loanable funds in the United States is put out at more or less stable rates of interest, stable in the sense that, as a rule, the rates vary slowly over a series of years and show little of the cyclical type of fluctuation. In turn, likewise, the great bulk of bank funds is loaned at rates of interest which vary within rather narrow limits. The rates which vary widely affect a relatively small portion of funds loaned, and the extremely variable rates an extremely small portion. From all this we may formulate a broad law to this effect:

The variability of interest rates, among the different groups or types of funds loaned, is, broadly speaking, in inverse proportion to the total amounts of the funds involved; that is, the greater the amount of funds loaned in each group, the less the variability, and vice versa.

We may perhaps go a step farther and parallel this law with another, dealing with the time relations of loans, viz.:

The variability of interest rates is, broadly speaking, in inverse proportion to the length of the term of the loan; that is to say, the least variability is in long-term mortgages and bonds, the extreme of variability in day-to-day call loans.

In a quite literal sense, then, the highly variable rates are on marginal loans, and to a far greater degree, possibly, than has been suspected. This is to say that there are fairly definite rates at which it is usually profitable to borrow money, as in the vast amounts loaned on mortgages and bonds, and these are rates which move but slowly and in response to influences which have little to do, relatively, with the trade cycle or what we call "business." In turn the great bulk of bank loans of the commercial sort are more or less equivalent to a banking partnership in the enterprises involved. Each bank gives to its more or less permanent customers a more or less permanent credit or line of credit, and the evidence appears to be that the line of credit so extended is used in a fairly regular fashion. That is to say, aside from the changes due to a changing general level of prices, bank loans grow along very steadily with the normal growth of business; and these likewise appear to change much less with the cyclical changes of trade than is generally supposed.

What do vary widely, both in volume and in rate, are the loans which belong in what are loosely termed the banks' "secondary reserves," that is, the most liquid types of loans obtainable, of which the great bulk are loans on stocks and bonds. Inasmuch as, generally, commercial loans cannot easily be contracted without serious injury to business, and inasmuch as it is the prime interest of the banks to accommodate their best and steady customers, who must always be protected as far as it is possible, it follows naturally that the marginal, and, to a great extent, the speculative type of loans are the most quickly affected by any expansion or contraction of the demands from business. Being relatively small in amount, as compared with the volume of commercial loans, it follows naturally that the relatively small fluctuations of trade may cause a variation as high as 50 per cent or more in the amount of funds available for the speculative markets.

Being the most liquid type of loans, brokers' loans, bankers' acceptances, commercial paper and the like pay normally the lowest rate of interest; the penalty for this very low rate being that in a pinch or when money grows tight they pay the highest. These loans may be likened to a small reservoir attached to a large body of water, in such fashion that a small rise or fall in the main body occasions a very heavy addition to or drain from the small reservoir.

Inasmuch as there is a more or less steady minimum demand for loans of this liquid type, and in times of speculative activity an intense demand, rates of this type will run up in a fashion out of all proportion to the normal run of business loans. On the one hand business men can pay high rates on a small amount of marginal loans, which they could not possibly afford to pay on the great bulk of their loans. And in turn the speculator, in anticipation of large profits or clinging desperately to commitments which have gone against him, is willing to pay temporary rates that may at times even be fantastically high.

These high rates have usually been due to the withdrawal of banking funds, and especially of the interior banks, and have often marked the climax of the security markets, while trade has continued high for some months longer. Under more ordinary conditions, when trade expansion gets well under way, it begins automatically to scrimp the funds available for speculation; and so the peak of a stock boom has often come some months ahead of a corresponding maximum of trade.

But it may actually happen that business may be at high tide, with a great wave of building construction, and all this accompanied by a tremendous boom in the stock markets, and interest rates nevertheless remain very low and funds abundant. Such has been the case in the activity of 1925-'26. It is undoubtedly an unusual situation and one that is rarely repeated; but we find closely similar conditions prevailing in 1891-'92, just before the panic of 1893 and the disastrous depression which followed. Interest rates continued to fall, in the face of a very large volume of business and very active stock markets.

Business and speculation are not always the controlling factors. The further fact we have to consider is that, again under exceptional conditions, forces may arise more potent in their influence upon interest rates than either, as has been notably the case in the last ten years. That is the changing value of money itself. Such an upheaval in price levels and money value as that brought on by the War and the post-war boom and collapse, sufficed to make clear the reality of this influence, so largely obscured in times of slower change. What is very clear is that when the currency of the country, or its equivalent, is debased in value, in due course interest rates will rise. And correspondingly, when the purchasing power of a currency is enhanced interest rates will, in due course, fall.

The modes in which these forces act are none too evident. It is clearly not a conscious action on the part of bankers or the holders of money. As a rule, even the more instructed business men are indifferent to, and it may be quite ignorant of, the changing value of the money standard. Certainly there are few to calculate closely, and profit by, the consequences it brings. The great majority of investors will continue to buy bonds, and seek low interest rates, because they are "safe," at times when the principal value of bonds is falling at such a rate as wholly to extinguish any real return in interest; i.e., when they receive only what Professor Fisher calls "negative" interest.

It has been equally clear that in such periods, alike in this and other countries, business men and investors will continue to find relative satisfaction in profits that may mean scarcely half or even a fraction of real profits, because in the nominal money units they seem large. Apparently only under extraordinary conditions of currency debasement, as in Germany, will a bold Stinnes and his like borrow huge sums at almost any rate of interest in anticipation of a still greater appreciation of their investments. For a long time after the headlong plunge of the mark, interest rates in Germany continued relatively low, although lenders were not only receiving no interest but losing heavily in the principal. For example, the larger German banks appear to have lost a large part of their capital because their directors were unable to grasp the meaning of the value of money, or at least to cope with the difficulties then presented.

On the other hand, it seems doubtful if many investors, in considering their commitments, will show a preference for fixed-rate securities or for loans, when the value of money is rising. Latterly there has been considerable education in this field; but the evidence seems abundant that neither the rise nor the fall of interest rates from these causes results from any intelligent effort to anticipate returns. The mode of action of these forces seems rather to be that a rapidly debased currency, evidenced in the corresponding rise in commodity values, brings an equivalently enlarged demand for loans, required to take care of a given volume of trade at the higher price levels; and vice versa. But it may happen, as, for example, was the case in this country in 1919, that the promoting cause of this currency debasement, a huge enlargement of the currency or credit supply, may for the time being operate to keep the interest rates down.

In whatever way these forces act, the drift of long-time interest rates, in the last twenty-five or thirty years, as of bond yields and even the long-term averages of commercial paper and other interest rates (chart 53), has corresponded more closely with changes in the general level of prices than to any other influence. For example, from 1917 to the end of 1920 we had the heaviest rise in general interest rates, to the highest yearly levels, within the last half century. This directly followed, at the usual lag of about a year, the most violent rise in price levels which we have known since the Civil War. But, on the other hand, the expansion of trade, from 1916 onward, was not, contrary to almost universal popular belief greater than other periods of active business in the last fifty years, and actually considerably less than that characteristic of the trade cycle prior to about 1900; and the same was true of stock market speculation. Neither of the latter could adequately explain the exceptional rise of interest rates in 1920.

These are facts which have been none too clear, since we have lacked, hitherto, reliable measures of the actual variations, at least in the total volume of trade. The measure of these variations has been a matter of rather extended investigation, with results that have been until recently difficult to reconcile. Some of these measures seemed to indicate variations of trade, within short periods of time, amounting to as much as 30 or 40 per cent and even much higher. So long as belief in variations of this extent was general, it did not seem difficult to account for corresponding changes in the interest rate, nor needful to seek the influence of other forces than those usually adduced in explanation.

The evidence presented in Chapters V and VI showed pretty conclusively that no such changes in the volume of trade or of business have taken place within at least the last quarter of a century. It is clear that, for example, the war did not bring a greater expansion, or subsequent contraction of the actual volume of trade than had occurred within recent years in peace times.

In Chart 56 comparison is made of the Clearings Index of Business with the 60 to 90 day rate on commercial paper in the New York Money market. This latter is not, indeed, as we have seen, the most typical or representative of interest rates; but it is the most accessible and the best long-range series we have; and while its fluctuations are much wider than those of the prevailing bank loan rates or other interest rates, it does provide an excellent survey of time relationships over a wide period; and it is this time relationship with which we are most concerned here. A review of the evidence here presented makes clear that something like the time relationships of trade and money rates, which Professor Warren M. Persons found for the period 1903-'13 inclusive,[2] have prevailed, with some notable exceptions, throughout the half century that is now available for definite investigation. It will be seen that in general the upward turns of business, following a decline, took place on a falling interest rate and often considerably before the lowest point in the interest curve had been reached. The corresponding upward turn of interest rates has come usually from ten to fifteen months later.

The peak of cyclical expansion, in turn, has usually been reached at an even earlier period before the extreme point of the interest rate, in some instances eighteen months or two years before, as, for example, in 1901-'03. It is striking how often this peak of trade has come close to the time at which the interest rate has risen to just about the average of the half century; i. e., when the interest rate "crosses" the average line. Now this fifty-year average on this type of bank paper has been just under 5 per cent—4.93 per cent. Barring the extreme periods of panic and depression, this rate has not often fallen below 3 per cent nor risen much above 6 per cent; and these are variations which, while considerable in percentages, do not represent any heavy penalty laid upon business.

Consider that these rates represent the extreme of fluctuations in commercial loans, and that the range of prevailing customers' rates at the banks lies well inside these limits. If the average rate paid by business concerns on bank loans

[2] W. M. Persons: "An Index of General Business Conditions," Harvard Rev. of Econ. Statistics, prel. vol. I, April, 1919.

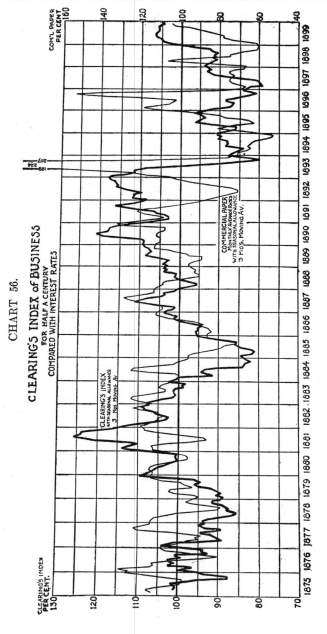

CHART 56.

CLEARING'S INDEX of BUSINESS
FOR HALF A CENTURY
COMPARED WITH INTEREST RATES

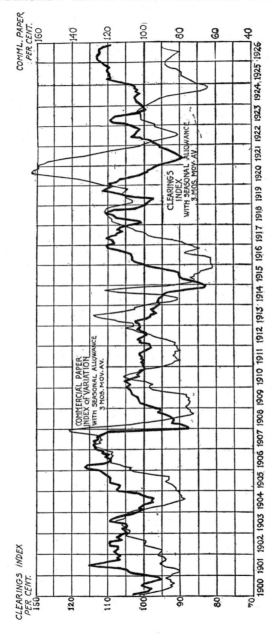

Clearings Index of Business, see Appendix, Table 24, p. 292.

Index of Commercial Paper Rates. Monthly average rates on prime commercial 60-90 day paper in New York City.

Seasonal: 1917-1923,			
J.	99	J.	99
F.	100	A.	97
M.	102	S.	100
A.	101	O.	101
M.	100	N.	101
J.	100	D.	101

Index: Percentage deviations of actual rates from 1875-1923 average (= 4.93%), seasonal allowed for. See Appendix, Table 33, p. 309.

lies, with rare exceptions, between 5½ and 7½ per cent (nominal rate 1 per cent to 1½ per cent less), this difference of 2 per cent can scarcely be a controlling influence in the trend of business generally. The experiences of 1906, of 1919-'20 and of practically every other boom period have shown clearly enough that in such times business men are not strongly deterred by high interest rates, nor in periods of depression will they, as a rule, borrow heavily because of cheap money. The case is different in the flotation of long-term securities, especially in the instance of great enterprises like the railways, where the capital investment is heavy, the rate of turnover very slow, and the interest such a large item in the conduct of the business. But even here it is scarcely true that such enterprises borrow heavily simply because money is cheap; the almost universal experience of railway executives is to the contrary, that they find it very difficult to induce a board of directors to borrow money when rates are low, since at such times it more often happens that trade is extremely dull and prospects far from bright.

So, broadly speaking, it seems clear that: The actual cost of money to merchants and manufacturers is not in itself a decisive factor in the business cycle.

And this conclusion seems abundantly confirmed by the vast amount of cost-accounting work, which shows that ordinarily the interest charge on borrowed capital is a relatively unimportant item. High money rates seem rather the sequelae or aftermath of business expansion and speculative activity, not, as a rule, in evidence until some time after the decline alike in business and in speculation has begun.

Whence comes, then, the almost universal and widely taught belief that the course of the business cycle is intimately bound up with the interest rate? A possible explanation may be that, first of all, under conditions long prevailing prior to the war, the interest rate was an extremely good guide to the trend of trade, and possibly one of the very best business "barometers" that business men had; and, secondly, that the interest rate is really one of the decisive factors in the course of stock speculation. One of our leading economists has recently noted how strong a factor in American business affairs has hitherto been the element of *fear*. For a long time we had in this country an abnormally high business mortality and a very high banking mortality; and the interest rate was an extremely good indicator of the general business situation. We now know that in the last fifty years the factor of risk in business loans has declined to not more than one-fourth what it was following the Civil War; and probably this amelioration has been going on for a long time. And corresponding to this were great ups and downs in the volume of trade, leading to such severe crises as those following 1873 and 1893.

All this has been slowly changing and, with the advent of the Federal Reserve System, quite decisively. But there is little question that the element of fear is still a potent influence, and a rising interest rate regarded as an ominous sign. This is especially true in the field of speculation; and for a long time the course of the stock market was, perhaps justly, likewise regarded as one of the most reliable guides or barometers which business men could employ. A shrewd coal merchant of former days was wont to say that, although he had never bought or sold a share of stock speculatively in his life, he would as soon think of neglecting the trend of the stock market as that of his own industry. And for this there was excellent reason. A rising stock market was an almost infallible indicator of expanding trade, and a stock market crisis almost always omen of a decline. In the absence of trustworthy measures of actual trade it was a wide belief that stock speculation distinctly preceded the ups and downs of business and was, therefore, an excellent "forecaster." It is now clear from our newer measures that this has been distinctly less true in the last ten or fifteen years than in former times. The stock markets latterly have seemed to swing more closely with the actual course of trade, and perhaps to lag behind as often as they lead.

Now, a strong movement of stock prices rarely ends in a cheap money market, or begins in a dear one; and it is easy to see from this how closely rates in New York money markets, and especially call rates on brokers' loans, have come to be associated with the actual trends of trade; the latter rates usually preceding the movement of longer-term interest rates, at least on the rise, by a distinct period.

To sum up, we find that new data compiled by the Federal Reserve Board have made it possible to compare the fluctuations of various types of interest rates with prevailing bank rates; and new measures of trade, whose reliability may be objectively tested, extending over the last half century, make it possible to compare the fluctuations of business with the course of interest rates. From these it seems clear that the more familiar datum lines of interest rates, such as the commercial paper rate, represent the marginal fluctuations and that the movement of the main body of loan rates is much less; and their variations, therefore, of correspondingly less importance in the conduct of business. The direct effect of interest rates upon the course of the business cycle seems less than many have supposed; and the importance of these fluctuations rather derived from their association with or use as business barometers, and especially as storm signals. In the main the more important changes in business seem to take place before the movement of interest rates could be of any material effect. All of which has an important bearing upon the problem of stabilizing trade or moderating the extremes of the business cycle by means of changes in the bank rate.

CHAPTER XIII

FORECASTING BUSINESS CYCLES

MEASUREMENT of business cycles derives its chief practical value if it leads to the possibility of forecasting, or predicting the future course of business. Scientific forecasting should have a degree of accuracy found in actuarial computations, and it will be interesting to note just how far the current methods of forecasting approach this standard.

Most business men use rough and ready means of forecasting. They learn to look out for certain danger signals, to watch the movement of the stock market or some such indicator, to keep informed as to the conditions existing in closely related lines of business, to weigh the many factors involved, and come to a conclusion by balancing the probabilities of the various factors. Such a method of forecasting is, of course, almost entirely subjective, and its value depends ultimately on the shrewdness of the business man's judgment. It corresponds to other types of intuitive forecasting, such as the sailor's weather predictions, which are often and amazingly right, but which have little scientific basis.

Of those methods in use which make any pretense of objectivity, the most common is the method of "correlation," i. e., of tracing out time relationships between various series, and using the ones which move earliest in the up or down grade as a forecaster of other series. The Harvard Committee has used a curve representing trading in stocks and several other factors to forecast general business.[1]

---

[1] For the pre-war period, they found five general groups of economic series, each of which could be used as a forecaster of another group. The

230

There are many relations of this sort between business series. Leonard Ayres found a close relationship between the number of pig iron furnaces in blast and the general tide of business.[2] He found the average percentage of furnaces in blast to be about sixty per cent capacity, and when it rises above this it forecasts generally a decline in business. Conversely, when the line of percentages crosses "normal" on the down-grade, it signifies a rise in business in the near future.

There is another correlation of some significance, and that is the relationship of the commercial paper interest rate to its average of the past fifty years. When it crosses the average line on the up-grade it often signals the peak of business. On the down-grade, the correlation is not so clear.

Another similar sort of indicator is obtained when there is a close relationship in the spread between two series. Thus, the normal spread between the price of raw cotton

first group, consisting of the rate of interest yielded by ten American railroad bonds, the average price of twenty railroad stocks, and the average price of industrial stocks, preceded the second group by two to four months. The second group, consisting of bank clearings in New York City, the value of building permits in twenty cities, and shares sold on the New York Stock Exchange, preceded the third group by two to four months. The third group, comprising pig iron production, bank clearings outside New York City, the value of merchandise imports, unfilled orders of the U. S. Steel Corporation and Bradstreet's index of business failures, preceded the fourth group by two to four months. The fourth group, comprising Bradstreet's index of commodity prices, gross earnings of ten leading railroads, index numbers of wholesale prices of all commodities (U. S. Bureau of Labor Statistics), and average reserves of New York City Clearing House Banks, preceded the fifth group by four to six months. The fifth group consisted of average loans and average deposits of the New York City Clearing House Banks, the rate of interest on four-to-six months and sixty-to-ninety day commercial paper in New York, and dividend payments by industrial corporations. (Review of Economic Statistics, April, 1919, W. M. Persons: "An Index of General Business Conditions," p. 111.)

For the post-war period, the lags and leads have not been so close as for the pre-war period. The curve used to forecast general business is a curve of speculative activity. General business consists of an average of bank debits outside New York City, and a ten commodity price index, and speculation is represented by New York City bank debits and the price of industrial stocks. (Review of Economic Statistics, April, 1925, p. 49).

[2] Leonard P. Ayres: "How a Big Bank Plans Its Investments." American Bankers' Association Journal, August, 1924.

and the standard grades of cotton cloth is relatively narrow. When this spread rises violently, it is a signal of approaching trouble. Copeland shows how good a forecaster this signal was in 1892 and 1907.[3] Other interesting relationships of the same sort can be worked out, as, for instance, the spread between crude copper and standard grades of manufactured articles, between certain standard grades of iron and steel, etc. This type of indicator is losing some of its value in many cases, however, due to the acceleration of the manufacturing processes. For instance, a very good indicator of the silk market was the spread between raw silk prices and manufactured silk, because the time element was considerable. But rayon, (a cellulose product silk), can be made and finished in as many days as the same process takes months for silk, and, to the degree that rayon supersedes silk, the spread becomes useless as an indicator. Similarly, the spread between pig iron and finished steel products is being eliminated by the acceleration of the refining process, so that there tends to be no period between the iron ore and finished steel when the metal turns cold and becomes pig iron.

The difficulty with all these interesting relationships is that none of them has been found to hold invariably. A clue to this situation lies in the constant changes in the underlying conditions of business. In the determination of the fluctuations of any one series, the behavior of a large number of economic and non-economic elements enters in. And the relative importance of these various elements must continually be in a state of flux, as new industries are developing, old processes are being superseded, wars and disasters with unforeseen effects, and many other changes are occurring. For instance, for many years before the War, a very excellent indicator of business cycles was the ratio of loans to deposits in national banks. As the ratio rose

[3] M. T. Copeland: "The Cotton Manufacturing Industry of the United States," 1917, p. 172, and chart facing p. 175.

sharply above its average, it offered an almost invariable danger signal, and, conversely, when the ratio fell very low, it indicated that business was about to improve. Then two events occurred which completely upset this ratio as an indicator. The first was the establishment of the Federal Reserve System. Now, when a bank is pressed for funds, it has simply to go to one of the twelve Federal Reserve Banks and rediscount its eligible paper. The second factor has been the increasingly important part that investments play in the banks' offerings of credit. Loans and investments, so far as credit is concerned, are essentially the same, but the one is optional to the bank, and the other optional to its customer, so now there would not be the tendency to an increase of investment when loans are pressing hard, and there would develop a tendency to sell investments in proportion as there was a pressure for loans. Thus two factors have developed, the one quite suddenly, and the other by a slow process extending over years, which have tended to invalidate this ratio as a business forecaster.

Other attempts to forecast general business take the form of some mechanical projection of the cycles. Were there a real periodicity in business cycles, any actual evidence that the several phases of the cycle recurred at regular intervals, this projection could be accomplished quite simply by mathematical formulæ dealing with such periodicities (Fourier series, etc.). There is no objective evidence, however, that the cycle recurs at regular intervals. Taking as a standard of measurement the point at which the index crosses "normal" on the upgrade, we get the following cycles in the clearings index of business:

Cycle beginning	and lasting
March, 1876	5 months
August, 1876	5 "
January, 1877	33 "
October, 1879	50 "
December. 1883	32 "

Cycle beginning   and lasting
August, 1886 .... 22 months
June, 1888 127   "
January, 1899 23   "
December, 1900 45   "
September, 1904 54   "
March, 1909 35   "
February, 1912 47   "
January, 1916 41   "
June, 1919 34   "
April, 1922 19   "
November, 1923 ....

There is little regularity shown by this method of measuring the length of cycles, and it is obvious that the average length of such a cycle would give a forecast subject to a very wide margin of error. This is, of course, an arbitrary way of determining the length of cycles. Other methods would be to measure from peak to peak, trough to trough, etc., but the subjective element very often invalidates such measures, as is evident by the lack of agreement among economists as to the length of cycles, what constitutes a cycle, etc.

Other methods of wave projection are not based on any assumption of periodicity in business cycles. The so-called "quadrature theory," developed by Edge and Karsten postulates the same idea that is fundamental in the correlation method; i. e., that there are close relationships of cause and effect between economic series. "Two forces are said by Mr. Edge to be in quadrature when they trace curves such that the fluctuations of one of the curves correspond to the fluctuations of a curve of the integration or cumulation of the data of the other curve. When a cause-and-effect relation exists between two such phenomena, the first may then be said to be cumulatively affected by the second." [4] Karsten applies this theory successfully in tracing the relationship of car shortage data to interest rates. The crude data show a moderate relationship between the two series,

[4] Karl G. Karsten: "The Theory of Quadrature in Economics," Journal of the American Statistical Association, March, 1924, p. 14.

with interest rates lagging several months irregularly. He then cumulates the deviations of the car shortage figures from their average and obtains a very close correspondence with the interest rate, and the interest rate can be forecast by projecting the cumulated curve of car shortages. This method is interesting and challenging, but much proof would be needed to show an inherent relationship between two such series, for it is possible that the mathematical abstractions bring to light economic coincidences rather than any invariable cause-and-effect relationships.

Fisher [5] uses a method of this same general class, but he deals with the rate of change in one series as related to the actual data in another series. He uses an ingenious method of distributing the lag in such a way as to bring about a close correspondence between the two series. The volume of trade (Harvard) is approximated by the "price-change shot forward." Here again some doubt must arise as to any inherent causal relation between the series investigated. Furthermore, the methods used have been chosen to bring about the desired results, so that there can be little objective validity to his conclusions.

Often a very practical sort of wave projection is obtained by applying this idea of the rate of change. Thus, in a series such as electric power production, a very smooth curve is obtained by plotting the ratio of each month to the corresponding month of the preceding year. This smooth curve can be readily projected graphically, and will usually give a very good forecast for a few months ahead. But the cycles in most economic series represent skew curves rather than this very even sine curve movement found in electric power production; i. e., there is a gradual process of recovery leading to the heights of prosperity, then usually a sudden and rapid decline. The upward movement, being slow and gradual, may often successfully be

[5] Irving Fisher: "Our Unstable Dollar and the So-called Business Cycle," Journal of the American Statistical Association, June, 1925, pp. 179-202.

projected by this method, but the precipitate downward movement is less readily foreseen, and more difficult to project. And, of course, from the practical point of view, it is the approach of "bad times" which it is most important to know about.

All things considered, then, the various methods of forecasting have not given highly satisfactory results. One reason for this was found in the continually changing underlying conditions in business. Another reason was found in the absence of regularity in the time movement of the phases of the business cycle. A glance at Chart 39 (Clearings Index of Business) will show that it is not only difficult to determine how long any phase of the cycle will continue, but also the degree of intensity which it will reach.

Although there have been notable brilliant forecasts of certain economic series by each of the methods considered, there have been also innumerable dismal failures. No method has given fool-proof results. But the importance of an intelligent analysis of the various factors of the business cycle, a measure of their intensity, an understanding of their changing relationships, and an exact quantitative expression of the measurement of economic events should lead to a much more intelligent prevision of business, and to a lessening of the severity of business cycles. Within reasonable limits we can now understand what is happening, and what has happened, and we can estimate roughly what is going to happen. And it is through measures of the type described in the preceding chapters, that much can be done towards the intelligent understanding that should eventually lead to control of the business cycle.

APPENDIX — TABLE 1

(CHART 2)

INDEX OF VOLUME OF CROP PRODUCTION

Each Crop Weighted by Its Average Price for Period 1909–1918

Base-average 1880–89 = $3,428,000

Year	Index	Year	Index	Year	Index
1870 . .	58.9	1890 . .	103.7	1910 . .	171.3
1871 . .	53.3	1891 . .	130.8	1911 . .	160.2
1872 . .	60.0	1892 . .	109.0	1912 . .	191.0
1873 . .	57.46	1893 . .	108.9	1913 . .	167.8
1874 . .	56.0	1894 . .	102.0	1914 . .	186.6
1875 . .	73.5	1895 . .	121.0	1915 . .	199.3
1876 . .	71.0	1896 . .	127.1	1916 . .	172.3
1877 . .	77.4	1897 . .	125.6	1917 . .	187.8
1878 . .	84.0	1898 . .	135.0	1918 . .	187.3
1879 . .	88.8	1899 . .	129.0	1919 . .	188.6
1880 . .	94.7	1900 . .	127.1	1920 . .	204.7
1881 . .	76.7	1901 . .	120.7	1921 . .	177.7
1882 . .	97.8	1902 . .	152.49	1922 . .	191.47
1883 . .	95.7	1903 . .	140.2	1923 . .	191.2
1884 . .	105.3	1904 . .	152.7	1924 . .	189.1
1885 . .	103.7	1905 . .	155.6	1925 . .	195.0
1886 . .	99.46	1906 . .	168.9	1926 . .	196.4
1887 . .	94.8	1907 . .	152.3	1927 . .	. . .
1888 . .	110.3	1908 . .	162.7	. . . .	. . .
1889 . .	125.3	1909 . .	166.6	. . . .	. . .

p - preliminary

237

APPENDIX — TABLE 1 — *Continued*

Cotton	crop multiplied by		$ .154	per	lb.
Wheat	"	"	" 1.187	"	bu.
Hay	"	"	" 13.14	"	ton
Oat	"	"	" .461	"	bu.
Rye	"	"	" .968	"	"
Corn	"	"	" .762	"	"
Tobacco	"	"	" .138	"	lb.
Potato	"	"	" .808	"	bu.
Barley	"	"	" .704	"	"
Buckwheat	"	"	" .944	"	"

Source: 1870–1880 Statistical Abstract 1887.
 1881–1923 Agricultural Year Book, 1919.
 1924–1925 Dec. 1 Crop Estimate.

APPENDIX — TABLE 2

(CHART 8)

Source, see p. 39

RAILWAY FREIGHT TRAFFIC

*Net Ton Miles of Freight (Revenue and non-revenue) Carried on
Class I Railroads in the United States**

(In 1,000,000)

1852	. .	1,101	1864	. .	6,178	1876	. .	23,148
1853	. .	1,158	1865	. .	5,729	1877	. .	23,182
1854	. .	1,490	1866	. .	6,946	1878	. .	28,297
1855	. .	1,719	1867	. .	8,019	1879	. .	34,625
1856	. .	2,193	1868	. .	9,105	1880	. .	38,375
1857	. .	2,200	1869	. .	11,170	1881	. .	42,556
1858	. .	2,306	1870	. .	13,041	1882	. .	43,012
1859	. .	2,521	1871	. .	14,768	1883	. .	44,065
1860	. .	3,282	1872	. .	17,008	1884	. .	44,725
1861	. .	4,061	1873	. .	19,825	1885	. .	49,152
1862	. .	5,328	1874	. .	20,490	1886	. .	52,802
1863	. .	5,504	1875	. .	20,776	1887	. .	62,061

* Estimated from reports of the varying number of railroads available.

APPENDIX — TABLE 3

(CHART 14)

PRODUCTION INDEXES (Snyder)

1910–1914 = 100. Unweighted average of relatives

	49 items	*87 items*		*49 items*	*87 items*
1870 . .	33.75	33.80	1900 . .	65.89	65.29
1871 . .	35.09	35.83	1901 . .	73.61	71.58
1872 . .	35.23	35.23	1902 . .	77.92	77.60
1873 . .	35.26	35.26	1903 . .	80.86	78.45
1874 . .	34.01	34.01	1904 . .	82.78	78.61
1875 . .	36.41	36.41	1905 . .	83.46	82.75
1876 . .	38.31	38.31	1906 . .	89.44	90.21
1877 . .	40.72	40.72	1907 . .	90.84	91.48
1878 . .	41.03	41.03	1908 . .	88.64	81.75
1879 . .	44.77	44.77	1909 . .	93.02	90.94
1880 . .	47.42	45.75	1910 . .	96.45	96.28
1881 . .	48.50	47.63	1911 . .	95.58	94.66
1882 . .	52.73	50.57	1912 . .	102.20	101.93
1883 . .	49.86	47.30	1913 . .	102.60	105.28
1884 . .	47.62	42.64	1914 . .	103.67	102.20
1885 . .	47.04	41.46	1915 . .	111.28	109.84
1886 . .	50.66	44.24	1916 . .	121.42	124.53
1887 . .	54.15	47.39	1917 . .	128.22	131.39
1888 . .	53.17	46.74	1918 . .	126.18	125.49
1889 . .	54.32	48.03	1919 . .	119.08	121.67
1890 . .	54.91	46.85	1920 . .	125.46	128.97
1891 . .	58.90	52.89	1921 . .	102.84	110.91
1892 . .	57.95	52.40	1922 . .	125.17	128.66
1893 . .	56.77	49.35	1923 . .	137.92	144.10
1894 . .	54.84	48.31	1924 . .	135.16	141.22
1895 . .	58.48	52.36	1925 . .	143.27	149.69
1896 . .	58.44	51.71			
1897 . .	59.46	53.04			
1898 . .	59.31	54.42			
1899 . .	64.42	61.22			

APPENDIX — TABLE 4

Sources, see p. 75

EMPLOYMENT IN NEW YORK STATE FACTORIES

AVERAGE

Unit = One hundred employed

	Data		Data
1910 . .	. . . .	1920 . . .	5,941
1911 . .	. . . .	1921 . . .	4,642
1912 . .	. . . .	1922 . . .	4,996
1913 . .	. . . .	1923 . . .	5,534
1914 . .	. . . .	1924 . . .	5,044
1915 . .	4,940	1925 . . .	5,009
1916 . .	5,793	1926 . . .	. . . .
1917 . .	6,042	1927 . . .	. . . .
1918 . .	6,137	1928 . . .	. . . .
1919 . .	5,730	1929 . . .	. . . .

Unit = One hundred employed

	1919		*1920*		*1921*		*1922*		*1923*		*1924*		*1925*	
	Data	*In-dex	Data	In-dex	Data	In-dex	Data	In-dex	Data	In-dex	Data	In-dex	Data	In-dex
Jan. . .	5705	112	6199	122	4670	92	4638	91	5470	108	5349	105	4965	98
Feb. . .	5636	111	6136	121	4756	94	4785	94	5539	109	5402	106	5053	100
Mar. . .	5608	109	6310	123	4803	94	4843	94	5670	110	5419	106	5107	99
Apr. . .	5597	110	6225	123	4708	93	4780	94	5658	111	5245	103	5016	99
May . .	5546	111	6131	122	4614	92	4823	96	5603	112	5028	100	4946	99
June . .	5531	110	6110	122	4528	90	4899	98	5553	111	4894	98	4910	98
July . .	5672	115	6076	123	4441	90	4899	99	5514	111	4698	95	4858	98
Aug. . .	5792	117	5953	120	4435	90	5013	101	5463	110	4710	95	4872	98
Sept. . .	5850	117	5876	117	4606	92	5112	102	5486	109	4892	98	4997	100
Oct. . .	5768	114	5767	114	4718	93	5277	104	5558	110	4951	98	5097	100
Nov. . .	5926	115	5454	106	4713	92	5399	105	5479	107	4954	96	5128	100
Dec. . .	6133	119	5055	98	4714	92	5479	107	5412	105	4990	97	5158	100
Aver. . .	5,730	113	5,941	118	4,642	92	4,996	99	5,534	110	5,044	100	5,009	99

* Index = percentage deviation of actual data from trend, seasonal allowed for.

APPENDIX — TABLE 5

(CHARTS 3, 4, 5, 6, 7, 10, 12, 19)

PRODUCTION OF PRODUCERS' GOODS AND CONSUMERS' GOODS

Sources, see pp. 85-91

COTTON CONSUMPTION

Unit = Thousand bales

Including linters, 1870–1903; excluding linters, 1904 to date

CROP YEARS

	Data		Data		Data		Data		Data		Data
1870	797	1880	1501	1890	2518	1900	3687	1910	4622	1920	6420
1871	1026	1881	1866	1891	2604	1901	3604	1911	4498	1921	4893
1872	1147	1882	1849	1892	2847	1902	4080	1912	5129	1922	5910
1873	1116	1883	2038	1893	2416	1903	4187	1913	5483	1923	6666
1874	1213	1884	1814	1894	2300	1904	3980	1914	5577	1924	5681
1875	1098	1885	1687	1895	2984	1905	4523	1915	5597	1925	6191
1876	1256	1886	2095	1896	2500	1906	4809	1916	6398	1926	....
1877	1314	1887	2050	1897	2841	1907	4985	1917	6789	1927	....
1878	1459	1888	2205	1898	3472	1908	4539	1918	6566	1928	....
1879	1457	1889	2309	1899	3672	1909	5092	1919	5766	1929	....

	1918–1919		1919–1920		1920–1921		1921–1922		1922–1923		1923–1924		1924–1925	
	Data	*Index	Data	Index	Data	Index	Data	Index	Data	Index	Data	Index	Data	Index
Aug. .	535	107	497	98	484	93	467	88	527	97	492	89	357	63
Sept. .	490	99	491	97	458	89	485	92	495	92	484	88	435	78
Oct. .	440	85	556	105	401	74	495	89	534	95	542	94	533	91
Nov. .	456	91	491	96	333	64	527	99	578	106	532	93	492	87
Dec. .	473	93	512	98	295	56	512	94	528	95	462	82	532	92
Jan. .	557	102	592	106	366	64	527	91	610	103	577	95	590	96
Feb. .	433	90	516	105	395	78	473	92	567	108	508	95	550	101
Mar. .	433	81	576	105	438	79	518	91	623	107	484	82	583	96
Apr. .	476	91	567	106	409	75	447	80	577	101	480	82	597	101
May .	488	92	541	100	441	80	496	88	621	108	414	70	531	89
June .	474	91	555	105	462	85	508	92	542	96	350	61	494	84
July .	510	99	525	100	410	76	459	84	462	83	347	61	484	83
Total	5766	..	6420	..	4893	..	5912	..	6665	..	5670	..	6178	..
Aver.	480	94	535	102	408	76	493	90	555	99	472	83	515	88

* Index = percentage deviation of actual data from trend, seasonal allowed for.

INDEX OF WOOL MILL ACTIVITY
Weighted Index of Percentage of Hours Active for Looms and Spindles

	1919		1920		1921		1922		1923		1924		1925	
	Data	*Index	Data	Index	Data	Index	Data	Index	Data	Index	Data	Index	Data	Index
Jan.	61.2	76	86.5	108	33.0	41	74.6	93	89.6	111	75.5	94	78.5	98
Feb.	52.4	65	88.5	110	38.9	48	73.6	91	86.8	108	76.9	96	77.8	97
Mar.	49.5	62	85.7	107	52.6	65	74.9	93	95.3	118	76.4	95	75.0	93
Apr.	60.6	75	88.0	109	60.8	76	71.6	89	96.5	120	69.7	87	71.4	89
May	71.0	88	86.6	108	74.3	92	66.0	82	95.3	118	67.3	84	67.1	83
June	75.9	94	77.8	97	79.5	99	69.3	86	90.7	113	61.3	76	65.6	81
July	82.0	102	62.2	77	82.0	102	71.3	89	84.0	104	56.6	70	62.3	77
Aug.	82.9	103	58.3	72	77.9	97	69.8	87	79.1	98	59.3	74	66.9	83
Sept.	83.6	104	56.8	71	78.1	97	79.5	99	80.4	100	70.3	87	70.9	88
Oct.	86.6	108	61.0	76	79.3	99	85.1	106	82.1	102	77.9	97	75.4	94
Nov.	87.8	109	53.1	66	80.3	100	84.9	105	81.4	101	79.1	98	74.7	93
Dec.	87.6	109	43.9	55	77.6	96	87.8	109	73.6	91	80.1	100	70.8	88
Total Aver.	73.4	91	70.7	88	67.9	84	75.7	94	86.2	107	70.9	88	71.4	89

* Index = percentage deviation of weighted index from trend, no seasonal allowed for.

PIG IRON PRODUCTION
Unit = Thousand gross tons

Data		Data		Data		Data		Data		Data	
1870	1,339	1880	3,355	1890	8,575	1900	13,405	1910	26,907	1920	36,603
1871	1,363	1881	3,574	1891	7,703	1901	15,495	1911	23,371	1921	16,593
1872	2,102	1882	4,000	1892	8,619	1902	17,431	1912	29,380	1922	26,995
1873	2,045	1883	4,085	1893	6,738	1903	17,504	1913	30,626	1923	40,059
1874	1,886	1884	3,689	1894	6,435	1904	16,160	1914	23,068	1924	31,108
1875	1,657	1885	3,688	1895	9,221	1905	22,639	1915	29,620	1925	36,398
1876	1,593	1886	5,273	1896	8,313	1906	24,874	1916	39,062	1926	....
1877	1,783	1887	5,901	1897	9,397	1907	25,344	1917	38,245	1927	....
1878	2,039	1888	5,955	1898	11,477	1908	15,687	1918	38,706	1928	....
1879	2,421	1889	7,028	1899	13,336	1909	25,419	1919	30,688	1929	....

	1919		1920		1921		1922		1923		1924		1925	
	Data	*Index	Data	Index	Data	Index	Data	Index	Data	Index	Data	Index	Data	Index
Jan.	3,302	120	3,015	106	2,416	82	1,645	54	3,230	103	3,019	94	3,370	102
Feb.	2,940	116	2,979	114	1,937	72	1,630	59	2,994	105	3,075	105	3,214	106
Mar.	3,090	109	3,376	115	1,596	53	2,036	65	3,524	110	3,466	105	3,565	105
Apr.	2,478	90	2,740	96	1,193	41	2,072	68	3,550	114	3,233	101	3,259	99
May	2,108	76	2,986	104	1,221	41	2,307	76	3,868	124	2,615	81	2,931	89
June	2,115	79	3,044	111	1,065	38	2,361	81	3,676	122	2,026	66	2,673	84
July	2,429	90	3,067	110	865	30	2,405	81	3,678	121	1,785	57	2,664	83
Aug.	2,743	98	3,147	109	954	32	1,816	59	3,449	110	1,886	58	2,704	81
Sept.	2,488	92	3,129	112	986	34	2,034	68	3,126	102	2,053	65	2,726	84
Oct.	1,864	65	3,293	111	1,247	41	2,638	84	3,149	98	2,477	75	3,023	89
Nov.	2,392	84	2,935	100	1,415	47	2,850	92	2,894	90	2,510	76	3,023	90
Dec.	2,633	94	2,704	94	1,649	55	3,087	101	2,921	93	2,962	92	3,250	98
Total	30,583		36,414		16,544		26,880		40,059		31,108		36,398	
Aver.	2,549	93	3,035	107	1,379	47	2,240	74	3,338	108	2,592	81	3,033	93

* Index = percentage deviation of actual data from trend, seasonal allowed for.

STEEL INGOT PRODUCTION

Unit = Thousand gross tons

	Data		Data		Data		Data		Data		Data
1870	..	1880	1,210	1890	4,149	1900	9,996	1910	25,154	1920	40,881
1871	..	1881	1,540	1891	3,787	1901	13,156	1911	23,029	1921	19,224
1872	..	1882	1,685	1892	4,780	1902	14,556	1912	30,285	1922	34,568
1873	..	1883	1,624	1893	3,899	1903	14,105	1913	30,280	1923	43,486
1874	..	1884	1,504	1894	4,280	1904	13,530	1914	22,820	1924	36,645
1875	..	1885	1,661	1895	5,932	1905	19,463	1915	31,284	1925	44,152
1876	..	1886	2,486	1896	5,124	1906	22,624	1916	41,402	1926	...
1877	..	1887	3,239	1897	6,942	1907	22,559	1917	43,619	1927	...
1878	710	1888	2,812	1898	8,801	1908	13,677	1918	43,051	1928	...
1879	907	1889	3,284	1899	10,459	1909	23,299	1919	33,695	1929	...

	1919		1920		1921		1922		1923		1924		1925	
	Data	Index*	Data	Index	Data	Index	Data	Index	Data	Index	Data	Index	Data	Index
Jan.	3,651	119	3,525	111	2,518	76	1,892	56	3,841	109	3,650	101	4,199	113
Feb.	3,178	118	3,403	119	1,999	67	2,072	68	3,472	110	3,826	118	3,756	113
Mar.	3,127	96	3,918	116	1,795	51	2,815	78	4,067	109	4,207	110	4,199	107
Apr.	2,632	88	3,133	101	1,387	43	2,902	88	3,964	117	3,348	96	3,588	100
May	2,266	77	3,424	113	1,447	46	3,219	99	4,216	126	2,640	77	3,458	99
June	2,607	91	3,540	120	1,146	37	3,128	99	3,767	116	2,066	62	3,207	94
July	2,946	102	3,329	111	918	30	2,953	92	3,531	107	1,878	55	3,088	89
Aug.	3,226	110	3,563	117	1,301	41	2,629	81	3,696	111	2,553	74	3,424	98
Sept.	s	..	3,563	123	1,343	45	2,818	91	3,357	106	2,828	87	3,493	105
Oct.	s	..	3,582	110	1,848	55	3,410	98	3,577	100	3,125	85	3,893	104
Nov.	s	..	3,134	101	1,897	59	3,430	104	3,134	93	3,121	90	3,907	110
Dec.	s	..	2,779	99	1,631	56	3,300	110	2,863	93	3,560	112	3,976	123
Total	...	..	40,893	..	19,230	..	34,568	..	43,486	..	36,811	..	44,152	..
Aver.	...	..	3,408	112	1,603	51	2,881	89	3,624	108	3,068	89	3,679	105

* Index = percentage deviation of actual data from trend, seasonal allowed for.
s = strike.

U. S. LUMBER PRODUCTION, REPORTED CUT

Unit = Million board feet

	Data		Data		Data		Data		Data		Data
1870	12,756	1880	18,091	1890	23,845	1900	...	1910	40,018	1920	33,799
1871	..	1881	...	1891	...	1901	...	1911	37,003	1921	26,961
1872	..	1882	...	1892	...	1902	...	1912	39,158	1922	31,569
1873	..	1883	...	1893	...	1903	...	1913	38,387	1923	37,166
1874	..	1884	...	1894	...	1904	34,135	1914	37,346	1924	35,931
1875	..	1885	...	1895	...	1905	30,503	1915	31,242	1925	37,500
1876	..	1886	...	1896	...	1906	37,551	1916	34,791	1926	..
1877	..	1887	...	1897	...	1907	40,256	1917	33,193	1927	..
1878	..	1888	...	1898	...	1908	33,224	1918	29,362	1928	..
1879	..	1889	...	1899	35,084	1909	44,510	1919	34,552	1929	..

LUMBER CUT OF NATIONAL LUMBER MFRERS'. ASS'N
Unit = Million board feet

	1919		1920		1921		1922		1923		1924		1925	
	Data	*In- dex	Data	In- dex	Data	In- dex	Data	In- dex	Data	In- dex	Data	In- dex	Data	In- dex
Jan. . .	835	88	1,021	107	598	62	937	96	1,066	108	1,155	116	1,225	122
Feb. . .	858	93	1,033	111	670	71	845	89	978	102	1,210	124	1,127	115
Mar. . .	1,036	96	1,182	108	798	72	970	87	1,355	121	1,275	112	1,285	112
Apr. . .	1,099	100	1,245	112	843	75	994	88	1,271	111	1,359	117	1,320	113
May . .	1,112	85	1,265	95	1,019	76	1,267	94	1,537	112	1,470	106	1,464	105
June . .	1,043	87	1,146	94	941	77	1,154	93	1,459	117	1,246	99	1,403	110
July . .	1,114	97	1,061	92	886	76	1,152	97	1,297	109	1,202	100	1,412	116
Aug. . .	1,276	101	1,174	92	974	75	1,323	101	1,519	115	1,260	94	1,389	103
Sept. .	1,197	100	1,092	90	917	75	1,207	97	1,404	112	1,259	100	1,352	106
Oct. . .	1,270	103	1,116	89	991	79	1,306	103	1,552	121	1,388	107	1,444	110
Nov. . .	1,029	97	885	83	922	85	1,236	113	1,332	121	1,126	101	1,143	102
Dec. . .	842	96	639	72	825	92	1,103	122	1,029	112	1,018	110	1,057	113
Total .	12,711	. .	12,859	. .	10,383	. .	13,495	. .	15,798	. .	14,967	. .	15,620	. .
Aver. .	1,059	95	1,072	95	865	76	1,125	98	1,317	113	1,247	107	1,302	110

* Index = percentage deviation of actual data from trend, seasonal allowed for.

SILK CONSUMPTION
APPROXIMATE DELIVERIES AT AMERICAN MILLS
Unit = Number of bales

	Data
1920	*198,692
1921	334,649
1922	367,620
1923	358,417
1924	365,937
1925	501,343
1926	. . . .
1927	. . . .
1928	. . . .
1929	. . . .

* Total 11 months.

	1920		1921		1922		1923		1924		1925	
	Data	* Index	Data	Index	Data	Index	Data	Index	Data	Index	Data	Index
Jan. . .	. . . .	. .	22,176	89	33,842	127	34,680	122	32,925	108	39,885	122
Feb. . .	30,071	128	16,725	67	22,107	82	36,231	126	29,804	97	37,529	114
Mar. . .	27,511	117	26,942	107	26,651	99	33,515	116	26,543	86	45,157	137
Apr. . .	25,336	107	31,933	126	24,247	89	38,193	132	25,985	84	40,040	121
May . .	22,325	94	31,307	123	33,284	122	24,509	84	28,272	91	38,266	115
June . .	14,869	62	32,217	126	29,529	108	27,824	95	23,164	74	39,575	118
July . .	10,846	45	33,762	131	24,996	91	28,573	97	30,952	98	44,013	130
Aug. . .	19,101	79	33,557	130	34,772	125	33,547	113	29,518	93	44,047	130
Sept. .	16,624	68	31,769	122	34,212	123	26,929	90	36,366	114	41,684	122
Oct. . .	11,112	45	26,816	102	37,471	134	25,917	86	35,508	111	46,815	136
Nov. . .	10,735	44	26,515	101	35,467	126	25,225	84	32,939	102	41,848	121
Dec. . .	10,162	41	20,930	79	31,042	109	23,274	77	33,961	105	42,484	122
Total .	198,692	. .	334,649	. .	367,620	. .	358,417	. .	365,937	. .	501,343	. .
Aver. .	18,063	76	27,887	109	30,635	111	29,868	102	30,495	97	41,779	124

* Index = percentage deviation of actual data from trend, no seasonal allowed for.

PRODUCTION OF CEMENT

Unit = Thousand barrels of 376 pounds

	Data		Data		Data		Data		Data
1880	2,073	1890	7,777	1900	17,231	1910	77,785	1920	100,023
1881	2,500	1891	8,223	1901	20,069	1911	79,548	1921	98,842
1882	3,250	1892	8,759	1902	25,754	1912	83,351	1922	114,790
1883	4,190	1893	8,002	1903	29,899	1913	92,949	1923	137,460
1884	4,000	1894	8,362	1904	31,675	1914	89,050	1924	148,859
1885	4,150	1895	8,731	1905	40,102	1915	86,708	1925	161,298
1886	4,500	1896	9,526	1906	51,000	1916	92,363	1926	....
1887	6,943	1897	11,038	1907	52,230	1917	93,454	1927	....
1888	6,503	1898	12,344	1908	52,911	1918	71,515	1928	....
1889	6,832	1899	15,855	1909	66,690	1919	80,778	1929	....

	1919		1920		1921		1922		1923		1924		1925	
	†Data	*Index	†Data	Index	Data	Index	Data	Index	Data	Index	Data	Index	Data	Index
Jan.	..	63	..	122	4,098	77	4,291	78	7,990	140	8,788	148	8,856	144
Feb.	..	64	..	106	4,379	74	4,278	69	8,210	128	8,588	129	8,255	119
Mar.	..	67	..	99	6,763	92	6,685	87	9,880	124	10,370	125	11,034	129
Apr.	..	73	..	88	8,651	94	9,243	97	11,359	115	11,726	114	13,807	129
May	..	77	..	87	9,281	87	11,176	101	12,910	112	13,777	116	15,503	125
June	..	80	..	89	9,296	90	11,245	105	12,382	111	13,538	118	15,387	128
July	..	87	..	87	9,568	94	11,557	109	12,620	115	14,029	123	15,641	132
Aug.	..	87	..	90	10,244	95	11,664	104	12,967	112	15,128	126	16,419	131
Sept.	..	92	..	93	10,027	96	11,424	106	13,109	117	14,519	124	15,939	131
Oct.	..	89	..	97	10,506	96	12,287	108	13,350	113	14,820	121	15,992	126
Nov.	..	88	..	102	8,921	93	11,349	114	12,603	122	13,141	123	13,656	123
Dec.	..	71	..	106	6,559	89	8,671	113	9,997	125	10,435	126	10,809	125
Total	..	..	..	..	98,293	..	113,870	..	137,377	..	148,859	..	161,298	..
Aver.	..	78	..	97	8,191	90	9,489	99	11,448	120	12,405	124	13,442	129

* Index = percentage deviation of actual data from trend, seasonal allowed for.
† Monthly data not available for publication prior to 1921.

COPPER PRODUCTION

Unit = Thousand pounds

	Data		Data		Data		Data		Data		Data
1870	28,224	1880	60,480	1890	259,763	1900	606,177	1910	1,088,237	1920	1,224,550
1871	29,120	1881	71,680	1891	284,122	1901	602,073	1911	1,114,764	1921	472,026
1872	28,000	1882	90 646	1892	344,999	1902	659,509	1912	1,249,095	1922	987,707
1873	34,720	1883	115,526	1893	329,354	1903	698,045	1913	1,235,570	1923	1,477,819
1874	39,200	1884	144,947	1894	354,188	1904	812,537	1914	1,148,431	1924	1,587,694
1875	40,320	1885	165,875	1895	380,613	1905	888,784	1915	1,488,072	1925	1,677,780
1876	42,560	1886	157,763	1896	460,061	1906	916,971	1916	2,005,875	1926	...
1877	47,040	1887	181,477	1897	494,078	1907	847,151	1917	1,895,434	1927	...
1878	48,160	1888	226,361	1898	526,513	1908	956,841	1918	1,910,023	1928	...
1879	51,520	1889	226,776	1899	568,667	1909	1,126,521	1919	1,212,334	1929	...

COPPER PRODUCTION — *Continued*
Unit = Million pounds

	1919 Data	*In-dex	1920 Data	In-dex	1921 Data	In-dex	1922 Data	In-dex	1923 Data	In-dex	1924 Data	In-dex	1925 Data	In-dex
Jan. . .	135.7	111	121.9	98	85.9	68	25.8	20	112.3	85	133.3	99	148.7	109
Feb. . .	111.7	100	117.5	103	76.5	66	37.4	32	102.7	85	131.4	107	137.6	111
Mar. .	102.0	81	120.3	94	89.1	68	62.3	47	121.6	89	130.4	94	149.8	107
Apr. . .	98.8	81	116.1	94	51.1	40	77.0	60	118.2	90	132.1	99	141.1	104
May .	92.7	73	115.0	89	24.2	18	92.0	69	125.4	92	131.2	94	140.1	99
June .	95.9	78	116.1	92	19.4	15	95.2	73	125.5	94	127.9	95	137.1	102
July .	100.4	86	109.7	92	17.8	15	93.5	75	126.1	100	129.6	101	137.0	105
Aug. .	108.0	88	112.5	90	21.4	17	99.7	77	131.7	100	133.5	100	136.2	100
Sept. .	108.7	92	104.9	87	20.9	17	95.0	76	124.5	98	127.6	99	135.4	103
Oct. .	115.1	94	105.2	84	24.6	19	103.4	79	132.1	100	137.9	103	141.2	104
Nov. .	117.3	100	106.7	90	22.3	18	101.6	82	127.8	101	136.6	107	134.8	104
Dec. .	103.0	84	95.7	77	18.6	15	104.7	81	129.7	99	136.2	102	138.4	102
Total .	1,289.2	..	1,341.7	..	472.0	..	987.7	..	1,477.5	..	1,587.7	..	1,677.4	..
Aver. .	107.4	89	111.8	91	39.3	31	82.3	64	123.2	94	132.3	100	139.8	104

* Index = percentage deviation of actual data from trend, seasonal allowed for.

ZINC PRODUCTION
Unit = Short tons

	Data		Data		Data		Data		Data
1880	....	1890	63,683	1900	123,886	1910	269,184	1920	463,377
1881	....	1891	80,873	1901	140,822	1911	286,526	1921	200,500
1882	33,765	1892	87,260	1902	156,927	1912	338,806	1922	354,277
1883	36,872	1893	78,832	1903	159,219	1913	346,676	1923	510,434
1884	38,544	1894	75,328	1904	186,702	1914	353,049	1924	517,339
1885	40,688	1895	89,686	1905	203,849	1915	489,519	1925	590,928
1886	42,641	1896	81,499	1906	224,770	1916	668,343	1926	.....
1887	50,340	1897	99,980	1907	249,860	1917	669,573	1927	.....
1888	55,903	1898	115,399	1908	210,424	1918	517,927	1928	.....
1889	58,860	1899	129,051	1909	255,760	1919	465,743	1929	.....

	1920 Data	*In-dex	1921 Data	In-dex	1922 Data	In-dex	1923 Data	In-dex	1924 Data	In-dex	1925 Data	In-dex
Jan. . .	43,441	104	25,916	59	23,706	52	46,317	97	49,709	100	50,386	97
Feb. . .	43,921	113	17,769	44	22,513	53	42,443	96	43,933	95	46,811	97
Mar. . .	48,256	112	15,741	35	26,532	56	48,731	99	47,775	93	51,485	96
Apr. . .	45,399	111	16,550	33	25,506	57	46,866	100	44,949	92	48,851	96
May . .	45,415	109	18,026	41	27,419	60	47,347	100	47,666	96	49,738	96
June .	41,009	108	19,443	49	28,547	69	42,840	99	43,442	96	45,921	98
July .	40,194	106	15,495	39	31,917	78	43,065	100	42,913	96	47,583	102
Aug. .	38,226	105	14,621	39	31,423	79	41,625	101	41,775	97	47,849	107
Sept. .	36,819	106	14,367	39	33,134	87	39,105	98	40,852	99	47,384	110
Oct. .	35,335	98	14,538	38	39,940	101	42,098	102	42,488	99	50,497	113
Nov. .	33,318	90	21,135	55	40,200	99	44,280	105	42,633	97	50,629	111
Dec. .	28,439	74	22,013	55	42,841	102	46,485	106	47,711	105	53,794	113
Total .	479,772	..	215,614	..	373,678	..	531,202	..	535,846	..	590,928	..
Aver. .	39,986	103	17,968	44	31,140	74	44,267	100	44,654	97	49,244	103

* Index = percentage deviation of actual data from trend, seasonal allowed for.

TIN DELIVERIES IN THE UNITED STATES AT BOTH ATLANTIC AND PACIFIC PORTS (Excl. of Bolivian Tin)

Unit = Long tons

	Data		Data		Data		Data
1890	....	1900	30,160	1910	47,250	1920	51,120
1891	....	1901	33,111	1911	46,332	1921	25,916
1892	....	1902	35,589	1912	51,395	1922	57,460
1893	....	1903	39,540	1913	45,551	1923	70,154
1894	....	1904	37,007	1914	43,308	1924	64,125
1895	....	1905	40,144	1915	50,387	1925	76,455
1896	....	1906	42,930	1916	56,216	1926	...
1897	....	1907	36,917	1917	57,881	1927	...
1898	....	1908	35,131	1918	58,339	1928	...
1899	31,499	1909	43,484	1919	32,301	1929	...

	1919		1920		1921		1922		1923		1924		1925	
	Data	*In-dex	Data	In-dex	Data	In-dex	Data	In-dex	Data	In-dex	Data	In-dex	Data	In-dex
Jan.	1,850	40	3,910	83	1,555	32	4,275	85	6,625	128	4,895	91	7,155	130
Feb.	2,450	49	5,200	100	1,585	30	3,215	58	6,185	109	8,845	151	7,205	119
Mar	2,070	39	5,130	93	1,683	30	6,030	103	6,634	110	4,560	73	7,100	111
Apr.	36	1	3,305	71	1,590	33	4,995	100	6,775	132	7,590	143	6,655	122
May	20	..	3,550	73	1,225	25	4,740	92	6,035	114	5,240	96	4,910	87
June	68	1	6,500	122	1,590	29	5,130	90	5,410	92	4,310	71	6,175	99
July	132	2	5,530	96	1,525	26	4,590	75	5,305	84	3,930	60	6,475	96
Aug.	4,345	88	3,745	74	3,320	63	4,150	77	5,510	99	4,805	84	6,520	110
Sept.	4,825	96	4,860	94	2,605	49	5,050	92	4,540	80	4,985	85	6,360	105
Oct.	2,875	58	3,415	67	2,280	43	5,603	103	5,540	98	5,090	88	6,070	101
Nov.	6,665	167	3,395	82	3,250	76	4,812	110	6,785	150	5,790	124	5,670	118
Dec.	6,965	149	2,580	53	3,710	74	4,870	95	4,810	91	4,085	75	6,160	109
Total	32,301	..	51,120	..	25,918	..	57,460	..	70,154	..	64,125	..	76,455	..
Aver.	2,692	58	4,260	84	2,160	42	4,788	90	5,846	107	5,344	95	6,371	109

* Index = percentage deviation of actual data from trend, seasonal allowed for.

PETROLEUM PRODUCTION

Unit = Thousand barrels

	Data		Data		Data		Data		Data		Data
1870	5,261	1880	26,286	1890	45,824	1900	63,621	1910	209,557	1920	442,929
1871	5,205	1881	27,661	1891	54,293	1901	69,389	1911	220,449	1921	472,183
1872	6,293	1882	30,350	1892	50,515	1902	88,767	1912	222,935	1922	557,531
1873	9,894	1883	23,450	1893	48,431	1903	100,461	1913	248,446	1923	732,407
1874	10,927	1884	24,218	1894	49,344	1904	117,081	1914	265,763	1924	713,940
1875	8,788	1885	21,859	1895	52,892	1905	134,717	1915	281,104	1925	755,852
1876	9,133	1886	28,065	1896	60,960	1906	126,494	1916	300,767	1926	....
1877	13,350	1887	28,283	1897	60,476	1907	166,095	1917	335,316	1927	....
1878	15,397	1888	27,612	1898	55,364	1908	178,527	1918	355,928	1928	....
1879	19,914	1889	35,164	1899	57,071	1909	183,171	1919	378,367	1929	....

PETROLEUM PRODUCTION — *Continued*

	1919 Data	*Index	1920 Data	Index	1921 Data	Index	1922 Data	Index	1923 Data	Index	1924 Data	Index	1925 Data	Index
Jan.	28,835	98	34,008	102	38,138	106	43,696	112	52,527	124	57,273	126	59,519	123
Feb.	26,549	95	33,193	107	35,524	107	41,314	114	48,588	126	55,889	134	54,045	121
Mar.	29,952	93	36,171	102	41,105	107	47,188	114	56,969	127	60,141	125	60,433	117
Apr.	29,628	92	34,945	103	40,233	108	45,167	111	59,008	134	59,830	127	61,431	122
May	30,587	91	36,622	103	42,189	110	47,002	113	62,377	139	61,834	129	68,082	132
June	30,878	97	36,663	105	40,548	106	46,087	111	62,845	139	59,583	124	66,675	129
July	34,020	100	37,746	105	40,461	102	47,134	110	65,925	142	61,932	123	67,318	126
Aug.	33,613	101	38,906	108	41,109	105	47,059	111	66,422	146	62,398	126	66,887	127
Sept.	33,893	102	37,521	106	36,763	95	45,805	109	65,306	144	60,376	124	64,708	121
Oct.	34,214	98	39,584	107	35,832	89	48,410	112	67,506	142	60,469	120	64,352	116
Nov.	33,026	98	38,609	110	38,108	99	48,027	116	65,388	145	56,782	118	61,658	146
Dec.	33,172	98	38,961	109	42,173	108	50,642	120	59,546	131	57,433	116	60,943	119
Total	378,367	..	442,929	..	472,183	..	557,531	..	732,407	..	713,940	..	755,852	..
Aver.	31,531	97	36,911	106	39,349	104	46,461	113	61,034	137	59,495	124	62,988	123

* Index = percentage deviation of actual data from trend, seasonal allowed for.

PRODUCTION OF GAS AND FUEL OIL

Unit = Million gallons

	Data		Data		Data		Data
1890	..	1900	..	1910	....	1920	8,861
1891	..	1901	..	1911	....	1921	9,664
1892	..	1902	..	1912	....	1922	10,706
1893	..	1903	..	1913	....	1923	12,074
1894	..	1904	360	1914	3,734	1924	13,460
1895	..	1905	..	1915	....	1925	15,278
1896	..	1906	..	1916	....	1926	...
1897	..	1907	..	1917	6,513	1927	...
1898	..	1908	..	1918	7,321	1928	...
1899	305	1909	1,702	1919	7,627	1929	...

	1919 Data	*Index	1920 Data	Index	1921 Data	Index	1922 Data	Index	1923 Data	Index	1924 Data	Index	1925 Data	Index
Jan.	590	103	618	96	837	116	858	107	989	112	1,063	109	1,171	111
Feb.	554	101	590	96	733	107	761	100	903	107	1,025	111	1,059	105
Mar.	575	97	687	103	758	101	849	102	971	106	1,114	111	1,204	110
Apr.	589	98	643	95	813	108	792	94	977	106	1,117	110	1,230	111
May	652	100	707	97	817	100	937	103	966	96	1,156	105	1,274	107
June	632	97	690	94	826	101	903	100	903	100	1,107	101	1,360	114
July	638	94	751	99	807	95	959	102	1,053	102	1,103	97	1,445	117
Aug.	686	96	834	104	784	87	944	95	1,011	92	1,167	97	1,404	108
Sept.	683	96	837	105	788	89	918	93	1,033	95	1,114	94	1,281	110
Oct.	680	96	823	103	834	94	922	94	1,070	99	1,161	98	1,322	103
Nov.	663	97	823	107	799	94	892	94	1,058	102	1,134	100	1,230	100
Dec.	685	101	859	113	866	102	972	104	1,073	105	1,199	107	1,298	107
Total	7,627	..	8,861	..	9,664	..	10,706	..	12,074	..	13,460	..	15,278	..
Aver.	636	98	738	101	805	99	892	99	1,006	102	1,122	103	1,273	108

* Index = percentage deviation of actual data from trend, seasonal allowed for.

SOLE LEATHER PRODUCTION

Unit = Thousand sides

	Data		Data
1910 . . .	. . . .	1920 . . .	18,393
1911 . . .	. . . .	1921 . . .	17,841
1912 . . .	. . . .	1922 . . .	17,554
1913 . . .	. . . .	1923 . . .	18,739
1914 . . .	. . . .	1924 . . .	14,638
1915 . . .	. . . .	1925 . . .	14,874
1916 . . .	. . . .	1926 . . .	. . . .
1917 . . .	. . . .	1927 . . .	. . . .
1918 . . .	19,837	1928 . . .	. . . .
1919 . . .	22,515	1929 . . .	. . . .

	1919		1920		1921		1922		1923		1924		1925	
	Data	*In-dex	Data	In-dex	Data	In-dex	Data	In-dex	Data	In-dex	Data	In-dex	Data	In-dex
Jan. . .	2,053	125	1,704	104	1,191	73	1,655	101	1,654	101	1,373	84	1,288	78
Feb. . .	1,707	118	1,532	106	1,178	81	1,466	101	1,449	100	1,213	84	1,203	83
Mar. . .	1,741	108	1,764	110	1,351	84	1,472	91	1,699	106	1,213	75	1,313	82
Apr. . .	2,039	123	1,590	96	1,423	86	1,327	80	1,681	101	1,173	71	1,320	80
May . .	1,995	115	1,706	98	1,561	90	1,321	76	1,674	96	1,147	66	1,286	74
June . .	2,039	116	1,786	102	1,522	87	1,408	80	1,629	93	1,063	61	1,331	76
July . .	1,873	119	1,514	96	1,431	91	1,398	89	1,647	105	1,151	73	1,293	82
Aug. . .	1,924	118	1,323	81	1,607	99	1,509	93	1,719	106	1,169	72	1,279	79
Sept. . .	1,914	123	1,376	88	1,507	97	1,491	95	1,411	90	1,225	78	1,111	71
Oct. . .	1,904	115	1,459	88	1,619	98	1,551	94	1,511	91	1,351	81	1,315	79
Nov. . .	1,640	111	1,316	89	1,705	115	1,482	100	1,369	92	1,198	81	1,074	73
Dec. . .	1,686	108	1,323	85	1,746	112	1,474	94	1,296	83	1,362	87	1,062	68
Total .	22,515	. .	18,393	. .	17,841	. .	17,554	. .	18,739	. .	14,638	. .	14,874	. .
Aver. .	1,876	117	1,533	95	1,487	93	1,463	91	1,562	97	1,220	76	1,240	77

* Index = percentage deviation of actual data from trend, seasonal allowed for

BITUMINOUS COAL PRODUCTION

Unit = Thousand net tons

	Data		Data		Data		Data		Data		Data
1870	17,371	1880	42,832	1890	111,302	1900	212,316	1910	417,111	1920	568,667
1871	27,543	1881	53,961	1891	117,901	1901	225,828	1911	405,907	1921	415,922
1872	27,220	1882	68,430	1892	126,857	1902	260,217	1912	450,105	1922	422,268
1873	31,450	1883	77,251	1893	128,385	1903	282,749	1913	478,435	1923	564,157
1874	27,787	1884	82,999	1894	118,820	1904	278,660	1914	422,704	1924	483,280
1875	29,863	1885	72,824	1895	135,118	1905	315,063	1915	442,624	1925	522,951
1876	30,487	1886	74,645	1896	137,640	1906	342,875	1916	502,520	1926	. . . .
1877	34,841	1887	88,562	1897	147,618	1907	394,759	1917	551,791	1927	. . . .
1878	36,246	1888	102,040	1898	166,594	1908	332,574	1918	579,386	1928	. . . .
1879	37,898	1889	95,683	1899	193,323	1909	379,744	1919	465,860	1929	. . . .

BITUMINOUS COAL PRODUCTION — *Continued*

	1919		1920		1921		1922		1923		1924		1925	
	Data	*In- dex	Data	In- dex	Data	In- dex	Data	In- dex	Data	In- dex	Data	In- dex	Data	In- dex
Jan . .	42,193	95	49,748	110	41,148	90	38,930	81	51,903	107	52,464	108	51,930	109
Feb. . .	32,103	84	41,055	105	31,524	80	42,425	102	43,610	104	47,262	113	38,987	96
Mar.. .	34,293	81	47,850	111	31,054	71	51,936	113	48,411	105	41,253	89	37,626	83
Apr. . .	32,712	95	38,764	110	28,154	79	16,335	44	44,028	117	30,404	81	33,702	92
May . .	38,186	100	39,841	102	34,057	86	21,005	52	47,660	114	32,248	77	35,474	87
June .	37,685	95	46,095	115	34,635	85	23,096	55	47,054	109	31,433	73	37,167	88
July .	43,425	107	45,988	112	31,047	74	17,602	41	46,678	106	33,317	75	39,582	92
Aug. . .	43,613	99	49,974	111	35,291	77	26,755	60	50,544	105	35,892	74	44,883	96
Sept. .	48,209	109	50,241	112	35,870	79	42,463	86	47,805	99	42,340	88	46,817	100
Oct. . .	57,200	122	53,278	111	44,687	92	46,733	91	50,869	99	48,373	94	53,203	106
Nov. . .	19,006	44	52,576	119	36,805	82	46,900	100	44,387	94	42,066	89	50,780	110
Dec. . .	37,235	87	53,257	122	31,650	72	48,088	106	41,208	89	46,228	98	52,816	116
Total .	465,860	..	568,667	..	415,922	..	422,268	..	564,157	..	483,280	..	522,951	..
Aver. .	38,822	93	47,389	112	34,661	81	35,189	77	47,013	104	40,273	88	43,579	98

* Index = percentage deviation of actual data from trend, seasonal allowed for.

LOCOMOTIVES BUILT BY PRINCIPAL LOCOMOTIVE COMPANIES

Unit = Number

	Data
1919 . . .	2,766
1920 . . .	2,394
1921 . . .	1,349
1922 . . .	1,274
1923 . . .	3,189
1924 . . .	1,465
1925 . . .	1,127
1926 . . .	..
1927 . . .	..
1928 . . .	..
1929 . . .	..

	1919		1920		1921		1922		1923		1924		1925	
	Data	*In- dex	Data	In- dex	Data	In- dex	Data	In- dex	Data	In- dex	Data	In- dex	Data	In- dex
Jan. .	366	166	196	32	220	104	74	34	229	107	151	71	90	43
Feb. .	299	135	126	58	177	82	44	20	207	97	99	47	85	40
Mar. .	386	175	105	48	161	74	39	18	282	132	132	62	109	52
Apr. .	233	105	132	60	185	84	21	10	217	102	73	34	92	44
May .	238	108	188	89	75	34	70	37	238	111	111	52	96	46
June .	204	92	174	78	80	36	114	53	232	109	145	63	110	52
July .	194	88	178	80	57	26	128	59	239	112	140	66	66	31
Aug. .	333	151	233	109	95	43	151	70	272	127	139	66	104	49
Sept. .	162	74	201	89	106	47	119	55	335	157	104	49	94	45
Oct. .	144	65	300	139	75	34	145	67	310	141	96	45	79	38
Nov. .	62	28	277	127	29	13	159	74	299	140	133	63	98	47
Dec. .	145	66	284	133	89	41	210	98	329	154	142	67	104	49
Total .	2,766	..	2,394	..	1,349	..	1,274	..	3,189	..	1,465	..	1,127	..
Aver. .	231	104	199	87	112	52	106	50	266	124	122	57	94	45

* Index = percentage deviation of actual data from trend, no seasonal allowed for, but gradual increase in locomotive capacity considered.

SWINE SLAUGHTERED UNDER FEDERAL INSPECTION

Unit = Thousand head

	Data		Data		Data
1900	. . . .	1910	26,014	1920	38,019
1901	. . . .	1911	34,133	1921	38,982
1902	. . . .	1912	33,053	1922	43,114
1903	. . . .	1913	34,199	1923	53,334
1904	. . . .	1914	32,532	1924	52,872
1905	. . . .	1915	38,381	1925	43,043
1906	. . . .	1916	43,084	1926	. . . .
1907	32,885	1917	33,910	1927	. . . .
1908	38,643	1918	41,214	1928	. . . .
1909	31,395	1919	41,812	1929	. . . .

	1919		1920		1921		1922		1923		1924		1925	
	Data	*In-dex	Data	In-dex	Data	In-dex	Data	In-dex	Data	In-dex	Data	In-dex	Data	In-dex
Jan. . .	5,846	124	5,079	106	4,347	89	3,985	79	5,134	100	5,911	113	5,979	112
Feb. . .	4,266	112	3,104	80	3,799	95	3,480	86	4,231	102	5,006	118	4,447	103
Mar. . .	3,443	104	3,482	103	3,047	89	3,350	95	4,838	134	4,536	123	3,299	88
Apr. . .	3,208	110	2,590	87	3,003	99	2,946	95	4,179	132	4,073	126	3 037	92
May .	3,743	115	3,585	108	3,274	97	3,716	107	4,325	122	4,278	118	3,186	86
June .	3,728	115	3,566	108	3,618	107	4,046	117	4,303	122	4,288	119	3,732	101
July .	2,884	106	2,644	95	2,821	100	3,104	107	3,983	135	4,114	136	2,819	91
Aug. .	1,949	89	2,191	98	2,530	111	2,888	124	3,556	149	3,070	126	2,453	99
Sept. .	1,997	99	1,979	96	2,422	115	2,747	128	3,212	146	2,857	127	2,598	113
Oct. . .	2,686	94	2,487	86	2,866	96	3,332	109	4,328	139	3,498	110	3,314	102
Nov. . .	3,270	87	3,329	86	3,447	88	4,318	108	5,341	130	4,641	110	3,646	85
Dec. . .	4,790	96	3,985	79	3,807	73	5,201	98	5,904	109	6,600	119	4,533	80
Total .	41,812	. .	38,019	. .	38,982	. .	43,114	. .	53,334	. .	52,872	. .	43,043	. .
Aver. .	3,484	104	3,168	94	3,249	96	3,593	104	4,445	127	4,406	121	3,587	96

* Index = percentage deviation of actual data from trend, seasonal allowed for.

CATTLE SLAUGHTERED UNDER FEDERAL INSPECTION

Unit = Thousand head

	Data		Data		Data
1900	. . . .	1910	7,808	1920. . . .	8,609
1901	. . . .	1911	7,619	1921	7,608
1902	. . . .	1912	7,253	1922	8,678
1903	. . . .	1913	6,978	1923	9,163
1904	. . . .	1914	6,757	1924	9,592
1905	. . . .	1915	7,153	1925	9,853
1906	. . . .	1916	8,310	1926	. . . .
1907	7,633	1917	10,350	1927	. . . .
1908	7,279	1918	11,829	1928	. . . .
1909	7,714	1919	10,091	1929	. . . .

CATTLE SLAUGHTERED UNDER FEDERAL INSPECTION — *Continued*

	1919		1920		1921		1922		1923		1924		1925	
	Data	*Index	Data	Index	Data	Index	Data	Index	Data	Index	Data	Index	Data	Index
Jan. . .	1,119	154	832	113	690	93	642	85	745	98	812	106	855	110
Feb. . .	701	116	631	103	526	85	569	91	634	100	669	105	656	102
Mar. . .	640	102	683	108	621	97	674	104	688	105	665	100	736	110
Apr. . .	622	101	638	103	591	94	590	93	697	109	689	106	731	112
May . .	721	116	626	100	570	88	702	110	762	118	773	118	749	113
June .	644	93	657	94	640	90	724	101	727	101	670	92	732	99
July . .	855	129	661	99	579	85	697	102	725	105	764	109	862	122
Aug. . .	859	119	686	94	680	92	761	102	821	109	786	103	811	105
Sept. .	855	108	825	103	689	85	796	97	810	98	870	104	866	102
Oct. . .	1,073	117	843	91	750	80	884	93	953	100	1,016	105	1,067	109
Nov. . .	1,040	120	859	98	686	78	859	96	846	94	952	104	861	93
Dec. . .	960	119	667	82	586	71	779	93	756	90	926	109	927	108
Total .	10,091	. .	8,609	. .	7,608	. .	8,678	. .	9,163	. .	9,592	. .	9,853	. .
Aver. .	841	116	717	99	634	87	723	97	764	102	799	105	821	107

* Index = percentage deviation of actual data from trend, seasonal allowed for.

CALVES SLAUGHTERED UNDER FEDERAL INSPECTION

Unit = Thousand head

	Data		Data		Data
1900	. . . .	1910	2,238	1920	4,058
1901	. . . .	1911	2,184	1921	3,808
1902	. . . .	1912	2,278	1922	4,182
1903	. . . .	1913	1,902	1923	4,500
1904	. . . .	1914	1,697	1924	4,935
1905	. . . .	1915	1,819	1925	5,352
1906	. . . .	1916	2,367	1926	. . . .
1907	2,024	1917	3,143	1927	. . . .
1908	1,958	1918	3,456	1928	. . . .
1909	2,189	1919	3,969	1929	. . . .

	1919		1920		1921		1922		1923		1924		1925	
	Data	*Index	Data	Index	Data	Index	Data	Index	Data	Index	Data	Index	Data	Index
Jan. . .	295	125	305	122	282	106	288	103	351	118	373	118	394	118
Feb. . .	210	97	283	123	254	104	279	108	297	108	346	119	378	122
Mar. . .	295	104	390	130	360	114	391	116	368	103	377	100	466	116
Apr. . .	383	116	382	109	366	98	365	93	400	96	466	105	496	106
May . .	391	112	369	100	367	93	401	96	467	106	470	100	481	97
June . .	327	103	431	128	370	104	389	103	388	97	408	96	473	105
July . .	400	137	343	110	324	98	329	94	379	102	421	107	473	114
Aug. . .	319	117	332	115	304	99	345	106	403	117	374	103	439	114
Sept. . .	318	114	348	118	321	102	353	106	338	96	419	112	423	107
Oct. . .	375	128	315	102	309	94	383	110	416	113	473	121	486	117
Nov. . .	344	127	316	110	292	96	348	108	370	109	392	108	398	104
Dec. . .	312	132	245	97	259	97	309	110	324	108	416	131	445	132
Total .	3,969	. .	4,058	. .	3,808	. .	4,182	. .	4,500	. .	4,935	. .	5,352	. .
Aver. .	331	118	338	114	317	101	349	104	375	106	411	110	446	113

* Index = percentage deviation of actual data from trend, seasonal allowed for.

SHEEP AND LAMBS SLAUGHTERED UNDER FEDERAL INSPECTION

Unit = Thousand head

	Data		Data		Data
1900	....	1910	11,408	1920	10,982
1901	....	1911	14,020	1921	13,005
1902	....	1912	14,979	1922	10,929
1903	....	1913	14,406	1923	11,529
1904	....	1914	14,229	1924	11,991
1905	....	1915	12,212	1925	12,000
1906	....	1916	11,941	1926	....
1907	10,252	1917	9,345	1927	....
1908	10,305	1918	10,320	1928	....
1909	11,343	1919	12,691	1929	....

	1919		1920		1921		1922		1923		1924		1925	
	Data	*In-dex	Data	In-*dex	Data	In-dex	Data	In-dex	Data	In-dex	Data	In-dex	Data	In-dex
Jan. . .	1,004	101	955	96	1,068	107	954	95	1,021	102	1,083	108	990	98
Feb. . .	754	88	828	96	958	111	776	90	836	97	912	105	854	99
Mar. . .	738	81	788	86	1,075	118	837	92	977	107	868	95	984	107
Apr. . .	808	93	714	82	1,041	119	739	85	960	110	860	98	1,012	115
May . .	894	96	671	72	985	106	872	93	972	104	959	103	1,030	110
June .	931	95	818	83	1,116	114	1,028	105	914	93	975	99	999	101
July .	1,160	113	1,048	102	1,060	103	964	93	962	93	1,051	101	1,071	103
Aug. .	1,234	112	1,042	95	1,237	112	1,024	93	957	87	1,063	96	1,031	93
Sept. .	1,292	113	1,151	100	1,249	109	1,013	88	990	86	1,150	100	1,086	94
Oct. .	1,414	125	1,068	95	1,285	114	981	87	1,046	92	1,148	101	1,083	95
Nov. .	1,227	125	968	99	1,040	106	882	90	915	93	950	96	879	89
Dec. .	1,235	131	932	99	890	94	858	91	978	104	972	103	981	104
Total .	12,691	..	10,982	..	13,005	..	10,929	..	11,529	..	11,991	..	12,000	..
Aver. .	1,058	106	915	92	1,084	109	911	92	961	97	999	100	1,000	101

* Index = percentage deviation of actual data from trend, seasonal allowed for.

CANE SUGAR MELTINGS AT UNITED STATES PORTS

(8 PORTS)

Unit = Thousand long tons

	Data		Data		Data		Data
1890 . .	...	1900 . .	1,706	1910 . .	2,186	1920 . .	3,582
1891 . .	...	1901 . .	1,690	1911 . .	2,114	1921 . .	3,584
1892 . .	...	1902 . .	1,796	1912 . .	2,214	1922 . .	5,084
1893 . .	*1,405	1903 . .	1,700	1913 . .	2,276	1923 . .	4,178
1894 . .	1,545	1904 . .	1,913	1914 . .	2,489	1924 . .	4,587
1895 . .	1,457	1905 . .	1,786	1915 . .	*2,624	1925 . .	5,015
1896 . .	1,508	1906 . .	1,992	1916 . .	3,505	1926 . .	....
1897 . .	1,597	1907 . .	1,948	1917 . .	3,308	1927 . .	....
1898 . .	1,502	1908 . .	1,985	1918 . .	3,086	1928 . .	....
1899 . .	1,681	1909 . .	2,077	1919 . .	3,903	1929 . .	....

* 1893-1915. Atlantic Ports' meltings only. About 73 % of 8 ports.

CANE SUGAR MELTINGS AT UNITED STATES PORTS — *Continued*

	1919 Data	*Index	1920 Data	Index	1921 Data	Index	1922 Data	Index	1923 Data	Index	1924 Data	Index	1925 Data	Index
Jan. . .	209.1	100	227.3	105	122.0	38	291.6	127	251.1	105	228.7	93	296.1	116
Feb. . .	341.3	113	318.4	102	240.0	74	415.7	125	342.7	99	426.9	120	313.2	85
Mar. . .	340.1	86	420.8	104	446.3	106	535.4	124	510.7	114	460.4	99	551.9	115
Apr. . .	407.2	103	411.8	101	355.4	84	532.0	123	486.4	108	427.0	92	545.1	113
May . .	432.1	108	362.5	88	314.2	74	577.3	132	474.2	104	432.2	92	450.7	93
June . .	438.8	110	419.9	102	320.2	75	532.1	121	396.3	87	468.3	99	478.8	98
July . .	430.9	112	434.3	109	321.6	78	530.3	125	259.7	59	503.5	111	482.8	103
Aug. . .	343.9	94	394.1	105	401.3	103	540.0	135	316.7	76	448.5	104	438.8	99
Sept. . .	383.3	143	222.0	80	244.1	85	312.9	106	268.4	88	422.7	134	459.9	141
Oct. . .	291.1	112	95.9	36	302.6	110	280.0	98	384.2	130	323.9	106	385.6	122
Nov. . .	171.0	78	148.3	66	276.1	118	309.3	128	288.0	116	288.1	112	262.9	99
Dec. . .	113.9	73	126.4	79	240.3	145	227.3	133	199.6	113	156.5	85	349.1	184
Total	3,902.8	..	3,581.7	..	3,584.2	..	5,083.9	..	4,178.0	..	4,586.7	..	5,014.9	..
Aver. .	325.2	103	298.5	90	298.7	91	423.7	123	348.2	100	382.2	102	417.9	114

* Index = percentage deviation of actual data from trend, seasonal allowed for

WHEAT FLOUR PRODUCTION
Unit = Thousand barrels

	Data		Data
1910 . . .	. . . .	1920 . . .	108,783
1911 . . .	. . . .	1921 . . .	121,014
1912 . . .	. . . .	1922 . . .	125,647
1913 . . .	. . . .	1923 . . .	125,758
1914 . . .	. . . .	1924 . . .	132,514
1915 . . .	114,632	1925 . . .	124,896
1916 . . .	119,947	1926 . . .	. . . .
1917 . . .	117,785	1927 . . .	. . . .
1918 . . .	110,610	1928 . . .	. . . .
1919 . . .	132,333	1929 . . .	. . . .

	1919 Data	*Index	1920 Data	Index	1921 Data	Index	1922 Data	Index	1923 Data	Index	1924 Data	Index	1925 Data	Index
Jan. . .	10,593	101	12,572	123	8,924	83	9,496	87	10,137	92	11,000	99	11,705	103
Feb. . .	7,736	85	9,252	104	8,087	76	9,232	98	9,425	99	10,286	107	10,189	104
Mar. . .	10,498	108	9,036	88	9,103	92	9,658	96	10,607	104	10,578	104	9,307	89
Apr. . .	11,274	135	7,375	87	8,516	110	7,823	90	8,969	102	9,521	107	8,183	90
May . .	10,463	125	8,244	95	8,406	96	8,073	90	9,007	100	9,765	107	8,151	88
June . .	7,405	88	6,800	91	8,087	98	8,136	97	8,331	98	9,332	109	8,617	99
July . .	7,899	85	8,200	90	10,280	117	10,311	110	10,408	110	10,395	109	10,377	107
Aug. . .	11,739	109	9,059	81	13,268	118	12,332	108	12,016	104	11,812	101	11,049	93
Sept. . .	14,087	121	9,650	82	13,349	113	12,540	104	11,995	98	13,798	112	12,501	100
Oct. . .	15,008	117	9,961	77	13,917	106	13,581	102	12,561	93	13,404	99	13,165	95
Nov. . .	13,518	112	9,889	81	10,221	82	13,424	107	11,524	91	11,616	90	10,869	83
Dec. . .	12,113	125	8,745	84	8,856	84	11,041	103	10,778	100	11,007	101	10,783	97
Total	132,333	..	108,783	..	121,014	..	125,647	..	125,758	..	132,514	..	124,896	..
Aver.	11,028	109	9,065	90	10,085	98	10,471	99	10,480	99	11,043	104	10,408	96

* Index = percentage deviation of actual data from trend, seasonal allowed for.

CIGAR CONSUMPTION

Includes Large and Small Cigars in United States and Porto Rico and Large Cigars in Philippines

Unit = Millions

	Data		Data		Data
1900 . . .	5,963	1910	8,213	1920	9,155
1901 . . .	6,455	1911	8,475	1921	7,636
1902 . . .	6,865	1912	8,350	1922	7,867
1903 . . .	7,427	1913	8,772	1923	7,901
1904 . . .	7,404	1914	8,443	1924	7,548
1905 . . .	7,589	1915	8,110	1925	7,382
1906 . . .	8,071	1916	8,582	1926	. . . .
1907 . . .	8,642	1917	9,251	1927	. . . .
1908 . . .	7,914	1918	8,320	1928	. . . .
1909 . . .	7,783	1919	7,975	1929	. . . .

	1919		1920		1921		1922		1923		1924		1925	
	Data	*In-dex	Data	In-dex	Data	In-dex	Data	In-dex	Data	In-dex	Data	In-dex	Data	In-dex
Jan. . .	618.2	96	763.4	120	564.2	87	520.0	85	644.2	107	574.1	98	536.5	102
Feb. . .	560.7	91	679.8	112	569.9	95	504.9	86	579.9	101	566.8	101	513.2	95
Mar. . .	660.9	96	851.5	126	641.3	96	606.9	93	657.5	103	593 5	96	578.6	96
Apr. . .	602.8	91	774.4	118	610.0	95	570.6	90	606.6	98	557.8	93	555.1	95
May . .	631.0	90	794.6	115	620.4	92	650.6	98	655.9	101	627.9	100	589.1	96
June .	648.7	90	802.4	113	689.2	99	700.6	103	667.0	100	630.0	97	647.7	103
July . .	643.3	91	786.0	113	626.3	92	655.4	98	650.0	100	675.8	107	648.5	105
Aug. . .	618.8	85	762.7	106	697.4	99	735.6	106	683.9	101	654.6	100	635.0	100
Sept. . .	673.3	93	791.3	111	690.0	99	715.2	104	669.2	100	687.7	106	660.7	105
Oct. . .	799.0	100	819.1	104	721.7	93	791.0	105	804.5	109	732.2	102	798.9	115
Nov. . .	760.2	102	756.5	103	691.1	96	772.6	110	728.1	106	674.0	101	677.3	105
Dec. . .	757.6	119	573.8	91	532.8	87	643.4	107	554.5	94	573.2	101	541.0	98
Total .	7,974.6	. .	9,155.3	. .	7,636.2	. .	7,867.0	. .	7,901.2	. .	7,547.5	. .	7,381 6	. .
Aver. .	664.5	95	762.9	111	636.4	94	655.6	99	658.4	102	629.0	100	615.1	101

* Index = percentage deviation of actual data from trend, seasonal allowed for.

CIGARETTE CONSUMPTION

Unit = Millions

	Data		Data		Data		Data		Data		Data
1870	14	1880	409	1890	2,233	1900	2,640	1910	7,874	1920	44,644
1871	19	1881	567	1891	2,685	1901	2,277	1911	9,254	1921	50,880
1872	21	1882	555	1892	2,893	1902	2,652	1912	11,240	1922	53,581
1873	27	1883	640	1893	3,177	1903	3,043	1913	15,811	1923	64,469
1874	29	1884	908	1894	3,184	1904	3,235	1914	16,513	1924	71,030
1875	41	1885	1,059	1895	3,328	1905	3,377	1915	17,954	1925	79,977
1876	77	1886	1,311	1896	4,044	1906	3,793	1916	25,255	1926	. . .
1877	149	1887	1,585	1897	4,153	1907	5,167	1917	34,833	1927	. . .
1878	165	1888	1,863	1898	3,754	1908	5,402	1918	37,929	1928	. . .
1879	238	1889	2,152	1899	2,805	1909	6,105	1919	44,805	1929	. . .

CIGARETTE CONSUMPTION — *Continued*

	1919 Data	*Index	1920 Data	Index	1921 Data	Index	1922 Data	Index	1923 Data	Index	1924 Data	Index	1925 Data	Index
Jan.	3,081	108	4,531	136	3,905	100	3,707	81	5,352	100	6,259	99	6,655	90
Feb.	3,128	112	3,538	108	4,123	107	3,126	69	4,625	88	4,856	79	5,682	78
Mar.	3,848	127	4,376	124	4,475	108	3,637	75	5,045	89	5,270	79	6,271	80
Apr.	2,652	93	3,766	113	3,805	98	3,454	76	4,712	88	5,326	85	6,050	82
May.	2,770	88	3,955	107	4,141	95	4,063	90	5,556	93	6,394	92	6,468	79
June	3,144	93	4,086	103	4,224	91	5,303	97	5,838	91	6,457	86	7,435	85
July	3,588	96	3,059	70	4,165	81	5,249	87	5,841	83	6,587	80	7,614	79
Aug.	3,921	107	3,573	84	5,135	102	6,375	108	5,859	85	6,316	78	6,984	74
Sept.	4,286	124	3,562	88	4,795	101	5,556	100	5,569	85	6,274	82	7,121	80
Oct.	5,032	133	3,844	87	4,881	94	4,499	74	6,279	88	6,491	78	6,929	71
Nov.	4,774	135	3,533	85	4,233	87	4,526	80	5,363	81	5,357	69	6,518	71
Dec.	4,581	155	2,821	82	2,998	74	3,546	75	4,430	80	5,443	84	6,251	82
Total	44,805	..	44,644	..	50,880	..	53,581	..	64,469	..	71,030	..	79,977	..
Aver.	3,734	114	3,720	99	4,240	95	4,465	84	5,372	87	5,919	82	6,665	79

* Index = percentage deviation of actual data from trend, seasonal allowed for.

MANUFACTURED TOBACCO CONSUMPTION

Unit = Thousand pounds

	Data		Data		Data		Data		Data		Data
1870	89,120	1880	132,310	1890	229,069	1900	278,977	1910	436,798	1920	363,309
1871	93,801	1881	142,706	1891	243,506	1901	294,102	1911	380,795	1921	350,705
1872	93,656	1882	156.458	1892	253,962	1902	298,048	1912	393,785	1922	382,071
1873	111,408	1883	165,077	1893	252,400	1903	310,668	1913	408,505	1923	372,650
1874	104,503	1884	168,593	1894	235,452	1904	328,651	1914	403,987	1924	374,023
1875	116,101	1885	174,416	1895	248,270	1905	334,849	1915	410,220	1925	372,432
1876	107,064	1886	185,426	1896	253,667	1906	354,915	1916	430,166	1926	....
1877	112,722	1887	199,938	1897	260,735	1907	369,186	1917	441,190	1927	....
1878	105,501	1888	201,926	1898	288,161	1908	364,109	1918	415,352	1928	....
1879	116,975	1889	213,461	1899	237,133	1909	388,757	1919	388,285	1929	....

	1919 Data	*Index	1920 Data	Index	1921 Data	Index	1922 Data	Index	1923 Data	Index	1924 Data	Index	1925 Data	Index
Jan.	29,309	89	33,608	104	24,750	78	30,938	99	33,546	110	34,217	115	32,054	111
Feb.	27,472	85	31,531	98	27,097	86	29,216	94	29,083	96	31,219	106	29,479	103
Mar.	29,228	81	38,422	108	32,210	93	34,396	101	32,269	97	31,356	96	30,880	98
Apr.	29,884	89	34,328	104	28,400	87	28,565	90	30,759	99	29,540	97	30,802	104
May.	33,340	97	34,876	102	28,671	86	32,511	99	32,997	103	31,737	101	31,626	104
June	31,312	93	34,231	103	31,738	98	35,099	110	32,539	104	31,032	102	32,025	109
July	33,839	101	30,989	94	29,226	90	32,591	102	31,210	100	31,311	103	32,590	111
Aug.	35,568	97	32,139	89	33,602	95	38,021	109	32,787	96	32,207	97	32,425	101
Sept.	36,623	106	32,095	94	31,489	94	33,807	103	30,804	96	33,522	107	32,917	108
Oct.	39,336	106	27,124	74	33,718	93	32,740	92	33,236	96	34,556	102	34,597	106
Nov.	32,965	101	18,514	58	27,747	88	30,641	99	30,148	100	27,416	93	27,309	96
Dec.	29,409	101	15,453	54	22,057	78	23,547	85	23,272	86	25,910	98	25,728	100
Total	388,285	..	363,309	..	350,705	..	382,071	..	372,650	..	374,023	..	372,432	..
Aver.	32,357	96	30,276	90	29,225	89	31,839	99	31,054	99	31,169	102	31,036	104

* Index = percentage deviation of actual data from trend, seasonal allowed for

TIRE PRODUCTION

CORD, BALLOON AND FABRIC CASINGS

Unit = Thousand casings

	Data		Data
1910 . . .	. . . .	1920 . . .	. . . .
1911 . . .	. . . .	1921 . . .	21,819
1912 . . .	. . . .	1922 . . .	30,699
1913 . . .	. . . .	1923 . . .	33,944
1914 . . .	8,021	1924 . . .	38,725
1915 . . .	. . . .	1925 . . .	45,631
1916 . . .	. . . .	1926 . . .	. . . .
1917 . . .	. . . .	1927 . . .	. . . .
1918 . . .	. . . .	1928 . . .	. . . .
1919 . . .	32,836	1929 . . .	. . . .

	1921		1922		1923		1924		1925	
	Data	*Index	Data	Index	Data	Index	Data	Index	Data	Index
Jan. . . .	703	34	2,055	92	3,127	130	3,220	127	3,554	134
Feb. . . .	820	38	2,084	90	3,218	131	3,278	126	3,680	135
Mar. . . .	1,163	44	2,646	92	3,866	126	3,428	106	3,957	117
Apr. . . .	1,651	67	2,401	90	3,539	125	3,308	111	4,005	128
May . . .	2,101	78	2,722	94	3,660	118	3,038	93	4,100	121
June . . .	2,313	91	2,839	104	2,957	102	2,630	86	4,063	128
July . . .	2,571	111	2,477	100	1,993	76	2,552	92	4,191	145
Aug. . . .	3,043	112	2,905	100	2,356	76	3,235	100	4,205	125
Sept. . . .	1,929	85	2,505	103	2,030	79	3,531	131	3,755	134
Oct. . . .	1,928	82	2,675	106	2,361	88	3,877	139	3,379	116
Nov. . . .	1,757	82	2,733	119	2,400	99	3,190	125	3,172	120
Dec. . . .	1,840	89	2,657	121	2,437	105	3,438	141	3,570	141
Total . .	21,819	. .	30,699	. .	33,944	. .	38,725	. .	45,631	. .
Aver. . .	1,818	76	2,558	101	2,829	105	3,227	115	3,803	129

* Index = percentage deviation of actual data from trend, seasonal allowed for.

GASOLINE PRODUCTION

Unit = Million gallons

	Data		Data		Data		Data
1890 . .	. . . .	1900 . .	. . . .	1910 . .	. . . .	1920 . .	4,883
1891 . .	. . . .	1901 . .	. . . .	1911 . .	. . . .	1921 . .	5,154
1892 . .	. . . .	1902 . .	. . . .	1912 . .	. . . .	1922 . .	6,202
1893 . .	. . . .	1903 . .	. . . .	1913 . .	. . . .	1923 . .	7,556
1894 . .	. . . .	1904 . .	291	1914 . .	1,500	1924 . .	8,960
1895 . .	. . . .	1905 . .	. . . .	1915 . .	. . . .	1925 . .	10,849
1896 . .	. . . .	1906 . .	. . . .	1916 . .	2,059	1926 . .	. . . .
1897 . .	. . . .	1907 . .	. . . .	1917 . .	2,851	1927 . .	. . . .
1898 . .	. . . .	1908 . .	. . . .	1918 . .	3,570	1928 . .	. . . .
1899 . .	281	1909 . .	540	1919 . .	3,958	1929 . .	. . . .

GASOLINE PRODUCTION — *Continued*

	1919		1920		1921		1922		1923		1924		1925	
	Data	*In-dex	Data	In-dex	Data	In-dex	Data	In-dex	Data	In-dex	Data	In-dex	Data	In-dex
Jan.	303.7	101	336.7	95	460.4	112	444 6	94	623.7	117	695.3	118	831.7	129
Feb.	283.5	102	322.6	99	388.2	102	398.2	92	568.7	116	683.7	125	790.4	134
Mar.	311.3	100	367.1	100	419.8	98	472.3	97	630.7	115	743.2	123	853.6	129
Apr.	319.8	101	355.6	95	426.2	99	472.9	96	619.0	112	754.8	124	860.5	129
May	354.5	104	381.1	95	448.6	97	513.7	97	631.7	107	779.2	119	922.0	130
June	338.3	100	415.2	104	430.3	94	525.9	101	636.7	109	737.1	114	944.2	135
July	342.5	100	423.4	105	419.6	90	569.7	108	636.9	108	742.0	114	966.9	137
Aug.	326.8	94	441.1	108	431.6	92	550.0	103	649.0	109	755.8	115	972.7	137
Sept.	339.6	98	453.9	112	416.9	89	536.5	102	623.7	106	750.3	116	906.1	130
Oct.	363.5	101	465.8	111	441.0	92	566.3	104	659.1	109	760.6	114	944.4	132
Nov.	338.7	97	452.6	111	431.9	92	567.1	107	617.6	105	762.0	118	922.1	133
Dec.	335.7	96	464.4	114	439.0	94	585.1	111	659.2	112	795.6	124	934.5	135
Total	3,957.9		4,882.5		5,153.5		6,202.2		7,556.0		8,959.7		10,849.1	
Aver.	329.8	100	506.9	104	429.5	96	516.9	101	629.7	110	746.6	119	904.1	132

* Index = percentage deviation of actual data from trend, seasonal allowed for.

NEWSPRINT PRODUCTION

Unit = Thousand tons

	Data		Data
1910	....	1920	1,512
1911	....	1921	1,226
1912	....	1922	1,448
1913	1,305	1923	1,489
1914	1,283	1924	1,461
1915	1,239	1925	1,526
1916	1,355	1926	....
1917	1,359	1927	....
1918	1,260	1928	....
1919	1,374	1929	....

	1919		1920		1921		1922		1923		1924		1925	
	Data	*In-dex	Data	In-dex	Data	In-dex	Data	In-dex	Data	In-dex	Data	In-dex	Data	In-dex
Jan.	116.2	98	129.7	110	123.8	105	105.8	90	127.5	108	128.8	109	129.0	109
Feb.	103.2	101	114.2	112	103.0	101	97.8	96	114.6	112	117.3	115	113.8	111
Mar.	114.7	102	127.8	114	107.5	96	117.5	105	129.3	115	119.1	106	127.5	113
Apr.	116.3	103	128.3	114	115.4	103	111.9	100	116.7	104	128.2	114	132.7	118
May	105 8	94	129.2	115	78.9	70	130.0	116	138.9	124	134.2	119	129.0	115
June	114.9	101	130.4	115	87.7	77	127.2	112	133.7	118	120.7	106	128.4	113
July	113.9	104	129.9	119	94.2	86	120.8	111	125.8	115	114.0	104	121.1	111
Aug.	113.4	101	128.8	115	102.3	91	133.2	119	132.6	118	116.5	104	120.9	108
Sept.	111.4	105	121.0	114	98.9	94	125.4	119	110.2	104	116.2	110	121.0	114
Oct.	125.2	109	124.8	109	101.9	89	130.7	114	122.1	107	129.4	113	135.2	118
Nov.	116.6	107	123.0	113	104.6	96	128.0	117	119.7	110	116.6	107	130.5	120
Dec.	122.8	108	124.9	110	107.9	95	119.4	105	117.8	104	120.3	106	136.7	120
Total	1,374.4		1,512.0		1,226.1		1,447.7		1,488.9		1,461.3		1,525.8	
Aver.	114.5	103	126.0	113	102.2	92	120.6	108	124.1	111	121.8	110	127.2	114

* Index = percentage deviation of actual data from trend, seasonal allowed for.

TOTAL PAPER PRODUCTION

Unit = Thousand short tons

	Data		Data		Data		Data
1890 . .	....	1900 . .	....	1910 . .	....	1920 . .	7,335
1891 . .	....	1901 . .	....	1911 . .	....	1921 . .	5,356
1892 . .	....	1902 . .	....	1912 . .	....	1922 . .	7,018
1893 . .	....	1903 . .	....	1913 . .	....	1923 . .	7,010
1894 . .	....	1904 . .	3,107	1914 . .	5,270	1924 . .	6,996
1895 . .	....	1905 . .	....	1915 . .	....	1925 . .	6,934
1896 . .	....	1906 . .	....	1916 . .	....	1926 . .	....
1897 . .	....	1907 . .	....	1917 . .	5,920	1927 . .	....
1898 . .	....	1908 . .	....	1918 . .	6,052	1928 . .	....
1899 . .	2,168	1909 . .	4,217	1919 . .	6,190	1929 . .	....

	1919		1920		1921		1922		1923		1924		1925	
	Data	*Index	Data	Index	Data	Index	Data	Index	Data	Index	Data	Index	Data	Index
Jan. . .	466.2	93	650.3	126	420.5	79	506.2	92	664.6	117	586.0	100	628.8	105
Feb. . .	415.1	91	564.5	120	408.0	84	501.8	100	614.4	119	570.2	107	577.9	106
Mar. . .	445.2	87	641.3	121	440.8	80	593.9	105	610.0	105	597.6	100	625.3	102
Apr. . .	451.9	92	634.4	126	422.0	81	528.5	98	605.5	109	607.8	107	623.4	106
May . .	480.2	94	645.4	122	384.0	70	590.0	105	659.0	114	604.8	102	594.1	97
June . .	498.0	95	657.3	122	403.7	72	593.3	103	600.0	101	545.2	90	542.4	87
July .	538.9	100	658.5	118	370.4	64	552.9	93	515.0	84	532.7	85	534.3	83
Aug. . .	573.7	102	654.2	113	442.5	74	635.1	103	593.0	93	570.5	87	546.1	81
Sept. . .	565.6	104	643.0	115	477.9	83	623.1	105	523.0	85	580.8	92	549.9	85
Oct. . .	616.8	107	622.0	105	542.4	88	644.3	102	585.8	90	638.3	95	596.1	87
Nov. . .	569.5	111	518.1	98	535.9	98	641.5	114	539.0	93	574.5	96	553.8	90
Dec. . .	569.4	115	445.5	87	508.3	96	607.2	112	501.0	90	587.7	102	561.8	95
Total .	6,190.5	..	7,334.5†	..	5,356.4	..	7,017.8	..	7,010.3	..	6,996.1	..	6,933.9	..
Aver. .	515.9	99	611.2	114	446.4	81	584.8	103	584.2	100	583.0	97	577.8	94

* Index = percentage deviation of actual data from trend, seasonal allowed for.
† From June 1923 production is estimated.

TOTAL BOOTS AND SHOES PRODUCED

Unit = Thousand pairs

	Data		Data		Data		Data
1890 . .	...	1900 . .	...	1910 . .	...	1920 . .	....
1891 . .	...	1901 . .	...	1911 . .	...	1921 . .	286,771
1892 . .	...	1902 . .	...	1912 . .	...	1922 . .	323,876
1893 . .	...	1903 . .	...	1913 . .	...	1923 . .	351,114
1894 . .	...	1904 . .	242,110	1914 . .	292,666	1924 . .	313,230
1895 . .	...	1905 . .	...	1915 . .	...	1925 . .	323,553
1896 . .	...	1906 . .	...	1916 . .	...	1926 . .	....
1897 . .	...	1907 . .	...	1917 . .	...	1927 . .	....
1898 . .	...	1908 . .	...	1918 . .	...	1928 . .	....
1899 . .	217,965	1909 . .	285,017	1919 . .	331,224	1929 . .	....

TOTAL BOOTS AND SHOES PRODUCED — *Continued*

Unit = Million pairs

	1921		1922		1923		1924		1925	
	Data	*Index	Data	Index	Data	Index	Data	Index	Data	Index
Jan.	...	..	25.12	94	30.71	114	26.50	97	26.08	94
Feb.	...	..	24.55	93	30.25	113	26.83	99	26.45	96
Mar.	...	..	29.35	98	35.84	117	28.86	93	29.89	95
Apr.	...	..	26.85	96	31.87	112	27.85	97	29.48	101
May	...	..	26.23	99	30.93	115	25.24	92	25.11	90
June	...	..	24.83	101	28.27	114	22.46	89	23.45	92
July	...	..	22.69	102	25.26	111	21.39	93	24.76	106
Aug.	...	..	27.68	103	30.03	110	25.47	92	28.49	101
Sept.	...	..	28.29	104	27.55	100	27.72	99	29.77	105
Oct.	...	..	30.37	102	30.70	102	30.83	100	31.06	100
Nov.	23.54	90	30.08	113	26.95	100	25.32	92	24.63	89
Dec.	24.13	100	27.85	114	22.68	91	24.60	98	24.40	95
Total	...	..	323.89	..	351.04	..	313.07	..	323.57	..
Aver.	...	..	26.99	102	29.25	108	26.09	95	26.96	97

* Index = percentage deviation of actual data from trend, seasonal allowed for.

PENNSYLVANIA ANTHRACITE COAL PRODUCTION

Unit = Thousand net tons

	Data		Data		Data		Data		Data		Data
1870	15,664	1880	28,650	1890	46,469	1900	57,368	1910	84,485	1920	89,598
1871	19,342	1881	31,920	1891	50,665	1901	67,472	1911	90,464	1921	90,473
1872	24,233	1882	35,121	1892	52,473	1902	41,374	1912	84,362	1922	54,683
1873	26,153	1883	38,457	1893	53,968	1903	74,607	1913	91,525	1923	93,339
1874	24,819	1884	37,157	1894	51,921	1904	73,157	1914	90,822	1924	90,214
1875	22,486	1885	38,336	1895	57,999	1905	77,660	1915	88,995	1925	62,974
1876	22,793	1886	39,035	1896	54,346	1906	71,282	1916	87,578	1926	....
1877	25,660	1887	42,088	1897	52,612	1907	85,604	1917	99,612	1927	....
1878	21,690	1888	46,620	1898	53,383	1908	83,269	1918	98,826	1928	....
1879	30,208	1889	45,547	1899	60,418	1909	81,070	1919	88,092	1929	....

	1919		1920		1921		1922		1923		1924		1925	
	Data	*In-dex	Data	In-dex	Data	In-dex	Data	In-dex	Data	In-dex	Data	In-dex	Data	In-dex
Jan.	7,819	104	7,459	99	7,681	101	6,566	85	8,521	112	7,924	102	7,419	94
Feb.	5,102	78	6,415	97	7,983	119	7,096	105	7,602	114	7,621	112	7,176	103
Mar.	5,190	65	7,935	99	7,677	95	9,181	112	9,175	114	8,114	98	7,058	85
Apr.	6,884	95	6,285	86	7,985	108	s 27	..	7,885	107	6,811	90	7,472	98
May	7,525	93	8,037	99	7,752	94	s 36	..	8,384	103	7,745	92	8,134	97
June	7,404	92	8,251	101	8,071	98	s 86	1	8,474	104	7,704	92	7,804	93
July	7,974	102	8,342	105	7,309	92	s 118	1	8,136	103	7,782	96	8,544	104
Aug.	8,096	102	8,105	101	7,459	92	s 164	2	8,672	108	7,086	86	8,624	104
Sept.	7,494	98	4,691	60	7,385	95	5,075	65	2,853	37	7,601	96	s 394	5
Oct.	8,645	102	8,148	95	7,858	91	8,896	102	8,532	100	7,674	87	s 68	s 1
Nov.	7,870	99	7,527	94	7,110	88	8,695	107	7,575	95	6,776	82	s 151	s 2
Dec.	8,089	103	8,403	106	6,203	77	8,743	108	7,530	98	7,376	88	s 224	s 3
Total	88,092	..	89,598	..	90,473	..	54,683	..	93,339	..	90,214	..	62,974	...
Aver.	7,341	94	7,467	95	7,539	96	4,557	58	7,778	100	7,518	93	5,248	66

* Index = percentage deviation of actual data from trend, seasonal allowed for.
s = strike.

APPENDIX — TABLE 6

(Charts 9 and 20)

AUTOMOBILE PRODUCTION (*Passenger Cars and Trucks*)

Sources, see p. 95

AUTOMOBILE PASSENGER CAR PRODUCTION

Unit = Thousand cars

		Data			Data			Data			Data
1890	. .	. .	1900	. .	5	1910	. .	181	1920	. .	1,883
1891	. .	. .	1901	. .	7	1911	. .	199	1921	. .	1,535
1892	. .	. .	1902	. .	9	1912	. .	356	1922	. .	2,340
1893	. .	. .	1903	. .	11	1913	. .	462	1923	. .	3,637
1894	. .	. .	1904	. .	22	1914	. .	544	1924	. .	3,145
1895	. .	. .	1905	. .	25	1915	. .	819	1925	. .	3,678
1896	. .	. .	1906	. .	34	1916	. .	1526	1926	. .	. .
1897	. .	. .	1907	. .	43	1917	. .	1741	1927	. .	. .
1898	. .	1	1908	. .	64	1918	. .	926	1928	. .	. .
1899	. .	3	1909	. .	128	1919	. .	1602	1929	. .	. .

	1919		1920		1921		1922		1923		1924		1925	
	Data	*In-dex	Data	In-dex	Data	In-dex	Data	In-dex	Data	In-dex	Data	In-dex	Data	In-dex
Jan. . .	73.8	56	165.3	111	43.1	26	81.7	45	223.8	115	284.0	139	204.6	94
Feb. . .	96.0	69	193.4	123	68.1	39	109.2	57	254.8	125	331.4	155	242.0	106
Mar. . .	117.5	73	231.5	127	130.3	65	153 0	69	319.8	135	341.9	138	319.1	121
Apr. . .	135.0	82	222.4	119	176.4	85	197.2	87	344.6	142	332.0	131	375.8	139
May . .	153.2	97	209.4	117	177.4	90	232.5	107	350.4	150	271.0	113	364.4	140
June . .	140.8	97	179.4	110	150.3	83	263.1	133	337.4	159	214.3	97	350.6	148
July . .	154.9	124	171.3	121	165.6	105	225.1	131	297.3	162	235.9	122	347.4	169
Aug. . .	130.3	96	171.3	111	167.8	98	249.5	133	314.4	157	249.8	118	214.4	96
Sept. .	139.3	102	142.3	92	144.7	85	187.7	101	298.9	149	256.9	122	262.1	117
Oct. . .	177.7	133	87.3	58	134.8	81	217.6	119	335.0	171	254.5	124	392.6	179
Nov. . .	158.8	139	62.1	48	106.1	74	215.4	138	284.9	170	198.4	112	327.6	175
Dec. . .	124.2	102	47.1	34	70.7	46	208.0	124	275.4	153	174.9	92	277.7	138
Total	1,601.5	. .	1,882.8	. .	1,535.3	. .	2,340.0	. .	3,636.7|	. .	3,145.0	. .	3,678.3	. .
Aver.	133.5	97	156.9	98	127.9	73	195.0	104	303.1	149	262.1	122	306.5	135

* Index = percentage deviation of actual data from trend, seasonal allowed for.

MOTOR TRUCK PRODUCTION

Unit = A truck

	Data		Data		Data
1900 . . .	....	1910. . . .	6,000	1920 . . .	322,039
1901 . . .	....	1911 . . .	10,655	1921 . . .	145,081
1902 . . .	....	1912 . . .	22,000	1922 . . .	246,281
1903 . . .	....	1913 . . .	23,500	1923 . . .	376,257
1904 . . .	411	1914 . . .	25,375	1924 . . .	359,863
1905 . . .	450	1915 . . .	74,000	1925 . . .	474,901
1906 . . .	500	1916 . . .	92,130	1926 . . .	....
1907 . . .	700	1917 . . .	128,157	1927 . . .	....
1908 . . .	1,500	1918 . . .	227,250	1928 . . .	....
1909 . . .	3,255	1919 . . .	316,364	1929 . . .	....

	1921		1922		1923		1924		1925	
	Data	*Index	Data	Index	Data	Index	Data	Index	Data	Index
Jan. . .	4,831	37	9,576	64	19,720	116	28,994	152	26,576	123
Feb. . .	7,830	51	13,350	75	22,161	109	31,231	137	32,717	127
Mar. . .	13,328	58	20,022	76	35,260	117	34,404	101	43,009	112
Apr. . .	18,070	75	22,640	81	38,056	120	36,015	102	46,247	115
May . .	18,070	70	24,097	82	43,678	130	33,561	89	41,415	97
June . .	14,328	58	26,298	92	41,145	126	28,117	76	36,260	87
July . .	10,766	50	22,046	89	30,663	109	25,284	80	39,992	111
Aug. . .	13,080	54	24,692	89	30,829	98	27,767	78	36,277	90
Sept. . .	13,648	64	19,462	79	28,638	104	30,609	99	57,888	163
Oct. . .	12,813	62	21,795	92	30,166	113	31,205	104	44,220	128
Nov. . .	10,010	57	21,949	109	28,066	125	26,824	104	37,758	130
Dec. . .	8,307	56	20,354	119	27,875	145	25,852	118	32,542	132
Total . .	145,081	..	246,281	..	376,257	..	359,863	..	474,901	..
Aver. . .	12,090	58	20,523	87	31,355	118	29,989	103	39,575	118

* Index = percentage deviation of actual data from trend, seasonal allowed for.

APPENDIX — TABLE 7

WHOLESALE TRADE IN SECOND FEDERAL RESERVE DISTRICT

(CHART 21)

Sources, see p. 97

WEIGHTED INDEX OF SALES

1919 = 100

	Annual Averages		Annual Averages
1910 . . .	....	1920 . . .	106
1911 . . .	....	1921 . . .	79
1912 . . .	....	1922 . . .	82
1913 . . .	....	1923 . . .	94
1914 . . .	....	1924 . . .	90
1915 . . .	....	1925 . . .	90
1916 . . .	....	1926 . . .	....
1917 . . .	....	1927 . . .	....
1918 . . .	....	1928 . . .	....
1919 . . .	100	1929 . . .	....

	1919		1920		1921		1922		1923		1924		1925	
	Data	*In-dex	Data	In-dex	Data	In-dex	Data	In-dex	Data	In-dex	Data	In-dex	Data	In-dex
Jan. . .	79.0	94	118.7	115	72.5	84	68.9	97	86.9	109	88.3	103	84.0	94.4
Feb. . .	78.2	92	102.4	93	77.3	88	72.4	96	94.5	113	96.8	103	92.5	99.6
Mar. . .	90.8	89	138.9	99	98.7	93	92.1	98	115.1	110	104.4	97	106.0	95.1
Apr. . .	89.1	105	108.7	93	77.0	94	73.1	101	88.7	107	89.8	100	87.2	92.6
May . .	85.6	113	105.0	104	68.4	100	68.1	99	81.2	103	72.2	91	73.8	91.3
June . .	87.2	120	105.8	102	69.3	101	68.0	101	78.3	103	64.9	88	74.6	89.5
July . .	103.5	127	103.7	96	67.1	99	66.2	96	80.4	105	73.6	91	81.1	93.8
Aug. . .	116.1	110	115.2	88	95.1	104	95.3	102	112.6	107	96.6	96	99.0	90.9
Sept. .	124.3	107	120.3	89	90.5	98	102.5	106	107.7	104	112.2	105	104.9	90.1
Oct. . .	125.2	102	103.6	79	93.1	101	108.3	111	120.2	109	111.9	99	113.5	93.6
Nov. . .	108.2	109	83.2	79	79.3	101	92.9	112	91.5	100	85.3	95	86.0	90.9
Dec. . .	112.7	124	68.7	80	65.3	99	77.1	112	73.4	97	78.9	99	81.0	96.9
Aver. .	100.0	108	106.2	93	79.47	97	82.1	103	94.2	105	89.6	97	90.4	93

* Index = percentage deviation of actual data from trend, seasonal and price changes allowed for.

APPENDIX — TABLE 8

(CHART 22)

CAR LOADINGS OF MISCELLANEOUS AND MERCHANDISE (L. C. L.) FREIGHT

Source, see p. 99

Unit = Thousand cars

	Data		Data
1910 . . .	. . . .	1920 . . .	25,687
1911 . . .	. . . .	1921 . . .	23,847
1912 . . .	. . . .	1922 . . .	26,751
1913 . . .	. . . .	1923 . . .	29,544
1914 . . .	. . . .	1924 . . .	30,007
1915 . . .	. . . .	1925 . . .	32,086
1916 . . .	. . . .	1926 . . .	. . . .
1917 . . .	. . . .	1927 . . .	. . . .
1918 . . .	. . . .	1928 . . .	. . . .
1919 . . .	24,216	1929 . . .	. . . .

	1919 Data	*In-dex	1920 Data	In-dex	1921 Data	In-dex	1922 Data	In-dex	1923 Data	In-dex	1924 Data	In-dex	1925 Data	In-dex
Jan. . .	1,756	101	2,027	112	1,617	89	1,743	92	2,164	106	2,209	104	2,306	104
Feb. . .	1,629	101	1,799	107	1,604	92	1,720	94	1,991	105	2,226	108	2,231	108
Mar. . .	1,894	97	2,288	109	1,977	90	2,199	96	2,501	105	2,486	104	2,628	105
Apr. . .	1,777	90	1,905	93	1,947	91	2,143	100	2,429	109	2,516	104	2,684	106
May .	1,943	96	2,076	103	1,913	91	2,343	103	2,585	109	2,510	101	2,627	106
June . .	1,884	95	2,269	105	2,051	91	2,448	105	2,569	105	2,342	96	2,719	103
July .	2,101	101	2,263	105	1,959	90	2,324	103	2,443	104	2,742	98	2,742	103
Aug. . .	2,219	104	2,316	104	2,202	91	2,467	98	2,663	105	2,592	98	2,831	103
Sept. .	2,324	106	2,317	102	2,224	94	2,389	97	2,549	103	2,743	102	2,957	106
Oct. . .	2,443	103	2,408	101	2,431	98	2,505	97	2,898	104	3,013	103	3,141	103
Nov. .	2,152	110	2,107	99	2,038	92	2,350	102	2,552	106	2,517	105	2,669	106
Dec. . .	2,094	111	1,912	97	1,884	92	2,120	103	2,200	103	2,359	102	2,551	106
Total .	24,216	. .	25,687	. .	23,847	.	26,751	. .	29,544	. .	30,007	. .	32,086	. .
Aver. .	2,018	101	2,141	103	1,987	92	2,229	99	2,462	105	2,501	102	2.674	105

* Index = percentage deviation of actual data from trend, seasonal allowed for.

APPENDIX — TABLE 9

(CHART 23)

CAR LOADINGS OF FREIGHT OTHER THAN MERCHANDISE (Less than Carload Lots) AND MISCELLANEOUS

Source, see p. 103

CAR LOADINGS OF GRAIN, GRAIN PRODUCTS, LIVESTOCK, COAL, COKE
FOREST PRODUCTS AND ORE

Unit = Thousand cars

	Data		Data
1910 . . .	. . . .	1920 . . .	19,728
1911 . . .	. . . .	1921 . . .	15,477
1912 . . .	. . . .	1922 . . .	16,456
1913 . . .	. . . .	1923 . . .	20,411
1914 . . .	. . . .	1924 . . .	18,840
1915 . . .	. . . .	1925 . . .	19,224
1916 . . .	. . . .	1926 . . .	. . . .
1917 . . .	. . . .	1927 . . .	. . . .
1918 . . .	. . . .	1928 . . .	. . . .
1919 . . .	17,681	1929 . . .	. . . .

	1919		1920		1921		1922		1923		1924		1925	
	Data	*In-dex	Data	In-dex	Data	In-dex	Data	In-dex	Data	In-dex	Data	In-dex	Data	In-dex
Jan. . .	1,392	96	1,550	106	1,324	93	1,292	89	1,643	108	1 633	105	1,686	107
Feb. .	1,127	89	1,305	102	1,137	87	1,323	100	1,398	104	1,559	110	1,388	101
Mar. . .	1,121	83	1,522	108	1,136	79	1,487	102	1,621	110	1,478	103	1,374	94
Apr. . .	1,305	110	1,313	109	1,097	90	858	72	1,495	124	1,297	102	1 385	108
May . .	1,468	106	1,504	111	1,265	92	1,129	78	1,759	120	1,508	101	1,573	108
June . .	1,502	106	1,765	119	1,360	90	1,192	78	1,851	119	1,435	95	1,583	99
July . .	1,733	113	1,787	115	1,298	86	1,212	79	1,842	119	1,511	92	1,670	101
Aug. . .	1,659	102	1,881	114	1,452	83	1,420	80	2,020	117	1,621	93	1,847	104
Sept. . .	1,838	112	1,868	112	1,422	84	1,618	94	1,781	107	1,762	100	1,712	96
Oct. . .	1,907	105	1,943	110	1,586	89	1,734	95	1,933	101	1,903	98	1,840	94
Nov. . .	1,233	87	1,723	115	1,250	82	1,656	108	1,653	106	1,561	103	1,596	104
Dec. . .	1,396	103	1,567	114	1,150	82	1,535	113	1,415	102	1,572	108	1,570	106
Total .	17,681	. .	19,728	. .	15,477	. .	16,456	. .	20,411	. .	18,840	. .	19,224	. .
Aver. .	1,474	101	1,644	111	1,290	87	1,371	91	1,701	111	1,570	101	1,602	102

* Index = percentage deviation of actual data from trend, seasonal allowed for.

APPENDIX — TABLE 10

(CHART 24)

EXPORTS AND IMPORTS OF MERCHANDISE

Source, see p. 105

UNITED STATES EXPORTS OF MERCHANDISE

Unit = Million dollars

	Data		Data		Data		Data		Data		Data
1870	403.6	1880	889.7	1890	857.5	1900	1477.9	1910	1866.3	1920	8228.0
1871	460.4	1881	833.5	1891	970.5	1901	1465.4	1911	2092.5	1921	4485.0
1872	468.8	1882	768.0	1892	938.4	1902	1360.7	1912	2399.2	1922	3831.8
1873	567.8	1883	795.2	1893	876.1	1903	1484.8	1913	2484.0	1923	4167.5
1874	569.9	1884	749.4	1894	825.1	1904	1451.3	1914	3113.6	1924	4591.0
1875	510.9	1885	688.2	1895	824.9	1905	1627.0	1915	3554.7	1925	4909.1
1876	590.7	1886	713.4	1896	1005.8	1906	1798.2	1916	5482.6	1926	...
1877	620.3	1887	715.3	1897	1099.7	1907	1923.4	1917	6233.5	1927	...
1878	737.1	1888	691.8	1898	1255.5	1908	1752.8	1918	6149.1	1928	...
1879	765.2	1889	827.1	1899	1275.5	1909	1728.2	1919	7920.4	1929	...

	1919		1920		1921		1922		1923		1924		1925	
	Data	*Index	Data	Index	Data	Index	Data	Index	Data	Index	Data	Index	Data	Index
Jan. . .	622.0	118	722.1	120	654.3	130	278.8	70	335.4	74	395.2	88	446.4	94
Feb. . .	585.1	131	645.1	122	486.5	121	250.6	74	307.0	79	365.8	95	370.7	90
Mar. . .	603.1	130	819.6	144	386.7	96	330.0	92	341.4	83	339.8	84	453.7	103
Apr. . .	714.8	160	684.3	123	340.5	92	318.5	91	325.5	82	346.9	90	398.3	95
May . .	604.0	138	745.5	137	329.7	96	307.6	90	316.4	83	335.1	91	370.9	94
June .	928.4	222	629.4	120	336.9	106	335.1	102	320.0	90	307.0	89	323.3	86
July .	568.7	146	651.1	138	325.2	114	301.2	98	302.2	95	276.6	89	339.6	99
Aug. .	646.1	151	578.2	116	366.9	121	301.8	90	311.1	92	330.7	98	379.9	102
Sept. .	595.2	116	604.7	105	324.9	91	313.2	79	381.4	95	427.5	106	420.4	95
Oct. .	631.6	106	751.2	117	343.3	82	370.7	79	399.2	85	527.2	111	490.6	95
Nov. .	740.0	122	676.5	110	294.1	70	380.0	81	401.5	83	493.6	102	447.0	86
Dec. .	681.4	108	720.3	124	296.2	69	344.3	71	426.7	88	445.7	89	468.3	89
Total	7,920.4	..	8,228.0	..	4,485.0	..	3,831.8	..	4,167.5	..	4,591.0	.	4,909.1	..
Aver.	660.0	137	685.7	123	373.8	99	319.3	85	347.3	86	382.6	94	409.1	94

* Index = percentage deviation of actual data from trend, seasonal and price change allowed for.

UNITED STATES IMPORTS OF MERCHANDISE

Unit = Million dollars

	Data		Data		Data		Data		Data		Data
1870	461.1	1880	696.8	1890	823.4	1900	829.1	1910	1562.9	1920	5278.5
1871	573.1	1881	670.2	1891	828.3	1901	880.4	1911	1532.4	1921	2509.1
1872	656.0	1882	752.8	1892	840.9	1902	969.3	1912	1818.1	1922	3112.7
1873	595.2	1883	687.1	1893	776.2	1903	995.5	1913	1792.6	1923	3792.1
1874	562.1	1884	629.3	1894	676.3	1904	1035.9	1914	1789.3	1924	3610.0
1875	503.2	1885	587.9	1895	801.7	1905	1179.1	1915	1778.6	1925	4224.3
1876	427.3	1886	663.4	1896	681.6	1906	1320.5	1916	2391.6	1926	...
1877	480.2	1887	708.8	1897	742.6	1907	1423.2	1917	2952.5	1927	...
1878	431.8	1888	725.4	1898	635.0	1908	1116.4	1918	3031.2	1928	...
1879	513.6	1889	770.5	1899	799.0	1909	1475.5	1919	3904.4	1929	...

	1919		1920		1921		1922		1923		1924		1925	
	Data	*Index	Data	Index	Data	Index	Data	Index	Data	Index	Data	Index	Data	Index
Jan. .	213.0	61	473.8	118	208.8	63	217.2	83	329.3	110	295.5	100	346.2	110
Feb. .	235.1	70	467.4	118	214.5	72	215.7	85	303.4	105	332.3	117	333.5	109
Mar. .	267.6	74	523.9	118	252.0	80	256.2	92	397.9	125	320.5	102	385.4	113
Apr. .	273.0	81	495.7	118	254.6	92	217.0	83	364.3	122	324.3	112	346.1	111
May .	328.9	100	431.0	105	204.9	79	252.8	99	372.5	130	303.0	110	327.5	110
June .	292.9	92	552.6	140	185.7	77	260.5	105	320.2	119	274.0	105	325.2	115
July .	343.7	107	537.1	137	178.2	76	251.8	99	287.4	110	278.6	108	325.6	115
Aug. .	307.3	87	513.1	125	194.8	78	281.4	102	275.4	99	254.5	92	340.1	114
Sept. .	435.4	126	363.3	94	179.3	75	229.5	111	253.6	94	287.1	106	350.0	118
Oct. .	401.8	109	333.2	84	188.0	72	345.1	96	308.3	106	310.8	106	374.1	118
Nov. .	424.8	115	321.2	86	210.9	82	291.8	102	291.3	100	296.1	101	376.6	120
Dec. .	380.7	98	266.1	75	237.5	90	293.8	100	288.3	97	333.2	108	394.0	122
Total	3,904.4	..	5,278.5	..	2,509.1	..	3,112.7	..	3,792.1	..	3,610.0	..	4,224.3	...
Aver.	325.4	93	439.9	110	209.1	78	259.4	96	316.0	110	300.9	106	352.0	115

* Index = percentage deviation of actual data from trend, seasonal and price change allowed for.

APPENDIX — TABLE 11

(CHART 25)

Source, see p. 107

PANAMA CANAL TRAFFIC

CARGO PASSING THROUGH CANAL IN BOTH DIRECTIONS

AMERICAN AND FOREIGN VESSELS

Unit = Thousand long tons

	Data		Data
1910 . . .	. . . .	1920 . . .	11,236
1911 . . .	. . . .	1921 . . .	10,707
1912 . . .	. . . .	1922 . . .	13,711
1913 . . .	. . . .	1923 . . .	25,161
1914 . . .	1,759	1924 . . .	25,892
1915 . . .	4,893	1925 . . .	23,701
1916 . . .	4,775	1926 . . .	. . . .
1917 . . .	7,444	1927 . . .	. . . .
1918 . . .	7,284	1928 . . .	. . . .
1919 . . .	7,478	1929 . . .	. . . .

	1919		1920		1921		1922		1923		1924		1925	
	Data	*In-dex	Data	In-dex	Data	In-dex	Data	In-dex	Data	In-dex	Data	In-dex	Data	In-dex
Jan. . .	561	86	895	114	1,117	118	807	70	1,592	115	2,427	146	1,908	95
Feb. . .	567	95	781	108	953	109	838	80	1,563	123	2,244	147	1,840	100
Mar. . .	516	80	855	110	1,085	115	960	85	1,941	142	2,272	138	2,104	106
Apr. . .	507	77	868	110	908	95	1,046	91	2,187	157	2,159	129	1,951	97
May . .	642	90	975	114	793	76	1,159	93	2,265	150	2,354	129	1,823	83
June .	587	92	834	109	695	75	978	88	2,096	156	2,023	125	1,920	98
July .	568	85	887	110	709	73	1,211	104	2,338	166	2,097	123	1,961	96
Aug. .	716	108	1,041	130	839	87	1,166	100	2,169	154	1,958	116	1,912	94
Sept. .	638	97	1,010	127	755	78	1,138	98	2,169	155	2,112	125	1,892	94
Oct. .	706	92	991	107	986	89	1,446	108	2,128	132	2,018	103	2,009	85
Nov. .	576	79	985	112	855	81	1,427	112	2,218	144	1,961	106	2,023	91
Dec. .	925	126	1,077	121	953	89	1,535	119	2,495	160	2,267	120	2,358	104
Total	7,508	. .	11,196	. .	10,647	. .	13,711	. .	25,161	. .	25,892	. .	23,701	. .
Aver.	626	92	933	114	887	90	1,143	96	2,097	146	2,158	126	1,975	95

* Index = percentage deviation of actual data from trend, seasonal allowed for.

APPENDIX — TABLE 12

(CHART 26)

ADVERTISING

Source, see p. 109

NEWSPAPER ADVERTISING IN 107 NEWSPAPERS IN 23 CITIES

Unit = Million agate lines

	Data		Data
1910 . . .	* 641	1920 . . .	1,175
1911 . . .	627	1921 . . .	1,068
1912 . . .	653	1922 . . .	1,113
1913 . . .	679	1923 . . .	1,191
1914 . . .	* 663	1924 . . .	1,182
1915 . . .	669	1925 . . .	1,238
1916 . . .	751	1926 . . .	....
1917 . . .	770	1927 . . .	....
1918 . . .	743	1928 . . .	....
1919 . . .	1,028	1929 . . .	....

* = estimated 1910–1914.

	1919		1920		1921		1922		1923		1924		1925	
	Data	*In-dex	Data	In-dex	Data	In-dex	Data	In-dex	Data	In-dex	Data	In-dex	Data	In-dex
Jan. . .	67.9	93	93.8	122	87.0	107	87.2	102	92.1	102	94.2	99	95.1	94
Feb. . .	66.4	100	89.3	128	77.6	105	77.1	99	85.2	104	90.7	104	87.7	96
Mar. .	81.1	100	105.4	123	94.3	104	95.2	100	106.9	106	106.3	100	108.4	97
Apr. .	86.1	103	101.9	115	92.4	99	99.6	101	110.8	107	109.3	100	110.0	95
May .	89.4	105	107.2	120	99.4	105	99.0	99	111.5	106	107.7	97	111.4	95
June .	88.3	113	98.5	119	88.7	103	95.5	104	100.3	103	98.4	96	98.1	91
July .	76.7	116	85.2	122	76.5	104	80.1	103	84.5	103	78.0	90	83.9	92
Aug. .	79.5	120	85.2	122	73.6	99	79.7	102	82.4	100	78.4	90	87.6	95
Sept. .	87.5	114	93.5	115	86.2	100	90.1	99	94.9	99	97.2	96	101.6	95
Oct. .	103.5	117	110.2	118	99.9	102	107.4	103	111.2	101	111.1	96	121.7	100
Nov. .	104.4	124	101.3	114	96.3	103	102.9	104	107.3	103	105.6	96	119.2	102
Dec. .	97.3	116	98.3	111	96.3	103	102.3	104	103.9	100	104.9	96	112.8	97
Total	1,028.0	..	1,175.0	..	1,068.0	..	1,113.0	..	1,190.9	..	1,181.8	..	1,237.5	..
Aver.	85.1	110	97.9	119	89.0	103	92.8	102	99.2	103	98.5	97	103.1	96

* Index = percentage deviation of actual data from trend, seasonal allowed for.

MAGAZINE ADVERTISING

Unit = Thousand agate lines

	Data		Data		Data
1900 . . .	. . . .	1910	15,319	1920	29,774
1901 . . .	. . . .	1911	15,250	1921	18,999
1902 . . .	. . . .	1912	15,598	1922	19,704
1903 . . .	. . . .	1913	15,375	1923	23,437
1904 . . .	. . . .	1914	14,534	1924	24,134
1905 . . .	. . . .	1915	14,298	1925	25,220
1906 . . .	. . . .	1916	17,626	1926	. . . .
1907 . . .	. . . .	1917	19,206	1927	. . . .
1908 . . .	11,052	1918	17,323	1928	. . . .
1909 . . .	14,152	1919	24,279	1929	. . . .

	1919		1920		1921		1922		1923		1924		1925	
	Data	*In-dex	Data	In-dex	Data	In-dex	Data	In-dex	Data	In-dex	Data	In-dex	Data	In-dex
Jan. . .	1,090	87	1,805	138	1,525	113	1,115	79	1,399	96	1,477	97	1,450	92
Feb. . .	1,447	92	2,426	148	1,700	100	1,389	79	1,730	94	1,867	98	1,934	98
Mar. . .	1,836	102	2,668	142	1,799	92	1,571	78	2,002	95	2,152	91	2,201	97
Apr. . .	2,257	113	2,914	141	1,805	84	1,788	80	2,298	99	2,468	102	2,436	97
May . .	2,368	119	2,931	142	1,876	87	1,940	87	2,270	98	2,452	102	2,442	97
June . .	2,367	130	2,846	150	1,730	88	1,776	87	2,108	99	2,268	103	2,300	100
July . .	1,871	133	2,070	142	1,323	87	1,436	91	1,726	105	1,678	99	1,703	96
Aug. . .	1,656	130	2,084	158	1,207	88	1,320	93	1,505	101	1,424	92	1,511	94
Sept. . .	2,152	143	2,353	150	1,370	84	1,537	91	1,780	101	1,800	99	1,983	105
Oct. . .	2,450	134	2,668	141	1,546	79	1,968	96	2,263	107	2,213	100	2,441	106
Nov. . .	2,325	126	2,637	138	1,602	81	1,938	94	2,247	105	2,201	99	2,514	109
Dec. . .	2,460	138	2,372	128	1,516	79	1,923	96	2,109	104	2,134	98	2,305	102
Total .	24,279	. .	29,774	. .	18,999	. .	19,704	. .	23,437	. .	24,134	. .	25,220	. .
Aver. .	2,023	121	2,481	143	1,583	88	1,642	88	1,953	100	2,011	98	2,102	100

* Index = percentage deviation of actual data from trend, seasonal allowed for.

APPENDIX — TABLE 13

(CHART 27)

Source, see p. 111

Source, see p. 111

SALES OF DEPARTMENT STORES, EXCLUDING APPAREL, IN SECOND FEDERAL RESERVE DISTRICT

Unit = Thousand dollars

	Data		Data
1910 . . .	. . . .	1920 . . .	365,754
1911 . . .	. . . .	1921 . . .	346,817
1912 . . .	. . . .	1922 . . .	354,351
1913 . . .	. . . .	1923 . . .	363,645
1914 . . .	. . . .	1924 . . .	378,398
1915 . . .	. . . .	1925 . . .	398,810
1916 . . .	. . . .	1926 . . .	. . . .
1917 . . .	. . . .	1927 . . .	. . . .
1918 . . .	. . . .	1928 . . .	. . . .
1919 . . .	307,130	1929 . . .	. . . .

	1919		1920		1921		1922		1923		1924		1925	
	Data	*In-dex	Data	In-dex	Data	In-dex	Data	In-dex	Data	In-dex	Data	In-dex	Data	In-dex
Jan. . .	19,556	93	28,738	106	26,866	102	24,890	99	26,060	98	28,456	100	28,843	96
Feb. . .	17,565	104	22,689	100	22,995	103	21,990	101	21,560	98	24,871	101	25,933	105
Mar. . .	21,017	99	31,336	106	29,693	106	27,584	101	29,263	103	27,848	98	29,358	97
Apr. . .	25,304	100	29,811	89	29,301	100	29,748	100	28,906	97	32,033	97	32,941	93
May . .	24,786	100	33,417	104	28,528	103	29,551	99	30,807	100	31,264	98	31,816	98
June . .	24,096	101	31,138	95	28,909	104	29,018	99	30,779	102	30,251	100	31,500	93
July . .	18,801	102	22,729	97	19,858	106	19,985	102	20,822	98	22,202	97	22,678	88
Aug. . .	17,901	110	20,630	95	19,503	98	20,492	100	21,809	104	20,114	101	22,093	103
Sept. . .	24,639	104	26,299	89	23,514	94	27,206	103	26,975	104	30,382	102	30,894	102
Oct. . .	33,130	99	34,597	89	35,145	103	36,635	103	38,291	100	38,831	98	44,715	106
Nov. . .	32,540	103	36,221	96	33,417	99	35,912	101	36,555	100	36,835	101	38,499	99
Dec. . .	47,795	100	48,149	93	49,088	101	51,340	103	51,818	102	55,311	100	59,540	100
Total .	307,130	. .	365,754	. .	346,817	. .	354,351	. .	363,645	. .	378,398	. .	398,810	. .
Aver. .	25,594	101	30,480	97	28,901	102	29,529	101	30,304	101	31,533	99	33,234	98

* Index = percentage deviation of actual data from trend, seasonal and price change allowed for.

APPENDIX — TABLE 14

(CHART 28)

CHAIN GROCERY STORE AND OTHER CHAIN STORE SALES

Sources, see p. 113

CHAIN GROCERY STORES

Unit = Thousand dollars

	Data		Data
1910 . . .	. . . .	1920 . . .	489,525
1911 . . .	. . . .	1921 . . .	436,207
1912 . . .	. . . .	1922 . . .	508,853
1913 . . .	. . . .	1923 . . .	632,787
1914 . . .	. . . .	1924 . . .	721,433
1915 . . .	. . . .	1925 . . .	888,490
1916 . . .	. . . .	1926 . . .	. . . .
1917 . . .	. . . .	1927 . . .	. . . .
1918 . . .	. . . .	1928 . . .	. . . .
1919 . . .	336,546	1929 . . .	. . . .

	1919		1920		1921		1922		1923		1924		1925	
	Data	*In-dex	Data	In-dex	Data	In-dex	Data	In-dex	Data	In-dex	Data	In-dex	Data	In-dex
Jan. . .	24,889	109	36,263	100	36,045	94	39,845	110	48,483	102	57,625	99	70,161	106
Feb. . .	23,804	109	35,602	102	34,592	92	37,903	104	47,820	105	56,233	97	65,368	104
Mar. . .	26,644	105	41,396	101	37,854	91	43,681	106	57,989	106	56,032	91	70,792	101
Apr. . .	26,146	99	43,898	110	35,099	92	40,811	104	50,741	99	59,028	99	72,412	105
May . .	27,002	100	42,708	103	34,015	95	40,705	98	53,334	100	60,071	102	71,315	106
June . .	25,258	102	43,594	102	34,171	100	41,064	102	51,694	99	56,002	101	71,105	107
July . .	28,186	103	44,354	102	33,248	100	40,165	97	50,185	96	57,887	98	72,649	103
Aug. . .	27,412	104	40,282	101	35,050	101	41,143	102	50,589	97	56,356	102	68,189	103
Sept. . .	27,610	102	40,136	96	34,669	99	42,359	104	51,594	102	58,816	101	68,636	101
Oct. . .	33,453	105	41,449	96	39,404	105	44,726	99	56,286	95	67,404	103	89,210	117
Nov. . .	31,635	103	39,969	94	39,242	104	46,865	100	57,094	98	65,031	104	76,230	106
Dec. . .	34,507	95	39,874	94	42,818	107	49,584	103	56,974	97	70,947	103	92,423	120
Total	336,546	. .	489,525	. .	436,207	. .	508,853	. .	632,787	. .	721,433	. .	888,490	. .
Aver.	28,046	103	40,794	100	36,351	98	42,404	102	52,732	100	60,119	100	74,041	107

* Index = percentage deviation of actual data from trend, seasonal and price change allowed for.

CHAIN STORE SALES

FIVE AND TEN CENT STORES, CANDY, APPAREL, DRUG, CIGAR AND SHOE STORES

Unit = Thousand dollars

	Data		Data
1910 . . .	. . . .	1920 . . .	476,787
1911 . . .	. . . .	1921 . . .	488,106
1912 . . .	. . . .	1922 . . .	524,915
1913 . . .	. . . .	1923 . . .	608,408
1914 . . .	. . . .	1924 . . .	673,463
1915 . . .	. . . .	1925 . . .	754,018
1916 . . .	. . . .	1926 . . .	. . . .
1917 . . .	. . . .	1927 . . .	. . . .
1918 . . .	. . . .	1928 . . .	. . . .
1919 . . .	382,085	1929 . . .	. . . .

Unit = Hundred thousand dollars

	1919		1920		1921		1922		1923		1924		1925	
	Data	*Index	Data	Index	Data	Index	Data	Index	Data	Index	Data	Index	Data	Index
Jan. . .	225	96	293	104	312	102	313	97	365	98	416	97	455	96
Feb. . .	228	100	282	101	318	105	324	99	361	98	431	99	464	99
Mar. . .	283	105	364	102	407	100	380	96	500	103	501	102	538	96
Apr. . .	300	95	372	103	392	105	431	100	450	100	551	97	600	93
May . .	312	100	396	107	388	101	419	96	491	99	548	98	590	96
June . .	285	98	381	104	383	100	408	97	495	103	508	98	552	94
July . .	288	98	388	109	367	103	398	101	441	99	490	95	552	93
Aug. . .	307	104	374	107	375	99	402	96	467	98	516	100	582	98
Sept. . .	308	98	395	104	384	98	441	101	493	103	532	95	597	94
Oct. . .	361	96	456	106	461	104	486	98	567	97	626	95	751	99
Nov. . .	369	108	428	104	423	98	477	99	549	100	623	104	676	99
Dec. . .	556	99	638	99	670	98	768	103	905	107	992	100	1,160	102
Total	3,821	. .	4,768	. .	4,881	. .	5,249	. .	6,084	. .	6,735	. .	7,540	. .
Aver.	318	100	397	104	407	101	437	99	507	100	561	98	628	97

* Index = percentage deviation of actual data from trend, seasonal and price change allowed for.

APPENDIX — TABLE 15

(CHART 29)

Source, see p. 115

MAIL ORDER HOUSE SALES

(Data confidential)

INDEX *

	1919	1920	1921	1922	1923	1924	1925
January . .	98	114	72	77	98	106	114
February . .	90	127	73	73	100	107	120
March . . .	81	101	85	79	103	98	107
April . . .	91	85	74	80	103	108	109
May . . .	97	88	73	85	113	105	111
June . . .	91	83	76	84	101	109	114
July . . .	105	90	73	88	107	95	117
August . . .	114	92	78	81	98	105	120
September . .	110	79	81	85	103	114	116
October . .	118	71	75	93	104	110	128
November . .	117	89	70	93	99	111	116
December . .	116	76	71	100	105	126	134
Average . .	102	91	75	85	103	108	117

* Index = percentage deviation of actual data from trend, seasonal and price change allowed for.

APPENDIX — TABLE 16

(CHART 30)

Source, see p. 117

LIFE INSURANCE SALES

Unit = Million dollars

	Data		Data		Data
1900 . . .	. . . .	1910	1,410	1920	6,138
1901 . . .	. . . .	1911	1,640	1921	5,101
1902 . . .	. . . .	1912	1,770	1922	5,511
1903 . . .	. . . .	1913	1,896	1923	6,592
1904 . . .	. . . .	1914	1,909	1924	7,094
1905 . . .	. . . .	1915	2,006	1925	8,056
1906 . . .	. . . .	1916	2,426	1926	. . . .
1907 . . .	1,020	1917	2,876	1927	. . . .
1908 . . .	1,110	1918	2,975	1928	. . . .
1909 . . .	1,310	1919	5,285	1929	. . . .

APPENDIX — TABLE 16 — *Continued*

	1919 (1)		1920 (1)		1921		1922		1923		1924		1925	
	Data	*In-dex	Data	In-dex	Data	In-dex	Data	In-dex	Data	In-dex	Data	In-dex	Data	In-dex
Jan. . .	154	92	214	99	427	95	407	98	467	105	539	111	560	107
Feb. . .	189	114	228	106	419	96	415	100	486	107	547	112	612	116
Mar. . .	233	119	310	120	478	96	481	•98	593	111	668	116	703	112
Apr. . .	223	116	309	120	461	97	456	96	567	109	663	120	712	117
May . .	247	119	275	99	483	98	508	101	626	113	633	108	733	114
June . .	201	102	264	101	454	99	489	103	590	113	597	108	689	112
July . .	213	117	249	104	390	93	444	102	534	112	591	118	688	123
Aug. . .	205	116	216	96	394	97	434	104	538	118	508	105	646	120
Sept ..	161	100	197	95	345	95	397	105	476	114	488	109	602	122
Oct. . .	185	95	225	95	399	94	461	103	555	113	572	110	669	116
Nov. . .	192	98	208	93	386	93	467	107	549	114	545	107	637	112
Dec. . .	208	87	216	81	467	91	553	102	611	103	744	117	805	113
Total	2,411	..	2,911	..	5,103	..	5,512	..	6,592	..	7,095	..	8,056	...
Aver.	201	106	243	101	425	96	459	102	549	111	591	112	671	115

* Index = percentage deviation of actual data from trend, seasonal and price change allowed for.
(1) 7 companies only.

APPENDIX — TABLE 17

(CHART 31)

BUILDING PERMITS AND REAL ESTATE TRANSFERS
Sources, see pp. 119 and 120

INDEX OF THE VOLUME OF BUILDING PERMITS IN 7 CITIES
1913 = 100

	Index		Index		Index		Index		Index
1880	...	1890	92.1	1900	58.7	1910	115.1	1920	68.0
1881	...	1891	87.2	1901	95.9	1911	114.2	1921	123.8
1882	42.6	1892	95.0	1902	85.3	1912	120.9	1922	192.4
1883	48.3	1893	67.2	1903	82.2	1913	100.0	1923	210.7
1884	48.8	1894	65.3	1904	97.8	1914	98.1	1924	221.6
1885	56.6	1895	91.7	1905	133.4	1915	111.4	1925	263.1
1886	63.2	1896	76.1	1906	128.9	1916	116.5	1926	...
1887	66.8	1897	85.9	1907	111.1	1917	54.6	1927	...
1888	60.2	1898	72.8	1908	102.5	1918	25.1	1928	...
1889	78.5	1899	90.8	1909	139.1	1919	84.4	1929	...

BUILDING PERMITS IN 158 CITIES

Unit = Thousand dollars

	1919		1920		1921		1922		1923		1924		1925	
	Data	*In-dex	Data	In-dex	Data	In-dex	Data	In-dex	Data	In-dex	Data	In-dex	Data	In-dex
Jan. .	23,307	22	123,022	78	58,599	44	139,713	118	193,519	141	218,747	151	209,079	141
Feb. .	33,854	33	108,911	64	81,074	62	133,735	112	219,461	154	271,093	184	247,135	159
Mar. .	62,938	38	155,981	57	121,095	59	242,771	128	369,414	162	410,095	175	343,268	143
Apr. .	84,555	50	182,338	64	143,936	71	217,084	113	322,940	137	291,900	124	396,637	169
May .	106,441	61	123,492	44	141,297	71	237,838	122	260 347	110	289,906	125	329,696	141
June .	130,658	73	126,661	50	143,849	80	251,001	135	237,653	110	258,743	123	331,260	155
July .	135,959	74	117,265	48	148,944	85	203,191	110	222,009	104	223,499	108	332,513	155
Aug. .	157,241	85	115,704	51	155,722	95	215,937	121	241,795	119	239,032	120	331,725	161
Sept. .	136,127	78	95,463	46	149,174	97	200,138	117	212,727	115	230,140	125	308,931	160
Oct. . .	148,915	86	92,160	47	169,714	110	204,889	119	271,425	148	269,724	146	342,876	178
Nov. .	137,752	87	69,957	42	146,031	103	202,534	129	252,670	151	226,410	136	290,037	166
Dec. .	144,382	90	69,616	45	139,250	105	243,002	162	242,819	152	242,913	149	273,967	160
Total .	1,300,341	...	1,373,189	...	1,598,685	...	2,482,833	...	3,046,779	...	3,172,204	...	3,737,124	...
Aver. .	108,362	65	114,432	53	133,224	82	206,903	124	253,898	134	256,017	139	311,427	157

* Index = percentage deviation of actual data from trend, seasonal and price change allowed for.

REAL ESTATE TRANSFERS IN ATLANTA, GA.

Unit = Number

	Data			Data			Data
1900 . . .	5,958	1910	16,166	1920	22,946
1901 . . .	6,356	1911	16,604	1921	24,787
1902 . . .	7,133	1912	17,809	1922	31,286
1903 . . .	8,044	1913	18,047	1923	35,926
1904 . . .	8,816	1914	17,841	1924	36,345
1905 . . .	9,998	1915	17,358	1925	....
1906 . . .	11,091	1916	18,205	1926	....
1907 . . .	11,663	1917	17,525	1927	....
1908 . . .	11,622	1918	14,654	1928	....
1909 . . .	14,341	1919	21,233	1929	....

REAL ESTATE TRANSFERS IN 41 CITIES

Unit = Hundreds

	1919		1920		1921		1922		1923		1924		1925	
	Data	*In-dex	Data	In-dex	Data	In-dex	Data	In-dex	Data	In-dex	Data	In-dex	Data	In-dex
Jan. . .	594	70	1,074	119	790	82	920	89	1,250	114	1,447	123	1,359	108
Feb. . .	595	79	936	117	739	86	816	89	1,085	111	1,326	127	1,248	112
Mar. . .	807	84	1,244	121	945	86	1,079	92	1,401	112	1,499	112	1,579	111
Apr. . .	911	92	1,300	123	991	88	1,050	87	1,417	110	1,530	112	1,697	116
May . .	964	95	1,185	110	966	84	1,187	97	1,562	119	1,488	106	1,670	112
June . .	937	97	1,117	109	961	88	1,155	98	1,516	121	1,402	105	1,564	110
July . .	990	109	1,036	106	902	87	1,106	100	1,413	119	1,380	109	1,624	120
Aug. . .	952	105	938	97	919	89	1,139	103	1,409	120	1,318	105	1,354	101
Sept. . .	1,051	116	996	103	937	91	1,141	104	1,319	113	1,314	105	1,492	112
Oct. . .	1,189	121	1,027	98	970	87	1,242	104	1,572	123	1,508	111	1,654	114
Nov. . .	1,022	112	890	91	933	90	1,193	107	1,399	118	1,308	103	1,492	110
Dec. . .	1,096	125	852	91	944	94	1,159	108	1,347	118	1,395	114	1,637	126
Total .	11,108	..	12,597	..	10,997	..	13,187	..	16,691	..	16,915	..	18,370	...
Aver. .	926	101	1,050	107	916	88	1,098	98	1,391	117	1,410	111	1,531	113

* Index = percentage deviation of actual data from trend, seasonal allowed for.

APPENDIX — TABLE 18

(CHART 32)

DEBITS OUTSIDE NEW YORK CITY AND IN NEW YORK CITY

Source, see p. 123

DEBITS TO INDIVIDUAL ACCOUNTS BY BANKS IN 140 CENTERS OUTSIDE NEW YORK CITY

Unit = Million dollars

	Data		Data		Data		Data		Data		Data
1870	....	1880	11,375	1890	23,088	1900	33,436	1910	66,821	1920	241,596
1871	....	1881	14,095	1891	22,908	1901	38,982	1911	67,857	1921	191,941
1872	....	1882	13,962	1892	25,257	1902	41,695	1912	73.209	1922	199,509
1873	....	1883	14,266	1893	22,882	1903	43,239	1913	75,181	1923	225,330
1874	....	1884	13,179	1894	21,072	1904	43,910	1914	72,227	1924	228,161
1875	....	1885	13,287	1895	23,339	1905	50,005	1915	77,253	1925	256,422
1876	....	1886	15,571	1896	22,376	1906	55,230	1916	102,275	1926	....
1877	....	1887	17,617	1897	23,802	1907	57,844	1917	129,540	1927	....
1878	*7,955	1888	18,384	1898	26,855	1908	53,133	1918	*153,817	1928	....
1879	9,291	1889	20,215	1899	33,286	1909	62,249	1919	211,175	1929	....

* 1878–1918 Bank clearings raised to be comparable with debits.

APPENDIX — TABLE 18 — Continued

	1919		1920		1921		1922		1923		1924		1925	
	Data	*In-dex	Data	In-dex	Data	In-dex	Data	In-dex	Data	In-dex	Data	In-dex	Data	In-dex
Jan. . .	16,810	101	21,731	111	17,996	93	15,879	97	19,666	108	19,384	100	22,277	111
Feb. . .	13,671	97	17,734	106	14,599	88	14,042	99	16,906	110	17,512	103	18,572	109
Mar. . .	15,472	97	21,146	105	16,550	88	16,535	100	19,644	107	19,193	104	21,219	110
Apr. . .	15,363	95	20,324	102	15,886	87	15,671	101	18,816	108	18,865	102	20,592	106
May . .	16,697	103	19,676	102	15,342	91	16,322	101	19,368	108	18,639	101	20,397	110
June . .	17,641	111	20,541	100	15,852	91	17,173	105	19,532	105	18,304	103	21,682	111
July . .	18,629	111	20,805	100	15,175	92	16,343	103	18,184	103	18,662	100	21,559	110
Aug. . .	17,668	113	18,904	99	14,911	93	15,849	100	17,307	99	17,776	104	19,848	109
Sept. . .	18,086	109	19,779	99	15,523	95	16,553	102	17,261	101	18,238	101	20,872	11u
Oct. . .	20,248	107	20,891	97	16,713	95	18,423	105	19,759	99	20,912	103	24,014	112
Nov. . .	19,185	112	19,525	96	15,949	97	17,133	100	18,521	100	18,846	104	21,334	111
Dec. . .	21,705	107	20,540	94	17,446	96	19,586	107	20,367	103	21,830	104	24,057	109
Total .	211,175	..	241,596	..	191,941	..	199,509	..	225,330	..	228,161	..	256,422	..
Aver. .	17,598	105	20,133	101	15,995	92	16,626	102	18,778	105	19,013	102	21,369	110

*Index = percentage deviation of actual data from trend, seasonal and price change allowed for.

DEBITS TO INDIVIDUAL ACCOUNTS BY BANKS IN NEW YORK CITY

Unit = Million dollars

	Data		Data		Data		Data		Data		Data
1870	....	1880	38,614	1890	37,459	1900	52,634	1910	97,275	1920	241,431
1871	....	1881	49,377	1891	33,749	1901	79,428	1911	92,373	1921	207,096
1872	....	1882	46,917	1892	36,662	1902	76,328	1912	100,744	1922	239,855
1873	....	1883	37,434	1893	31,261	1903	65,970	1913	94,634	1923	238,396
1874	....	1884	30,986	1894	24,388	1904	68,649	1914	83,019	1924	263,531
1875	....	1885	28,152	1895	29,842	1905	93,822	1915	110,564	1925	313,372
1876	....	1886	33,677	1896	28,871	1906	104,676	1916	159,581	1926	....
1877	....	1887	33,475	1897	33,427	1907	87,182	1917	177,405	1927	....
1878	*19,859	1888	31,100	1898	41,972	1908	79,276	1918	* 178,533	1928	....
1879	29,236	1889	35,895	1899	60,762	1909	103,589	1919	244,119	1929	....

* 1878–1918 Bank clearings raised to be comparable with debits.

	1919		1920		1921		1922		1923		1924		1925	
	Data	*In-dex	Data	In-dex	Data	In-dex	Data	In-dex	Data	In-dex	Data	In-dex	Data	In-dex
Jan. . .	18,119	98	23,636	106	20,033	103	19,065	107	22,087	108	22,114	104	27,682	122
Feb. . .	14,492	95	18,054	98	15,130	92	16,543	107	19,019	112	19,886	108	22,924	122
Mar. . .	16,698	94	22,285	100	17,353	90	20,397	110	22,541	109	21,546	107	26,382	121
Apr. . .	17,323	97	21,320	98	16,349	91	20,717	121	20,479	109	20,654	105	23,945	113
May . .	20,330	110	19,581	91	17,171	98	21,654	116	20,704	103	21,406	107	26,179	124
June .	21,570	116	19,806	85	17,755	97	22,063	114	21,041	103	21,926	110	26,930	119
July .	22,427	120	19,063	89	16,340	99	19,673	112	18,321	100	21,469	109	25,458	118
Aug. . .	20,276	122	17,371	93	15,186	97	18,287	109	16,189	93	20,916	119	23,265	122
Sept. . .	20,446	116	17,600	91	16,102	102	19,215	113	16,799	99	20,734	113	24,369	122
Oct. . .	24,226	115	20,137	93	17,610	98	22,322	115	19,152	100	22,506	103	28,916	121
Nov. . .	23,351	121	20,171	99	17,492	101	19,027	100	19,983	101	23,047	117	27,009	125
Dec. . .	24,860	109	22,408	103	20,575	105	20,851	102	22,081	104	27,327	116	30,313	123
Total .	244,119	..	241,431	..	207,096	..	239,855	..	238,396	..	263,531	..	313,372	..
Aver. .	20,343	109	20,119	96	17,258	98	19,988	110	19,866	103	21,961	110	26,114	121

* Index = percentage deviation of actual data from trend, seasonal and price change allowed for.

APPENDIX — TABLE 19
(Chart 33)
ELECTRIC POWER PRODUCTION AND POSTAL RECEIPTS

Sources, see p. 125

PRODUCTION OF ELECTRICITY IN THE UNITED STATES
Unit = Million kilowatt hours

	Data		Data		Data
1900 . . .	. . . .	1910	. . . .	1920	43,555
1901 . . .	. . . .	1911	. . . .	1921	40,976
1902 . . .	. . . .	1912	17,572	1922	47,659
1903 . . .	. . . .	1913		1923	55,674
1904 . . .	. . . .	1914	. . . .	1924	59,014
1905 . . .	. . . .	1915	. . . .	1925	65,517
1906 . . .	. . . .	1916	. . . .	1926	. . . .
1907 . . .	10,621	1917	32,679	1927	. . . .
1908 . . .	. . . .	1918		1928	. . . .
1909 . . .	. . . .	1919	38,921	1929	. . . .

	1919		1920		1921		1922		1923		1924		1925	
	Data	*In-dex	Data	In-dex	Data	In-dex	Data	In-dex	Data	In-dex	Data	In-dex	Data	In-dex
Jan. . .	3,395	104	3,856	107	3,541	90	3,806	89	4,754	103	5,189	105	5,592	106
Feb. . .	2,976	101	3,480	107	3,166	89	3,468	90	4,324	104	4,834	108	4,982	104
Mar. . .	3,138	99	3,746	108	3,395	90	3,821	93	4,728	106	4,985	105	5,362	105
Apr. . .	3 015	99	3,578	108	3,239	89	3,597	91	4,473	105	4,739	104	5,152	106
May . .	3,115	100	3,583	105	3,264	88	3,824	95	4,653	107	4,794	102	5,189	104
June . .	3,015	98	3,569	106	3,244	88	3,835	96	4,523	105	4,554	99	5,203	106
July . .	3,129	101	3,627	107	3,270	88	3,871	96	4,536	105	4,613	99	5,347	108
Aug. . .	3,162	100	3,717	107	3,411	91	4,075	100	4,670	106	4,735	100	5,376	107
Sept. . .	3,166	100	3,632	105	3,688	98	4,049	100	4,535	104	4,803	102	5,483	110
Oct. . .	3,419	102	3,751	103	3,574	90	4,332	101	4,950	107	5,192	105	5,936	112
Nov. . .	3,570	105	3,706	100	3,639	90	4,414	101	4,838	103	5,051	100	5,787	108
Dec. . .	3,850	110	3,761	99	3,820	92	4,611	103	4,956	103	5,545	107	6,108	111
Total .	38,950	. .	44,006	. .	41,251	. .	47,703	. .	55,940	. .	59,034	. .	65,517	. .
Aver. .	3,246	102	3,667	105	3,438	90	3,975	96	4,662	105	4,920	103	5,460	107

* Index = percentage deviation of actual data from trend, seasonal allowed for.

POSTAL RECEIPTS IN 50 SELECTED CITIES

Unit = Thousand dollars

	Data		Data
1910 . . .	....	1920 . . .	248,243
1911 . . .	....	1921 . . .	249,100
1912 . . .	....	1922 . . .	274,535
1913 . . .	....	1923 . . .	301,024
1914 . . .	....	1924 . . .	316,024
1915 . . .	....	1925 . . .	345,975
1916 . . .	....	1926 . . .	....
1917 . . .	....	1927 . . .	....
1918 . . .	204,780	1928 . . .	....
1919 . . .	220,651	1929 . . .	....

	1919		1920		1921		1922		1923		1924		1925	
	Data	*In-dex	Data	In-dex	Data	In-dex	Data	In-dex	Data	In-dex	Data	In-dex	Data	In-dex
Jan. . .	18,592	104	19,659	102	20,007	96	20,956	94	24,935	104	26,031	101	27,271	98
Feb. . .	17,100	102	18,345	101	19,115	98	20,339	97	23,082	102	25,264	104	25,644	98
Mar. . .	19,222	97	23,009	108	22,720	99	24,237	98	27,870	105	27,463	96	29,085	95
Apr. . .	19,191	105	22,441	114	20,593	97	22,099	97	24,374	99	26,918	102	29,083	103
May .	18,890	106	19,786	103	19,504	94	22,317	100	24,902	104	25,914	101	27,455	99
June .	17,012	98	19,790	106	19,752	98	22,231	103	23,802	102	23,524	94	26,987	100
July .	15,879	100	18,486	108	17,509	95	19,543	99	21,046	99	22,728	99	25,707	105
Aug. . .	15,675	96	18,446	105	19,290	102	21,372	105	22,624	103	22,545	96	25,085	99
Sept. .	17,534	98	20,034	104	20,407	98	22,764	102	23,272	97	25,898	100	28,551	103
Oct. . .	20,331	102	22,080	102	21,670	93	24,777	99	27,235	101	29,119	101	32,489	104
Nov. . .	18,086	93	21,166	101	21,806	97	24,812	102	26,531	102	26,471	94	29,962	99
Dec. . .	23,139	101	25,001	101	26,727	100	29,150	102	31,351	102	34,149	103	38,656	108
Total .	220,651	..	248,243	..	249,100	..	274,535	..	301,024	..	316,024	..	345,975	..
Aver. .	18,388	100	20,687	105	20.758	97	22,878	100	25,085	102	26,335	99	28,831	101

* Index = percentage deviation of actual data from trend, seasonal allowed for.

APPENDIX — TABLE 20
(CHART 34)

NEW CORPORATE FINANCING AND SHARES SOLD ON THE NEW YORK STOCK EXCHANGE

Sources, see p. 127

NEW CORPORATE FINANCING
(FOREIGN AND DOMESTIC, INCLUDING REFUNDING)

Unit = Million dollars

	Data		Data
1910 . . .	....	1920 . . .	2,966.3
1911 . . .	....	1921 . . .	2,414.9
1912 . . .	....	1922 . . .	3,073.3
1913 . . .	....	1923 . . .	3,265.4
1914 . . .	....	1924 . . .	3,838.7
1915 . . .	....	1925 . . .	4,763.3
1916 . . .	....	1926 . . .	....
1917 . . .	....	1927 . . .	....
1918 . . .	....	1928 . . .	....
1919 . . .	2,739.7	1929 . . .	....

	1919		1920		1921		1922		1923		1924		1925	
	Data	*Index	Data	Index	Data	Index	Data	Index	Data	Index	Data	Index	Data	Index
Jan. . .	254.3	109	376.7	162	284.6	122	252.9	108	623.4	†191	304.7	131	508.6	218
Feb. . .	216.4	93	223.3	96	229.6	98	165.9	71	258.2	111	265.6	114	503.6	216
Mar. . .	100.6	43	303.4	130	134.4	58	310.9	133	296.3	127	266.1	114	352.6	151
Apr. . .	56.9	24	331.9	142	393.8	†70	337.6	145	286.6	123	275.7	118	482.6	207
May . .	170.5	73	354.1	152	189.8	81	362.8	156	201.7	86	496.0	213	295.9	127
June . .	317.5	136	278.3	119	88.2	38	330.5	142	288.4	124	316.1	136	379.3	163
July . .	302.1	130	190.5	82	198.9	85	234.2	100	132.1	57	279.2	120	241.0	103
Aug. . .	267.5	115	124.7	53	72.9	31	124.7	53	133.0	57	287.8	123	423.1	181
Sept. .	275.4	118	112.6	48	242.3	104	368.7	158	141.3	61	312.4	134	310.7	133
Oct. . .	335.4	144	297.9	128	70.9	30	244.9	105	230.4	99	418.5	179	371.3	159
Nov. . .	249.5	107	148.0	63	207.8	89	132.7	57	387.0	166	243.4	104	376.2	161
Dec. . .	193.6	83	225.0	96	301.7	129	207.3	89	287.0	123	373.2	160	518.4	222
Total .	2,739.7	..	2,966.3	..	2,414.9	..	3,073.3	..	3,265.4	..	3,838.7	..	4,763.3	..
Aver. .	228.3	98	247.2	106	201.2	78	256.1	110	272.1	110	319.9	137	396.9	170

* Index = percentage deviation of actual data from trend, no seasonal allowed for.
† Allowance made for large refunding operations.

NUMBER OF SHARES SOLD ON THE NEW YORK STOCK EXCHANGE

Unit = Thousand shares

	Data		Data		Data		Data		Data
1880	...	1890	71,283	1900	138,380	1910	164,051	1920	226,640
1881	...	1891	69,032	1901	265,945	1911	127,208	1921	170,849
1882	...	1892	85,875	1902	188,503	1912	131,128	1922	256,693
1883	...	1893	80,978	1903	161,102	1913	83,471	1923	236,116
1884	...	1894	49,075	1904	187,312	1914	47,901*	1924	281,932
1885	...	1895	66,583	1905	263,081	1915	173,145	1925	454,405
1886	...	1896	54,654	1906	284,298	1916	233,312	1926	....
1887		1897	77,324	1907	196,439	1917	185,629	1927	....
1888	65,179	1898	112,700	1908	197,206	1918	144,118	1928	....
1889	72,015	1899	176,421	1909	214,632	1919	316,788	1929	....

* Exchange closed 4 months.

	1919		1920		1921		1922		1923		1924		1925	
	Data	*In-dex	Data	In-dex	Data	In-dex	Data	In-dex	Data	In-dex	Data	In-dex	Data	In-dex
Jan. . .	11,858	71	19,880	117	16,145	95	16,472	96	19,914	115	26,857	154	41,571	237
Feb. . .	12,211	73	21,865	129	10,170	60	16,175	94	22,979	133	20,722	119	32,794	187
Mar. . .	21,404	127	29,009	171	16,321	96	22,820	133	25,965	150	18,316	105	38,294	218
Apr. . .	28,587	170	28,447	168	15,530	91	30,634	178	20,092	116	18,117	104	24,844	141
May . .	34,414	204	16,642	98	17,237	101	28,921	168	23,156	134	13,514	77	36,648	208
June . .	32,860	195	9,354	55	18,265	107	24,081	140	19,754	114	17,003	97	30,751	175
July . .	34,502	204	12,542	74	9,288	54	15,118	88	12,522	72	24,318	139	32,813	186
Aug. . .	24,433	145	13,729	81	11,117	65	17,863	104	13,145	76	21,809	125	33,047	188
Sept. . .	24,142	143	15,296	90	12,924	75	21,712	126	14,643	84	18,185	104	37,109	210
Oct. . .	37,355	221	13,667	80	13,130	77	25,763	149	15,803	91	18,333	105	54 092	307
Nov. . .	30,169	178	22,069	130	15,439	90	19,407	112	22,589	130	41,657	238	49,177	279
Dec. . .	24,853	147	24,139	142	17,148	100	19,686	114	25,524	147	43,101	246	43,265	245
Total	316,788	..	226,640	..	170,849	..	256,693	..	236,116	..	281,932	..	454,405	..
Aver. .	26,399	156	18,887	111	14,237	84	21,391	125	19,676	113	23,494	134	37,868	215

* Index = percentage deviation of actual data from trend, no seasonal allowed for.

APPENDIX — TABLE 21

(CHARTS 13 AND 35)

GRAIN EXPORTS AND FUTURE SALES OF GRAIN

Sources, see p. 129

GRAIN EXPORTS

CORN, OATS, RYE, BARLEY, WHEAT AND WHEAT FLOUR

Unit = Million bushels

	Data		Data		Data		Data
1890 . .	...	1900 . .	419.7	1910 . .	115.0	1920 . .	413.2
1891 . .	...	1901 . .	406.1	1911 . .	150.9	1921 . .	543.7
1892 . .	...	1902 . .	250.2	1912 . .	179.5	1922 . .	489.9
1893 . .	...	1903 . .	267.3	1913 . .	220.3	1923 . .	259.5
1894 . .	...	1904 . .	121.1	1914 . .	308.3	1924 . .	288.9
1895 . .	...	1905 . .	226.0	1915 . .	469.1	1925 . .	236.1
1896 . .	...	1906 . .	270.9	1916 . .	411.4	1926 . .	....
1897 . .	...	1907 . .	251.9	1917 . .	351.0	1927 . .	....
1898 . .	...	1908 . .	199.5	1918 . .	389.7	1928 . .	....
1899 . .	462.8	1909 . .	134.7	1919 . .	403.5	1929 . .	....

	1919		1920		1921		1922		1923		1924		1925	
	Data	*In-dex	Data	In-dex	Data	In-dex	Data	In-dex	Data	In-dex	Data	In-dex	Data	In-dex
Jan. . .	35.6	142	18.5	74	41.1	164	34.8	139	24.0	96	15.5	62	16.9	67
Feb. . .	24.5	110	16.5	74	36.4	163	34.9	157	28.7	129	14.2	64	14.4	65
Mar. . .	29.5	148	27.8	140	37.6	189	41.0	206	21.0	106	14.5	73	20.7	104
Apr. . .	39.9	227	22.0	125	38.1	216	35.4	201	18.9	107	13.2	75	25.7	146
May . .	43.2	248	39.0	224	42.8	246	34.4	198	24.9	143	11.3	65	24.6	141
June . .	52.9	256	30.0	145	48.1	232	42.5	205	19.1	92	15.4	74	15.9	77
July . .	26.0	104	44.8	178	48.7	194	42.9	171	18.2	73	10.5	42	19.0	76
Aug. . .	32.0	109	41.6	142	89.3	305	59.6	203	25.2	86	24.7	84	24.2	83
Sept. . .	37.4	113	41.4	125	66.8	201	60.6	183	28.5	86	28.6	86	29.6	89
Oct. . .	29.0	81	50.1	139	39.2	109	43.4	121	20.8	58	72.4	201	17.1	48
Nov. . .	30.3	89	39.7	116	27.4	80	34.7	101	14.2	42	40.7	119	13.8	40
Dec. . .	23.2	77	41.8	139	28.2	94	25.7	86	16.0	53	27.9	93	14.2	47
Total .	403.5	..	413.2	..	543.7	..	489.9	..	259.5	..	288.9	..	236.1	..
Aver. .	33.6	142	34.4	135	45.3	183	40.8	164	21.6	89	24.1	86	19.7	82

* Index = percentage deviation of actual data from trend, seasonal allowed for.

GRAIN FUTURE SALES AT CHICAGO

Unit = Million bushels

	Data		Data
1910 . . .	. . . .	1920 . . .	12,105 e
1911 . . .	. . . .	1921 . . .	20,954
1912 . . .	. . . .	1922 . . .	17,494
1913 . . .	. . . .	1923 . . .	13,931
1914 . . .	. . . .	1924 . . .	17,828
1915 . . .	. . . .	1925 . . .	26,897
1916 . . .	. . . .	1926 . . .	. . . .
1917 . . .	. . . .	1927 . . .	. . . .
1918 . . .	. . . .	1928 . . .	. . . .
1919 . . .	10,489 e	1929 . . .	. . . .

	1919e		1920e		1921		1922		1923		1924		1925	
	Data	*In-dex	Data	In-dex	Data	In-dex	Data	In-dex	Data	In-dex	Data	In-dex	Data	In-dex
Jan. . .	1,164	124	517	53	1,697	136	1,043	80	1,287	95	796	57	2,791	191
Feb. . .	1,122	132	619	70	1,623	117	2,027	141	1,202	80	707	45	2,597	160
Mar. . .	1,265	120	744	68	1,734	109	2,216	134	982	57	996	55	3,220	172
Apr. . .	1,040	91	924	78	2,120	158	1,471	105	1,666	115	730	48	2,216	141
May . .	984	95	825	76	1,928	158	1,280	101	1,561	118	637	46	2,005	140
June . .	786	77	994	93	2,110	141	1,555	100	1,387	85	1,261	75	2,414	137
July . .	820	75	1,084	96	1,721	130	1,226	89	1,063	74	1,962	131	1,836	118
Aug. . .	1,033	91	1,200	102	1,582	120	1,398	102	987	69	2,158	145	1,893	122
Sept. . .	929	93	1,116	107	1,812	139	1,204	88	927	65	1,826	124	1,788	116
Oct. . .	601	57	1,389	126	1,658	115	1,288	86	1,141	73	2,412	149	1,705	101
Nov. . .	663	68	1,233	122	1,572	118	1,283	93	968	67	1,899	127	1,671	107
Dec. . .	82	9	1,460	158	1,397	102	1,503	105	760	51	2,444	157	2,761	171
Total .	10,489	. .	12,105	. .	20,954	. .	17,494	. .	13,931	. .	17,828	. .	26,897	. .
Aver. .	874	86	1,009	96	1,746	129	1,458	102	1,161	79	1,486	97	2,241	140

* Index = percentage deviation of actual data from trend, seasonal allowed for.
e = estimated from tax on sales of grain futures in 1919 and 1920.

APPENDIX — TABLE 22

(Chart 36)

COTTON — FUTURE SALES

Source, see p. 131

TAX RECEIPTS ON COTTON FUTURE SALES AT NEW YORK AND NEW ORLEANS EXCHANGES

Unit = Thousand dollars

	Data		Data
1910 . . .	....	1920 . . .	3,342
1911 . . .	....	1921 . . .	1,636
1912 . . .	....	1922 . . .	2,700
1913 . . .	....	1923 . . .	5,492
1914 . . .	....	1924 . . .	3,483
1915 . . .	....	1925 . . .	1,610
1916 . . .	....	1926 . . .	....
1917 . . .	....	1927 . . .	....
1918 . . .	....	1928 . . .	....
1919 . . .	3,708	1929 . . .	....

TAX RECEIPTS AND INDEX OF ESTIMATED VOLUME OF SALES

	1919		1920		1921		1922		1923		1924		1925	
	Data	*In-dex	Data	In-dex	Data	In-dex	Data	In-dex	Data	In-dex	Data	In-dex	Data	In-dex
Jan. . .	240.7	107	309.6	97	150.0	106	139.1	84	406.8	150	523.0	147	111.1	83
Feb. . .	189.1	112	293.6	111	101.1	105	130.6	94	392.3	166	493.8	173	122.3	106
Mar. . .	181.9	105	361.0	129	76.5	91	99.5	71	419.6	169	371.7	150	151.8	127
Apr. . .	208.0	112	417.2	145	68.9	78	93.7	67	436.1	185	405.0	150	118.6	104
May . .	314.3	153	288.1	98	60.6	63	184.7	111	406.3	175	295.8	103	114.6	100
June . .	345.4	155	233.2	82	80.9	88	259.2	143	348.5	140	251.1	90	124.8	104
July . .	334.0	140	239.7	81	55.2	57	215.6	118	256.4	111	203.9	136	131.3	108
Aug. . .	270.4	98	319.5	96	125.5	87	222.6	98	275.2	99	191.9	112	107.0	71
Sept. .	299.2	98	292.0	93	319.9	142	265.8	104	465.8	128	205.8	125	177.3	104
Oct. . .	473.9	116	254.4	92	247.4	97	315.7	98	517.8	116	208.5	108	180.0	99
Nov. . .	492.0	111	193.1	85	193.4	86	411.7	118	811.9	165	176.5	95	151.4	87
Dec. . .	358.8	99	140.1	93	157.0	81	361.8	127	755.3	178	156.3	104	119.3	90
Total .	3,707.7	..	3,341.5	..	1,636.4	..	2,700.0	..	5,492.0	..	3,483.3	..	1,609.6	..
Aver. .	309.0	117	278.5	100	136.4	90	225.0	103	457.7	149	290.3	125	134.1	99

* Index = percentage deviation of actual data from trend, seasonal and price changes allowed for.

APPENDIX — TABLE 23

(CHARTS 37 AND 38)

INDEX OF GENERAL PRICE LEVEL

1913 = 100

Sources, see p. 137

	Weight
Wholesale prices . .	2.0
Wages	3.5
Cost of living . . .	3.5
Rents	1.0

Years	Jan.	Feb.	Mar.	Apr.	May	June	July	Aug.	Sept.	Oct.	Nov.	Dec.	Average
1875	84	84	84	84	84	84	84	84	84	83	82	82	84
1876	82	82	81	81	80	79	80	80	79	79	79	79	80
1877	79	79	79	78	79	78	78	77	76	76	75	74	77
1878	74	74	73	72	71	70	71	71	70	70	70	69	71
1879	69	70	70	69	69	70	70	70	70	72	73	74	71
1880	77	77	77	76	76	75	75	75	76	76	77	77	76
1881	77	77	77	77	78	78	78	79	79	81	81	81	79
1882	80	80	81	82	82	82	82	83	81	80	80	79	81
1883	79	80	80	80	79	79	78	78	78	77	77	77	79
1884	78	78	77	77	76	76	76	76	76	75	74	74	76
1885	73	73	73	73	74	73	74	74	74	74	73	73	73
1886	72	72	72	72	72	72	72	72	72	72	72	73	72
1887	72	73	73	73	73	73	73	73	73	73	74	75	73
1888	75	75	75	75	75	75	75	75	76	76	76	75	75
1889	75	74	74	74	74	74	74	74	74	74	74	74	74
1890	75	75	75	75	75	75	75	75	76	76	76	75	75
1891	76	76	76	76	76	76	75	75	75	75	75	75	76
1892	75	75	75	75	75	74	74	74	74	74	74	74	74
1893	75	75	75	75	75	75	75	75	75	75	75	74	75
1894	73	73	73	72	72	72	72	72	72	72	72	72	72
1895	72	72	72	72	72	72	72	72	72	72	72	71	72
1896	71	71	71	71	71	71	71	71	71	71	71	71	71
1897	71	71	71	71	71	70	70	71	71	71	71	71	71
1898	71	71	71	71	71	71	71	71	71	71	72	72	71
1899	73	73	74	74	74	74	74	74	75	75	75	75	74
1900	76	76	76	76	76	76	76	76	76	76	76	76	76
1901	76	76	77	77	76	77	77	77	77	77	78	78	77
1902	78	78	79	79	79	79	80	80	80	80	80	80	79
1903	81	81	81	81	80	80	80	80	80	80	80	80	80
1904	81	81	81	81	81	81	81	81	81	81	81	81	81
1905	81	81	81	82	82	82	82	82	82	82	83	83	82
1906	83	84	84	85	85	85	85	85	86	86	87	87	85
1907	88	88	88	88	89	89	89	89	90	90	90	90	89
1908	90	89	89	89	89	89	89	89	89	90	91	90	89
1909	90	90	91	91	92	92	93	93	94	94	95	95	93
1910	96	96	96	96	96	95	96	96	96	96	96	95	96
1911	95	95	95	95	95	95	96	96	97	97	97	97	96
1912	99	99	99	99	100	99	99	99	100	100	100	100	99
1913	98	98	100	100	100	100	100	101	101	101	101	101	100
1914	100	101	100	100	99	100	101	102	102	101	101	101	101

APPENDIX — TABLE 23 — *Continued*

Years	Jan.	Feb.	Mar.	Apr.	May	June	July	Aug.	Sept.	Oct.	Nov.	Dec.	Average
1915	102	102	101	101	102	102	102	103	103	105	106	106	103
1916	109	109	111	112	113	114	115	116	119	121	124	126	116
1917	128	129	131	135	139	141	141	142	145	147	148	149	140
1918	151	153	155	157	159	163	166	169	174	176	175	175	164
1919	179	176	177	178	180	181	185	189	189	193	198	201	186
1920	207	207	210	215	219	219	221	218	218	213	208	201	213
1921	196	190	186	182	179	172	173	174	173	172	171	171	178
1922	167	166	167	167	168	169	170	171	172	173	175	176	170
1923	177	178	179	180	182	182	183	182	183	184	183	183	181
1924	182	182	182	180	180	180	179	181	182	182	182	184	181
1925	185	185	186	183	184	185	186	186	186	187	187	188	186
1926	188	187	186	186	...	...	...	...	...	...	...	...	...
1927	...	...	...	...	...	...	...	...	...	...	...	...	...
1928	...	...	...	...	...	...	...	...	...	...	...	...	...
1929	...	...	...	...	...	...	...	...	...	...	...	...	...

APPENDIX — TABLE 23 A

INDEX OF WHOLESALE PRICES

1913 = 100

Sources, see p. 137

Years	Jan.	Feb.	Mar.	Apr.	May	June	July	Aug.	Sept.	Oct.	Nov.	Dec.	Average
1875	115	114	115	117	116	114	115	116	113	109	108	107	113
1876	106	106	107	105	103	99	103	102	101	100	100	103	103
1877	105	103	101	102	104	101	99	94	93	92	89	88	99
1878	89	88	87	87	82	79	80	81	79	79	77	75	82
1879	75	78	78	74	76	78	80	78	80	90	94	99	82
1880	104	104	103	100	96	93	92	94	95	95	97	97	98
1881	98	99	99	99	99	100	102	105	108	112	109	109	103
1882	108	108	109	113	114	114	115	120	110	108	105	102	111
1883	104	105	105	103	104	101	98	98	97	96	95	96	100
1884	97	98	97	94	94	92	93	93	95	91	87	84	93
1885	84	84	84	84	75	84	85	85	85	75	74	84	82
1886	82	80	87	81	79	80	87	87	80	79	79	80	80
1887	79	80	80	79	79	80	80	80	81	81	84	88	81
1888	87	86	87	86	86	85	86	87	93	90	88	86	87
1889	84	82	82	80	79	78	79	78	78	77	80	78	80
1890	82	82	82	82	81	81	80	81	82	83	82	81	82
1891	80	80	80	80	80	79	78	78	78	78	78	78	79
1892	77	77	77	76	76	76	76	76	76	76	76	77	76
1893	78	78	78	77	77	76	75	75	75	75	74	73	76
1894	72	72	71	70	70	70	70	70	70	70	70	69	70
1895	68	68	68	68	68	68	68	68	69	70	70	69	69
1896	68	68	67	66	66	65	65	65	66	66	66	66	66
1897	66	66	66	65	65	64	64	65	66	67	67	67	66
1898	67	67	67	67	67	67	67	67	67	67	68	69	67
1899	70	71	72	73	73	74	75	76	77	78	79	80	75
1900	82	83	84	84	82	82	81	80	80	80	81	81	82
1901	80	80	80	80	79	79	80	80	81	81	81	82	80
1902	82	82	82	83	84	84	84	83	83	85	85	85	84
1903	86	86	86	85	84	84	83	83	84	83	83	83	84
1904	84	85	85	84	84	84	83	83	83	83	83	84	84
1905	84	85	85	85	84	84	85	86	86	87	88	89	86
1906	89	90	90	90	90	90	90	90	91	91	93	94	91
1907	95	95	96	95	96	96	96	96	97	97	95	93	96
1908	93	92	92	92	91	90	90	90	90	90	90	91	91
1909	92	92	92	92	93	93	93	93	95	95	97	98	94
1910	98	98	99	99	98	97	97	97	97	97	96	96	97
1911	95	95	95	95	95	95	95	96	96	96	96	96	95
1912	97	97	98	100	100	99	99	99	100	100	100	100	99
1913	100	100	100	100	99	99	100	100	102	101	100	99	100
1914	98	99	98	98	97	97	97	101	102	97	97	97	98
1915	98	99	99	99	100	99	100	100	100	102	104	108	101
1916	113	115	119	121	122	123	123	126	130	136	146	149	127
1917	153	157	162	173	183	185	188	189	187	183	183	182	177
1918	184	186	187	190	190	191	196	200	204	202	203	202	195
1919	199	193	196	199	202	203	212	216	210	211	217	223	207
1920	233	232	234	245	247	243	241	231	226	211	196	179	227
1921	170	160	155	148	145	142	141	142	141	142	141	140	147
1922	138	141	142	143	148	150	155	155	153	154	156	156	149
1923	156	157	159	156	153	153	151	150	154	153	152	151	154
1924	151	152	'50	148	147	145	147	150	149	152	153	157	150
1925	160	161	161	156	155	157	160	160	160	158.	158	156	159
1926	156	155	152	151	152	...	...	...	...	...	...	...	...

APPENDIX — TABLE 23 B
INDEX OF WAGE LEVEL
1913 = 100
Sources, see p. 137

	Weight
Factory	1.0
Unskilled labor . . .	1.0
Teachers and clerks . .	0.5

Years	Jan.	Feb.	Mar.	Apr.	May	June	July	Aug.	Sept.	Oct.	Nov.	Dec.	Average
1875	69	69	69	69	69	69	69	69	69	69	69	69	69
1876	69	69	69	68	68	68	68	68	68	68	68	68	68
1877	67	67	67	66	66	66	66	66	66	65	65	65	66
1878	64	64	64	64	64	64	64	64	64	64	64	64	64
1879	64	64	64	64	64	64	64	64	64	64	64	64	64
1880	69	69	69	69	69	69	69	69	69	69	69	69	69
1881	70	70	70	70	70	70	70	70	70	70	71	71	70
1882	71	71	72	72	72	72	72	72	72	72	73	73	72
1883	73	73	74	74	74	74	74	74	74	74	74	74	74
1884	75	75	75	75	75	75	75	75	75	75	75	75	75
1885	74	74	74	74	74	74	74	74	74	74	74	74	74
1886	73	73	73	73	73	73	73	73	73	73	74	74	73
1887	74	74	75	75	75	75	75	75	75	75	75	75	75
1888	75	75	75	75	75	75	75	75	75	75	75	75	75
1889	75	75	75	75	75	75	75	75	75	75	75	75	75
1890	75	75	75	75	75	75	75	75	75	75	75	75	75
1891	76	76	76	76	76	76	76	76	76	76	76	76	76
1892	76	76	76	76	76	76	76	76	76	76	76	76	76
1893	76	76	76	76	76	76	76	76	76	76	76	76	76
1894	75	75	75	75	75	75	75	75	75	75	75	75	75
1895	75	75	75	75	75	75	75	75	75	75	75	75	75
1896	76	76	76	76	76	76	76	76	76	76	76	76	76
1897	76	76	76	76	76	76	76	76	76	76	76	76	76
1898	75	75	75	75	75	75	75	75	75	75	76	76	75
1899	76	76	77	77	77	77	77	77	77	77	77	77	77
1900	77	77	77	77	77	77	77	77	77	77	77	77	77
1901	78	78	78	78	78	78	78	78	78	78	79	79	78
1902	79	79	80	80	80	80	80	80	80	80	80	80	80
1903	81	81	81	81	81	81	81	81	81	81	81	81	81
1904	82	82	82	82	82	82	82	82	82	82	82	82	82
1905	82	82	82	83	83	83	83	83	83	83	84	84	83
1906	84	85	85	86	86	86	87	87	87	87	88	88	86
1907	89	89	89	90	90	90	91	91	91	91	92	92	90
1908	92	92	92	92	92	92	92	92	92	93	93	93	92
1909	92	92	93	93	93	93	93	93	93	93	93	93	93
1910	94	94	94	94	94	94	94	94	94	94	95	95	94
1911	95	95	95	96	96	96	96	96	96	96	96	96	96
1912	97	97	97	97	97	97	97	97	97	98	98	98	97
1913	99	99	99	100	100	100	100	100	100	100	100	100	100
1914	100	100	100	100	100	102	101	101	100	100	100	101	100
1915	101	101	102	102	102	103	103	104	103	106	107	107	103
1916	108	108	110	110	111	112	113	114	117	118	118	120	113
1917	119	120	122	121	124	125	125	127	131	133	135	136	127
1918	134	138	142	146	150	154	156	160	166	168	164	165	154
1919	174	171	172	172	173	174	176	182	188	188	193	196	180
1920	198	200	205	206	212	116	218	220	220	221	220	219	213
1921	216	213	212	209	204	191	193	194	192	190	187	186	199
1922	181	180	181	180	182	183	183	186	190	192	194	196	186
1923	197	198	202	204	210	214	214	212	212	213	212	213	208
1924	213	212	214	213	212	212	211	212	214	212	212	214	213
1925	213	213	215	212	214	213	213	214	214	215	215	217	214
1926	218	217	218	218	...	...	...	...	...	...	...	...	...

APPENDIX — TABLE 23 c

INDEX OF COST OF LIVING

1913 = 100

Sourecs, see p. 137

Years	Jan.	Feb.	Mar.	Apr.	May	June	July	Aug.	Sept.	Oct.	Nov.	Dec.	Average
1875	82	82	81	81	81	81	81	81	81	81	80	80	81
1876	80	80	79	79	78	78	78	78	78	78	78	78	79
1877	77	77	77	77	77	77	77	77	76	76	76	75	77
1878	74	74	73	72	71	70	70	70	70	70	69	69	71
1879	69	69	69	69	69	69	69	69	69	69	69	69	69
1880	69	69	69	69	69	70	70	70	70	71	71	71	70
1881	71	71	71	71	72	72	72	72	72	73	73	73	72
1882	73	73	73	74	74	74	74	73	73	72	72	72	73
1883	71	71	71	71	70	70	70	70	69	69	69	69	70
1884	68	68	67	67	66	66	66	66	65	65	65	65	66
1885	65	65	65	65	65	65	65	65	65	65	65	65	65
1886	65	65	65	65	65	65	65	65	65	65	65	65	65
1887	65	65	65	65	65	65	65	65	65	66	66	66	65
1888	66	66	66	66	67	67	67	67	67	68	68	68	67
1889	68	68	68	68	68	68	68	68	69	69	69	69	68
1890	70	70	70	70	71	71	71	71	71	71	71	71	71
1891	72	72	72	72	72	72	72	72	72	72	72	72	72
1892	71	71	71	71	71	70	70	70	70	70	70	70	70
1893	71	71	71	72	72	72	72	72	72	72	72	72	72
1894	71	70	70	69	69	69	69	69	69	69	69	69	69
1895	68	68	68	68	68	68	68	68	68	68	67	67	68
1896	66	66	66	66	66	66	66	66	66	66	66	66	66
1897	66	66	66	66	66	66	66	66	66	66	67	67	66
1898	67	67	68	68	68	68	68	68	68	68	68	68	68
1899	69	69	69	69	69	69	69	69	69	69	69	69	69
1900	69	69	69	69	69	70	70	70	70	70	71	71	70
1901	71	71	72	72	72	73	73	73	73	73	74	74	73
1902	74	74	75	75	75	76	76	76	76	76	76	76	75
1903	76	76	76	76	76	76	76	76	76	76	76	76	76
1904	76	76	76	76	76	77	77	77	77	77	77	77	77
1905	77	77	77	77	77	77	77	77	77	77	78	78	77
1906	78	78	79	79	79	80	80	80	80	80	81	81	80
1907	81	81	82	82	82	83	83	83	83	84	84	84	83
1908	84	84	84	84	84	85	85	85	85	86	86	86	85
1909	85	86	87	88	89	90	91	92	93	94	95	96	91
1910	96	96	97	96	96	96	97	97	97	97	97	95	96
1911	96	96	95	94	94	94	96	96	98	98	98	98	96
1912	102	103	102	101	103	101	101	101	102	103	103	102	102
1913	95	94	100	101	100	101	102	102	101	102	102	102	100
1914	103	103	103	101	101	102	104	105	105	106	105	104	104
1915	104	104	102	102	103	103	103	103	104	105	106	105	104
1916	108	109	109	111	111	113	113	113	116	117	120	122	114
1917	125	126	127	131	134	138	136	137	141	146	147	149	136
1918	155	157	156	156	159	164	167	170	175	178	179	180	166
1919	182	179	179	181	184	185	187	191	189	197	202	203	188
1920	211	210	213	217	221	221	224	219	221	215	211	202	215
1921	196	188	181	178	175	172	174	175	173	173	172	174	178
1922	170	168	167	167	167	167	167	167	166	166	168	170	168
1923	170	171	169	171	172	170	173	172	172	175	173	173	172
1924	171	171	170	168	168	169	168	169	171	171	171	173	170
1925	173	172	173	172	173	174	175	176	176	177	178	178	175
1926	179	179	176	176	174	...	...	...	...	...	...	...	...

APPENDIX — TABLE 23 D

INDEX OF RENTS

1913 = 100

Sources, see p. 137

Years	Jan.	Feb.	Mar.	Apr.	May	June	July	Aug.	Sept.	Oct.	Nov.	Dec.	Average
1875	...	...	...	...	...	...	84	...	...	...	...	...	...
1876	...	...	...	...	...	...	82	...	...	...	...	...	...
1877	...	...	...	...	...	...	80	...	...	...	...	...	...
1878	...	...	...	...	...	...	82	...	...	...	...	...	...
1879	...	...	...	...	...	...	80	...	...	...	...	...	...
1880	...	...	...	...	...	...	84	...	...	...	...	...	...
1881	...	...	...	...	...	...	84	...	...	...	...	...	...
1882	...	...	...	...	...	...	84	...	...	...	...	...	...
1883	...	...	...	...	...	...	84	...	...	...	...	...	...
1884	...	...	...	...	...	...	84	...	...	...	...	...	...
1885	...	...	...	...	...	...	84	...	...	...	...	...	...
1886	...	...	...	...	...	...	84	...	...	...	...	...	...
1887	...	...	...	...	...	...	84	...	...	...	...	...	...
1888	...	...	...	...	...	...	84	...	...	...	...	...	...
1889	...	...	...	...	...	...	84	...	...	...	...	...	...
1890	...	...	...	...	...	...	84	...	...	...	...	...	...
1891	...	...	...	...	...	...	84	...	...	...	...	...	...
1892	...	...	...	...	...	...	84	...	...	...	...	...	...
1893	...	...	...	...	...	...	84	...	...	...	...	...	...
1894	...	...	...	...	...	...	84	...	...	...	...	...	...
1895	...	...	...	...	...	...	86	...	...	...	...	...	...
1896	...	...	...	...	...	...	86	...	...	...	...	...	...
1897	...	...	...	...	...	...	86	...	...	...	...	...	...
1898	...	...	...	...	...	...	86	...	...	...	...	...	...
1899	...	...	...	...	...	...	86	...	...	...	...	...	...
1900	...	...	...	...	...	...	86	...	...	...	...	...	...
1901	...	...	...	...	...	...	86	...	...	...	...	...	...
1902	...	...	...	...	...	...	88	...	...	...	...	...	...
1903	...	...	...	...	...	...	90	...	...	...	...	...	...
1904	...	...	...	...	...	...	90	...	...	...	...	...	...
1905	...	...	...	...	...	...	92	...	...	...	...	...	...
1906	...	...	...	...	...	...	92	...	...	...	...	...	...
1907	...	...	...	...	...	...	94	...	...	...	...	...	...
1908	...	...	...	...	...	...	96	...	...	...	...	...	...
1909	...	...	...	...	...	...	96	...	...	...	...	...	...
1910	...	...	...	...	...	...	96	...	...	...	...	...	...
1911	...	...	...	...	...	...	96	...	...	...	...	...	...
1912	...	...	...	...	...	...	98	...	...	...	...	...	...
1913	...	...	...	...	...	...	100	...	...	...	...	...	...
1914	...	...	...	...	...	...	100	...	...	...	...	...	...
1915	...	...	...	...	...	...	102	...	...	...	...	...	...
1916	...	...	...	...	...	...	104	...	...	...	...	...	...
1917	102	102	102	102	102	102	100	100	100	100	100	100	101
1918	102	102	104	104	106	106	108	108	108	110	110	110	107
1919	110	111	112	112	113	114	115	117	119	121	123	125	116
1920	127	129	131	133	135	135	138	140	142	145	148	151	138
1921	152	154	155	157	159	159	160	160	160	161	161	161	158
1922	161	161	161	161	161	161	161	161	161	161	162	162	161
1923	162	162	162	163	163	163	164	164	164	165	166	167	164
1924	167	167	167	167	167	168	168	168	168	168	168	168	168
1925	168	168	168	168	168	167	167	167	167	167	167	167	167
1926	167	167	167	167	...	...	...	...	...	...	...	...	...

APPENDIX — TABLE 24

(CHART 39)

CLEARINGS INDEX OF BUSINESS

Computed normal = 100

Sources, see p. 123

BANK CLEARINGS, OUTSIDE OF NEW YORK CITY, 1875–1918; DEBITS, OUTSIDE OF NEW YORK CITY, 1919–1926

3 months moving average. Seasonal variation and price changes allowed for

Years	Jan.	Feb.	Mar.	Apr.	May	June	July	Aug.	Sept.	Oct.	Nov.	Dec.	Average
1875	....	....	101.1	100.8	100.9	101.6	98.0	95.3	87.9	88.0	94.0	95.1	96.3
1876	99.9	96.8	102.4	101.0	102.0	102.3	99.2	100.6	92.9	94.4	93.9	99.1	98.7
1877	104.0	101.1	95.2	89.4	91.7	92.2	94.6	89.4	92.6	94.1	95.1	93.5	94.4
1878	94.1	92.7	89.5	86.8	85.8	88.0	87.8	88.4	89.6	91.9	91.5	89.6	89.6
1879	88.9	90.4	89.5	90.4	91.8	95.2	96.0	94.3	95.6	100.9	106.7	109.9	95.8
1880	106.9	106.7	106.1	105.4	103.6	102.1	100.3	100.4	100.9	100.3	103.3	108.2	103.7
1881	112.9	114.2	111.2	110.2	112.3	120.3	123.4	126.1	124.2	123.9	119.3	116.3	117.9
1882	113.3	110.4	105.6	103.1	102.8	104.3	105.6	105.9	108.2	108.5	109.5	107.4	107.0
1883	108.1	106.3	104.8	101.3	100.9	101.3	101.47	101.0	99.2	99.7	98.1	102.9	102.1
1884	100.4	100.0	91.9	92.7	94.5	93.6	90.2	84.2	83.6	83.5	82.3	83.5	90.0
1885	84.5	84.8	81.9	81.1	81.7	84.9	85.7	86.1	85.7	87.5	91.9	95.6	86.0
1886	95.7	95.7	95.2	95.2	94.5	96.1	99.4	101.2	101.46	100.7	102.5	104.0	98.47
1887	103.3	101.2	101.2	104.3	108 3	111.46	110.1	108.2	104.6	103.8	104.0	101.8	105.2
1888	100.0	98.2	95.7	95.9	97.3	100.4	101.4	101.1	101.0	104.2	103.4	104.4	100.3
1889	103.2	104.7	104.0	103.0	104.8	105.9	108.9	107.7	107.3	107.5	108.1	109.2	106.2
1890	109.4	109.3	109.1	109.7	115.7	119.4	121.1	118.1	118.0	117.7	116.0	112.7	114.7
1891	108.8	105.9	102.9	103.1	104.2	106.3	106.6	110.9	115.3	116.6	112.4	109.9	108.6
1892	108.7	112.5	111.9	112.1	109.9	113.4	114.7	116.5	115.9	116.6	116.7	117.7	113.9
1893	118.2	117.3	113.7	111.6	111.7	108.9	102.2	89.5	82.6	80.0	83.2	85.7	100.4
1894	88.0	86.4	85.1	84.1	87.4	88.7	88.1	88.1	88.2	90.4	89.9	90.9	87.9
1895	91.0	88.2	86.0	85.7	90.9	94.0	96.4	95.0	94.0	94.46	95.0	96.5	92.3
1896	93.7	91.8	87.8	87·0	86.7	88.8	88.5	85.3	82.3	80.6	81.9	84.2	86.6
1897	83.2	82.3	79.6	80.3	80.9	83.46	85.6	88.2	91.9	92.6	93.5	92.7	86.2
1898	93.3	94.2	93.1	91.8	91.0	92.2	91.2	91.6	90.4	91.9	92.7	96.1	92.5
1899	100.4	103.4	104.9	105.2	106.4	106.6	106.5	105.8	105.6	105.9	105.1	104.46	105.0
1900	103.1	101.3	99.0	98.3	99.46	100.7	100.1	98.2	95.3	95.6	97.1	100.3	99.0
1901	103.46	104.3	104.6	106.8	112.46	115.3	112.6	109.2	106.6	107.46	106.4	107.3	108.1
1902	108.5	108.1	107.3	107.4	109.7	109.7	109.2	106.1	108.0	106.8	106.2	104.9	107.7
1903	105.1	106.0	103.2	104.7	105.0	107.8	109.7	109.0	107.1	104.6	102.7	101.9	105.7
1904	100.0	101.5	100.1	100.0	97.6	98.0	97.5	99.4	100.8	101.9	104.6	107.0	100.7
1905	107.8	106.6	106.46	107.6	109.8	109.8	109.6	109.6	110.3	111.2	111.4	112.0	109.4
1906	115.8	116.46	116.0	111.4	109.9	109.2	109.6	109.6	110.9	109.7	111.5	111.1	112.0
1907	113.3	113.5	114.4	113.5	114.1	112.8	112.9	112.2	111.0	110.4	101.6	93.8	110.3
1908	87.6	89.9	92.6	92.4	91.9	92.3	93.6	94.2	96.3	95.6	95.8	96.4	93.2
1909	98.3	99.9	100.6	101.5	101.5	101.9	101.7	102.9	103.4	103.6	103.8	104.3	102.0
1910	104.4	103.9	104.8	105.6	104.9	103.1	101.46	101.7	100.8	100.2	99.9	100.0	102.6
1911	100.5	100.2	101.0	100.2	100.8	100.8	101.5	101.5	101.0	99.7	99.0	98.1	100.4
1912	98.6	101.4	101.0	101.8	100.8	100.0	99.4	99.8	100.7	101.9	101.3	101.3	100.7
1913	101.6	102.7	102.6	100.8	99.1	98.5	98 3	97.0	97.8	98.1	97.2	96.4	99.2
1914	95.7	96.4	96.2	96.1	95.1	94.9	94.7	93.3	90.1	85.4	83.1	83.0	92.0
1915	83.8	86.1	87.5	89.3	89.7	90.0	90.0	90.3	91.2	92.7	96.1	99.1	90.5
1916	100.2	102.2	102.9	103.4	103.3	103.4	103.5	104.4	106.1	108.3	110.3	110.4	104.9
1917	110.4	108.2	108 5	108.5	110.3	109.6	108.0	107.7	106.0	107.4	107.0	106.7	108.2
1918	104.1	100.4	101.1	103.7	107.5	108.0	108.4	110.3	110.0	109.0	103.5	101.4	105.6
1919	99.7	98.8	98.1	97.2	99.4	104.1	108.4	108.4	111.6	110.9	109.5	109.1	104.6

APPENDIX — TABLE 24 — *Continued*

Years	Jan.	Feb.	Mar.	Apr.	May	June	July	Aug.	Sept.	Oct.	Nov.	Dec.	Average
1920	109.8	107.8	107.2	105.4	104.1	102.2	100.4	99.6	99.3	98.2	97.3	95.7	102.3
1921	94.3	91.7	90.7	88.9	89.8	90.0	91.7	92.1	93.4	94.3	95.6	95.9	92.4
1922	96.6	97.4	98.5	100.7	101.4	103.2	102.9	102.4	101.6	102.4	102.6	104.0	101.1
1923	105.1	108.3	109.5	109.5	109.0	108.1	106.4	103.3	101.2	99.8	100.0	100.8	105.1
1924	101.0	102.1	102.3	103.9	103.2	102.7	101.3	102.3	101.7	102.5	102.5	103.3	102.4
1925	106.1	108.0	110.2	109.4	109.6	109.9	110.3	110.1	109.5	110.4	111.1	111.6	109.7
1926	112.2	112.8	113.4	113.7	....	....	....	....	....	....	....	....	....
1927	....	....	....	....	....	....	....	....	....	....	....	....	....
1928	....	....	....	....	....	....	....	....	....	....	....	....	....
1929	....	....	....	....	....	....	....	....	....	....	....	....	....

APPENDIX — TABLE 25

(CHARTS 40 AND 41)

VELOCITY OF BANK DEPOSITS — ANNUAL RATE OF TURNOVER — ACTUAL FIGURES

Sources, see p. 147

141 CITIES

	1919	1920	1921	1922	1923	1924	1925	1926
J	40.0	45.2	41.9	40.7	42.1	43.0	44.1	....
F	38.7	42.5	38.1	40.9	43.0	43.9	43.9	....
M	36.5	41.6	36.0	39.8	41.9	42.2	43.1	....
A	37.1	41.6	36.2	41.5	40.8	40.9	40.7	....
M	40.8	40.9	38.0	40.4	41.6	41.0	44.3	....
J	45.1	40.4	37.8	40.9	42.3	41.6	44.3	....
J	44.5	40.1	37.4	39.2	39.5	38.8	42.4	....
A	40.4	37.0	33.5	34.7	35.6	36.5	39.2	....
S	42.0	39.7	37.9	39.0	39.1	37.5	42.6	....
O	45.9	43.4	40.5	43.8	40.8	39.3	47.2	....
N	48.8	45.0	42.4	43.9	43.5	42.3	48.3	....
D	47.6	45.8	42.6	43.8	46.2	43.6	49.8	....
T	507.4	503.2	462.3	485.6	496.4	490.6	529.9	....
A	42.3	41.9	38.5	40.5	41.4	40.9	44.2	....
7-yr. av.	....	....	....	41.4	....	....	....	....

CHICAGO, ILLINOIS

	1919	1920	1921	1922	1923	1924	1925	1926
J	47.2	50.0	46.4	47.3	47.0	43.5	46.0	....
F	45.0	44.1	42.4	49.7	50.3	45.5	45.6	....
M	41.3	45.3	41.3	49.3	46.4	46.2	48.2	....
A	44.4	46.3	42.7	47.1	47.1	44.4	44.1	....
M	44.1	47.0	43.3	44.5	44.5	42.0	44.6	....
J	47.8	49.7	42.0	45.6	45.8	42.7	44.1	....
J	50.2	48.2	43.6	41.7	43.3	42.1	43.5	....
A	44.3	46.3	41.5	38.4	39.9	38.7	38.1	....
S	46.4	51.5	44.1	41.9	43.2	38.4	41.1	....
O	47.0	50.8	46.6	43.7	43.3	39.6	43.1	....
N	46.5	46.9	47.4	41.4	44.0	43.9	42.8	....
D	51.3	49.4	48.4	45.9	47.9	45.0	46.7	....
T	555.5	575.5	529.7	536.5	542.7	512.0	527.9	....
A	46.3	48.0	44.1	44.7	45.2	42.7	44.0	....
7-yr. av.	....	....	....	45.0	....	....	....	....

APPENDIX — TABLE 25

VELOCITY OF BANK DEPOSITS — ANNUAL RATE OF TURNOVER — ACTUAL FIGURES

NEW YORK, N. Y.

	1919	1920	1921	1922	1923	1924	1925	1926
J	64.7	83.1	76.3	74.2	79.9	86.4	87.4	....
F	63.6	77.0	68.0	75.2	82.3	87.3	88.1	....
M	62.1	76.6	64.1	75.4	84.0	83.6	86.5	....
A	63.7	77.3	62.9	79.9	83.1	79.2	79.4	....
M	72.4	70.6	68.7	77.8	79.8	79.8	88.5	....
J	81.2	68.7	66.2	75.7	80.2	80.6	88.9	....
J	81.3	67.1	66.2	74.2	73.6	74.5	82.5	....
A	72.6	62.7	58.7	65.2	65.3	70.6	76.4	....
S	74.5	66.0	65.7	68.6	72.4	71.6	83.6	....
O	85.4	77.5	70.4	86.3	74.6	72.6	93.7	....
N	91.3	79.1	75.7	77.4	83.8	83.2	97.8	....
D	89.5	83.8	77.1	79.9	89.9	85.4	99.3	....
T	902.3	889.5	820.0	909.8	948.9	954.8	1,052.1	....
A	75.2	74.1	68.3	75.8	79.1	79.6	87.7	....
7-yr. av.	....	....	....	77.1	....	....	....	....

BOSTON, MASS.

	1919	1920	1921	1922	1923	1924	1925	1926
J	31.7	42.5	33.5	32.4	34.7	37.1	42.6	....
F	30.5	37.4	30.9	29.6	35.7	35.9	38.9	....
M	31.4	38.0	30.0	32.7	38.0	36.4	35.3	....
A	31.2	39.4	30.0	33.6	39.3	36.9	38.6	....
M	34.2	38.0	31.1	31.4	35.1	33.7	36.7	....
J	37.3	36.1	30.4	33.4	36.7	34.7	35.0	....
J	38.2	36.2	29.3	32.3	32.8	32.9	36.0	....
A	33.8	30.8	25.9	24.7	27.4	31.6	31.7	....
S	35.4	34.4	28.2	28.6	32.2	32.3	33.4	....
O	42.9	37.0	32.2	34.3	31.2	34.4	43.6	....
N	45.1	38.0	33.6	32.5	34.8	38.5	43.5	....
D	47.6	39.0	32.8	35.4	39.3	38.1	43.9	....
T	439.3	446.8	367.9	380.9	417.2	422.5	459.2	....
A	36.6	37.2	30.7	31.7	34.8	35.2	38.3	....
7-yr. av.	....	....	....	34.9	....	....	....	....

APPENDIX — TABLE 25

VELOCITY OF BANK DEPOSITS — ANNUAL RATE OF TURNOVER — ACTUAL FIGURES

SAN FRANCISCO, CALIFORNIA

	1919	1920	1921	1922	1923	1924	1925	1926
J	35.5	40.9	39.4	43.9	39.0	36.4	34.2	....
F	39.6	42.6	37.7	37.7	39.7	41.2	39.4	....
M	39.0	43.1	42.8	41.2	42.6	44.0	41.5	....
A	34.0	40.3	42.4	39.4	41.6	39.0	35.4	....
M	38.0	40.7	40.2	37.3	39.4	39.2	38.0	....
J	38.5	39.4	42.3	37.6	41.5	35.8	39.2	....
J	41.9	38.5	38.9	37.1	38.0	37.8	37.1	....
A	43.1	35.4	36.7	34.4	36.3	34.8	39.1	....
S	44.2	41.6	38.6	40.7	42.7	37.5	41.4	....
O	42.8	41.6	42.2	37.4	39.8	36.3	41.8	....
N	42.5	40.2	37.4	39.7	40.7	36.6	42.0	....
D	44.9	41.8	42.8	39.9	41.5	37.5	38.3	....
T	484.0	486.1	481.4	406.3	482.8	456.1	467.4	....
A	40.3	40.5	40.1	38.9	40.2	38.0	39.0	....
7-yr. av.				39.6				

ALBANY, NEW YORK

	1919	1920	1921	1922	1923	1924	1925	1926
J	33.0	24.6	26.4	28.5	23.5	26.8	24.9	....
F	29.1	28.7	24.8	25.4	26.0	30.4	23.6	....
M	27.4	25.7	27.0	22.4	23.9	28.0	32.1	....
A	34.2	32.2	27.4	29.4	26.3	24.2	28.1	....
M	40.6	34.6	36.8	28.6	22.8	23.4	28.9	....
J	49.0	32.9	30.5	26.2	29.6	24.3	28.0	....
J	43.1	35.0	28.1	24.3	26.4	25.5	26.4	....
A	28.9	32.1	22.5	22.1	25.8	23.8	30.7	....
S	30.3	31.8	24.4	21.6	27.0	24.9	28.3	....
O	35.0	32.6	26.0	24.0	27.7	27.2	30.9	....
N	33.8	31.8	27.7	25.8	26.9	28.2	29.1	....
D	39.2	35.9	30.5	31.4	29.0	30.0	30.5	....
T	423.6	377.9	332.1	309.7	314.9	316.7	341.5	....
A	35.3	31.5	27.7	25.8	26.2	26.4	28.5	....
7-yr. av.				28.8				

APPENDIX — TABLE 25

VELOCITY OF BANK DEPOSITS — ANNUAL RATE OF TURNOVER — ACTUAL FIGURES

ROCHESTER, NEW YORK

	1919	1920	1921	1922	1923	1924	1925	1926
J	16.7	20.0	21.7	21.7	21.4	23.0	31.5	.....
F	17.0	19.6	20.3	18.9	21.4	21.9	27.8	.....
M	16.7	19.2	19.3	19.2	21.4	22.7	28.3	.....
A	18.4	20.9	21.5	19.9	22.0	21.8	28.9	.....
M	17.5	20.5	19.8	19.1	22.2	21.5	27.5	.....
J	18.9	20.6	21.4	22.0	24.3	26.1	33.4	.....
J	18.5	20.4	19.6	19.7	22.6	23.3	30.4	.....
A	17.7	19.8	18.3	17.8	20.6	18.0	26.5	.....
S	19.2	21.4	21.4	21.1	22.8	26.0	33.1	.....
O	20.6	21.9	21.8	23.6	22.9	25.8	34.1	.....
N	19.6	21.9	22.0	22.3	21.9	24.8	31.2	.....
D	20.4	22.5	21.8	22.7	26.6	30.7	31.3	.....
T	221.2	248.7	248.9	248.0	270.1	285.6	364.0	.....
A	18.4	20.7	20.7	20.7	22.5	23.8	30.3	.....
7-yr. av.	.....	.....	.....	22.4				

SYRACUSE, NEW YORK

	1919	1920	1921	1922	1923	1924	1925	1926
J	11.9	11.6	10.1	8.3	8.7	9.2	9.1	.....
F	9.9	10.8	9.2	8.2	8.6	9.5	8.2	.....
M	9.0	10.0	8.6	8.1	9.7	9.0	7.9	.....
A	8.5	11.7	9.1	9.2	10.0	9.0	8.5	.....
M	8.6	11.4	8.9	8.4	9.7	9.1	8.8	.....
J	9.7	11.7	8.6	8.5	10.0	9.3	9.1	.....
J	10.2	12.8	8.8	8.8	10.0	8.6	9.7	.....
A	9.9	11.4	7.0	7.3	8.7	7.9	8.6	.....
S	10.4	11.6	8.1	8.4	9.5	8.9	8.4	.....
O	11.5	13.2	9.0	8.8	10.2	8.7	10.1	.....
N	12.2	11.6	9.8	9.7	10.3	8.7	9.4	.....
D	12.1	11.5	9.1	9.6	9.4	8.4	8.6	.....
T	123.9	139.3	106.3	103.3	114.8	106.3	106.4	.....
A	10.3	11.6	8.9	8.6	9.6	8.9	8.9	.....
7-yr. av.	.....	.....	.....	9.5				

APPENDIX — TABLE 25

VELOCITY OF BANK DEPOSITS — ANNUAL RATE OF TURNOVER — ACTUAL FIGURES

Binghamton, New York

	1919	1920	1921	1922	1923	1924	1925	1926
J	20.4	26.2	24.6	22.9	22.0	22.5	21.1	....
F	18.9	24.0	21.6	23.4	22.3	22.4	20.4	....
M	17.1	23.4	21.9	21.6	21.4	20.0	19.0	....
A	21.5	25.4	23.7	24.3	24.9	22.4	20.0	....
M	19.2	26.4	22.6	24.6	23.7	21.8	20.7	....
J	20.2	26.7	23.0	23.0	25.4	21.7	21.6	....
J	20.9	26.5	24.0	21.5	24.4	21.4	20.6	....
A	19.7	26.4	19.8	18.5	21.7	18.1	18.4	....
S	20.4	23.8	21.0	19.6	20.6	19.7	18.7	....
O	22.4	26.3	23.5	20.8	22.0	19.6	21.8	....
N	25.7	23.9	23.2	21.4	23.1	19.6	23.0	....
D	25.0	25.2	23.5	23.6	24.3	20.1	21.5	....
T	251.4	298.2	272.4	265.2	275.8	249.3	246.8	....
A	21.0	24.9	22.7	22.1	23.0	20.8	20.6	....
7-yr av.				22.2				

Buffalo, New York

	1919	1920	1921	1922	1923	1924	1925	1926
J	16.5	21.0	20.9	20.1	24.6	27.0	27.4	....
F	17.0	19.4	19.2	18.9	25.1	25.6	25.0	....
M	17.8	18.6	16.9	18.0	24.2	24.3	23.3	....
A	18.8	18.8	18.2	19.5	27.8	24.9	25.2	....
M	18.4	19.9	18.0	19.7	25.4	25.9	27.1	....
J	19.4	19.4	18.3	20.2	26.6	26.1	25.0	....
J	17.9	22.3	19.2	21.9	26.5	25.2	26.3	....
A	17.5	19.9	16.1	18.3	24.8	21.5	24.8	....
S	16.5	21.1	17.8	20.4	25.9	22.5	25.6	....
O	18.4	22.8	19.9	22.6	27.2	25.2	29.2	....
N	19.0	22.2	19.9	23.0	27.7	26.2	28.9	....
D	19.7	23.1	20.2	24.5	28.8	24.5	26.0	....
T	216.9	248.5	224.6	247.1	314.6	298.9	313.8	....
A	18.1	20.7	18.7	20.6	26.2	24.9	26.2	....
7-yr av.				22.2				

APPENDIX — TABLE 26

(CHARTS 40 AND 42)

INDEX OF BUSINESS ACTIVITY FROM VARIATIONS IN RATE OF DEPOSITS TURNOVER

(Percentage of Deviations from Average)

THREE MONTHS MOVING AVERAGE. SEASONAL ALLOWED FOR

1875–1918. Velocity based on relation of total clearings to total individual deposits in National Banks. 100 = seven years moving average

Years	Jan.	Feb.	Mar.	Apr.	May	June	July	Aug.	Sept.	Oct.	Nov.	Dec.	Average
1875	...	115	116	113	110	105	104	95	94	99	97	101	104
1876	99	108	106	101	97	93	96	93	95	95	93	99	98
1877	98	96	93	95	95	100	97	100	100	98	94	91	96
1878	91	89	92	89	89	86	88	88	90	90	89	86	89
1879	92	97	100	103	104	101	101	105	112	118	120	116	106
1880	111	114	118	120	115	106	100	98	97	102	106	117	109
1881	125	130	126	123	122	123	119	113	109	104	103	105	117
1882	108	115	117	113	106	103	109	114	112	111	105	103	110
1883	101	102	102	99	98	97	100	101	103	96	95	94	99
1884	101	99	99	100	99	95	88	86	83	78	77	79	90
1885	83	83	81	79	78	82	84	86	88	95	101	101	87
1886	103	104	101	94	95	98	104	105	104	104	107	107	102
1887	106	103	105	104	105	102	103	101	100	100	96	95	102
1888	94	93	94	94	96	95	97	99	101	98	96	97	96
1889	102	103	103	101	100	101	103	104	101	100	99	101	101
1890	103	104	104	109	113	114	110	110	109	106	101	101	107
1891	99	99	100	100	101	100	100	108	108	107	100	103	102
1892	111	112	110	102	101	99	100	100	99	98	100	107	103
1893	111	113	109	106	104	103	98	93	88	88	87	88	99
1894	86	86	85	85	84	83	84	84	84	82	83	87	84
1895	87	89	90	97	100	103	102	101	100	98	98	96	97
1896	98	96	97	93	95	97	97	95	92	94	95	96	95
1897	93	92	91	89	91	96	105	113	110	105	99	100	99
1898	103	102	98	92	92	93	99	101	99	95	95	106	98
1899	113	121	119	117	110	106	105	106	106	105	104	103	109
1900	100	99	100	101	98	93	90	86	85	91	98	109	96
1901	111	114	122	134	134	124	109	101	98	100	103	105	113
1902	102	100	104	107	105	102	101	108	106	106	101	100	103
1903	98	99	98	97	98	98	97	92	87	84	85	84	93
1904	85	84	84	83	83	84	86	88	91	98	103	105	89
1905	105	108	114	114	109	103	103	104	104	104	108	116	108
1906	119	118	115	114	112	108	110	111	114	109	109	110	112
1907	111	115	112	109	100	99	101	100	100	92	86	80	100
1908	82	85	84	85	86	89	89	93	90	92	95	99	89
1909	99	98	100	101	105	104	109	107	108	105	105	108	104
1910	109	111	108	104	102	100	100	96	93	94	96	98	101
1911	101	103	100	98	100	100	103	100	98	97	96	98	100
1912	100	102	105	105	104	101	100	99	102	102	103	100	102
1913	100	100	100	98	98	97	98	98	98	98	96	94	98
1914	95	96	97	94	94	93	89	81	72	72	74	76	86
1915	80	84	90	92	93	92	94	98	101	104	104	100	94
1916	101	103	105	104	103	102	104	107	111	113	113	110	106
1917	106	103	105	106	109	109	111	107	105	101	98	94	104
1918	90	92	96	101	105	108	112	111	109	103	101	100	102

APPENDIX — TABLE 26 (*Continued*)

1919 to date (*revised*). Velocity based on relation of debits to individual account in 141 cities to individual demand deposits in weekly Reporting Member Banks (about 700). 100 = 1919–1925 average.

Years	Jan.	Feb.	Mar.	Apr.	May	June	July	Aug.	Sept.	Oct.	Nov.	Dec.	Average
1919	97	94	92	92	95	101	108	112	110	109	109	110	102
1920	108	104	101	100	101	100	99	100	102	103	103	103	102
1921	101	97	91	88	89	90	92	92	94	95	97	96	94
1922	96	95	95	97	98	99	98	97	98	100	99	99	98
1923	97	99	100	101	101	101	100	99	98	98	98	100	99
1924	101	102	101	101	100	100	99	101	100	99	97	98	99
1925	100	102	103	101	103	104	106	106	107	109	109	110	105
1926	...	...	...	...	...	...	...	...	...	...	...	...	...

APPENDIX — TABLE 27

(CHART 45)

PIG IRON PRODUCTION INDEX

THREE MONTHS MOVING AVERAGE. TREND AND SEASONAL ALLOWED FOR

100 = Computed normal

Sources, see p. 85

	1877	1878	1879	1880	1881
January	83	85	78	116	118
April	81	82	79	125	121
July	82	81	87	111	119
October	74	67	102	98	106

	1882	1883	1884	1885	1886
January	112	114	93	76	91
February	...	...	...	76	92
March	...	...	...	79	97
April	120	103	96	78	101
May	...	...	...	77	111
June	...	...	...	76	115
July	104	98	91	75	114
August	...	...	87	74	110
September . . .	...	...	81	72	107
October	101	92	79	72	108
November . . .	...	...	78	76	109
December . . .	...	...	75	83	111

APPENDIX — TABLE 27 (*Continued*)

PIG IRON PRODUCTION INDEX

	1887	1888	1889	1890	1891
January	118	110	121	128.8	112.2
February	120	99	119	129.6	101.4
March	123	93	118	130.7	89.2
April	120	91	113	128.0	79.0
May	111	96	111	130.1	83.7
June	103	96	110	129.5	97.2
July	94	96	108	125.0	108.9
August	103	97	109	121.5	113.1
September	110	100	108	119.3	112.4
October	118	104	113	120.9	115.2
November	119	109	118	119.8	118.1
December	116	115	123	116.8	119.7

	1892	1893	1894	1895	1896
January	122.7	106.4	57.7	91.0	105.8
February	121.3	104.6	58.9	87.5	99.4
March	120.6	105.3	64.1	85.5	95.8
April	114.8	104.1	64.0	81.5	91.3
May	112.4	105.5	55.9	82.9	91.7
June	109.3	101.1	48.3	85.7	90.8
July	104.2	86.1	49.1	89.4	84.8
August	102.1	87.2	65.1	95.2	75.0
September	94.4	50.2	75.6	98.3	62.4
October	96.7	44.6	83.3	103.5	56.8
November	104.1	47.1	85.8	106.0	58.3
December	103.8	52.2	88.8	106.6	65.6

	1897	1898	1899	1900	1901
January	73.8	102.1	100.7	117.1	94.9
February	76.8	101.5	98.2	114.6	100.8
March	78.9	102.3	98.5	113.8	106.2
April	77.7	99.5	96.9	109.6	104.7
May	79.1	99.8	102.1	112.0	109.4
June	78.4	97.8	104.8	111.7	111.7
July	77.1	93.3	106.4	104.7	111.6
August	78.9	90.7	107.3	95.3	108.9
September	82.2	88.6	107.0	85.7	106.2
October	88.7	91.1	108.7	81.4	107.3
November	93.6	93.3	111.1	80.1	108.9
December	97.3	96.8	112.8	83.4	107.7

APPENDIX — TABLE 27 (*Continued*)

PIG IRON PRODUCTION INDEX

	1902	*1903*	*1904*	*1905*	*1906*
January	112.1	112.2	73.2	115.9	132.1
February	110.0	113.2	85.9	121.0	132.1
March	114.3	116.4	100.7	124.0	132.0
April	112.0	120.9	105.6	128.5	132.1
May	116.5	125.2	103.7	127.6	130.7
June	115.4	124.3	93.6	124.2	130.3
July	117.1	120.2	84.7	121.0	126.2
August	115.1	116.2	85.3	122.3	125.0
September . . .	111.9	110.9	91.4	126.5	126.0
October	111.1	97.3	98.0	129.2	130.4
November . . .	110.8	78.9	103.0	131.0	134.7
December . . .	110.6	66.9	110.3	131.1	134.7

	1907	*1908*	*1909*	*1910*	*1911*
January	135.3	66.7	99.2	137.8	92.0
February	132.8	65.4	99.2	135.1	97.2
March	132.8	67.3	98.0	132.9	102.2
April	133.8	67.0	98.2	128.7	101.0
May	136.5	65.6	102.0	125.1	96.2
June	138.1	67.4	109.2	119.9	92.2
July	136.7	70.5	115.4	114.5	92.3
August	134.6	76.3	122.9	110.0	94.7
September . . .	133.4	81.2	129.3	106.8	97.8
October	124.3	84.8	133.7	102.8	98.3
November . . .	104.2	90.0	136.8	96.9	98.4
December . . .	79.4	94.3	136.8	91.3	97.6

	1912	*1913*	*1914*	*1915*	*1916*
January	102.0	128.5	87.1	69.7	132.3
February	106.0	126.2	90.9	76.1	132.0
March	110.9	125.5	96.4	83.3	132.6
April	114.2	125.3	96.7	89.3	132.3
May	116.9	129.0	92.3	95.6	133.3
June	118.3	123.6	88.3	102.6	134.1
July	118.0	119.0	86.6	109.4	131.6
August	117.6	116.2	85.6	115.4	130.6
September . . .	119.6	113.7	81.3	120.9	131.7
October	120.5	108.3	74.0	123.6	132.3
November . . .	124.3	99.4	67.9	127.2	130.7
December . . .	125.8	89.8	65.5	128.0	126.1

APPENDIX — TABLE 27 — *Continued*

PIG IRON PRODUCTION INDEX

	1917	1918	1919	1920	1921
January	120.4	99	124	99	97
February	119.3	101	123	109	87
March	121.7	101	118	117	73
April	128.4	112	108	114	59
May	131.3	123	95	110	48
June	132.3	127	85	109	42
July	129.7	130	85	114	39
August	127.1	129	93	116	35
September . . .	124.1	129	97	116	34
October	122.8	127	88	117	38
November . . .	118.4	126	84	114	44
December . . .	107.3	125	85	108	51
	1922	1923	1924	1925	1926
January	56	108	102	101	109
February	60	112	108	113	111
March	64	116	112	118	111
April	69	120	115	117	113
May	75	127	107	110	. . .
June	81	132	92	103	. . .
July	86	134	76	97	. . .
August	80	129	67	94	. . .
September . . .	76	122	67	94	. . .
October	77	114	74	97	. . .
November . . .	89	107	81	100	. . .
December . . .	100	104	91	105	. . .

APPENDIX — TABLE 28

(Chart 46)

Sources, see Chart 8, p. 39

RAILWAY FREIGHT TRAFFIC — TON MILES —

PER CENT DEVIATION — FROM 10-YEAR MOVING AVERAGE

1852	100.0	1870	103.2	1889	101.3	1907	113.2
1853	100.0	1871	105.0	1890	106.7	1908	99.4
1854	107.1	1872	108.3	1891	108.1	1909	94.1
1855	106.3	1873	114.5	1892	111.4	1910	104.6
1856	115.8	1874	106.8	1893	113.5	1911	100.4
1857	100.0	1875	96.7	1894	91.5	1912	99.4
1858	88.5	1876	95.9	1895	91.3	1913	107.1
1859	80.6	1877	86.6	1896	95.5	1914	96.0
1860	94.3	1878	96.3	1897	89.4	1915	87.6
1861	105.1	1879	108.5	1898	100.7	1916	103.3
1862	120.5	1880	112.0	1899	102.0	1917	116.9
1863	110.0	1881	114.8	1900	108.3	1918	118.4
1864	108.8	1882	107.2	1901	104.5	1919	105.6
1865	87.7	1883	100.2	1902	102.9	1920	112.3
1866	92.0	1884	94.5	1903	103.7	1921	82.5
1867	93.0	1885	97.0	1904	98.3	1922	89.0
1868	93.8	1886	96.9	1905	99.7	1923	105.4
1869	100.0	1887	106.5	1906	108.9	1924	97.8
....	...	1888	97.6	....	....	1925	101.6

APPENDIX — TABLE 29

(CHART 53)

AVERAGE YIELD OF 45 HIGH GRADE BONDS

Sources, see p. 203

Three Months Moving Average

Years	Jan.	Feb.	Mar.	Apr.	May	June	July	Aug.	Sept.	Oct.	Nov.	Dec.
1900	....	....	3.91	3.89	3.88	3.89	3.90	3.91	3.92	3.93	3.92	3.83
1901	3.87	3.85	3.83	3.81	3.81	3.81	3.82	3.83	3.84	3.85	3.85	3.85
1902	3.84	3.83	3.82	3.81	3.80	3.80	3.81	3.83	3.84	3.86	3.87	3.89
1903	3.89	3.90	3.91	3.93	3.95	3.97	4.01	4.05	4.09	4.11	4.11	4.10
1904	4.09	4.08	4.09	4.08	4.08	4.05	4.03	4.00	3.98	3.97	3.95	3.94
1905	3.92	3.91	3.90	3.90	3.90	3.90	3.91	3.91	3.90	3.90	3.91	3.92
1906	3.92	3.93	3.95	3.96	3.99	4.00	4.03	4.05	4.09	4.11	4.11	4.11
1907	4.12	4.13	4.16	4.19	4.22	4.24	4.28	4.32	4.37	4.43	4.54	4.61
1908	4.62	4.56	4.51	4.48	4.46	4.42	4.39	4.36	4.35	4.32	4.29	4.25
1909	4.22	4.19	4.18	4.17	4.16	4.17	4.17	4.18	4.19	4.20	4.21	4.22
1910	4.22	4.23	4.24	4.26	4.28	4.31	4.33	4.35	4.36	4.35	4.33	4.33
1911	4.32	4.32	4.32	4.32	4.30	4.29	4.28	4.30	4.31	4.32	4.32	4.32
1912	4.32	4.31	4.31	4.31	4.32	4.32	4.32	4.33	4.34	4.35	4.37	4.38
1913	4.39	4.40	4.41	4.44	4.48	4.52	4.57	4.59	4.59	4.57	4.57	4.58
1914	4.56	4.53	4.48	4.46	4.45	4.44	4.44	4.45	4.48	4.52	4.56	4.67
1915	4.67	4.65	4.55	4.55	4.55	4.56	4.58	4.61	4.62	4.61	4.56	4.50
1916	4.45	4.43	4.41	4.41	4.42	4.43	4.43	4.43	4.43	4.41	4.38	4.36
1917	4.34	4.34	4.36	4.43	4.52	4.61	4.68	4.73	4.80	4.86	4.93	5.00
1918	5.06	5.09	5.10	5.15	5.18	5.13	5.20	5.22	5.24	5.25	5.16	5.06
1919	5.01	5.04	5.09	5.12	5.13	5.13	5.13	5.18	5.24	5.26	5.29	5.35
1920	5.43	5.53	5.58	5.68	5.80	5.94	6.04	6.04	5.99	5.87	5.80	5.82
1921	5.86	5.87	5.84	5.84	5.75	5.79	5.81	5.90	5.80	5.70	5.58	5.42
1922	5.24	5.11	5.04	4.97	4.90	4.85	4.82	4.78	4.72	4.71	4.74	4.77
1923	4.78	4.77	4.80	4.85	4.87	4.87	4.88	4.89	4.92	4.93	4.94	4.93
1924	4.90	4.87	4.84	4.84	4.81	4.77	4.71	4.68	4.66	4.66	4.64	4.65
1925	4.66	4.66	4.64	4.62	4.59	4.56	4.55	4.57	4.59	4.60	4.62	4.62

APPENDIX — TABLE 30

(Chart 53)

PRICE INDEX OF 12 EARLY-MOVING COMMODITIES

1913 = 100 — weighted

	1919	1920	1921	1922	1923	1924	1925	1926
J	153	212	99	96	128	115	129	128
F	140	204	92	98	133	115	123	123
M	136	199	88	97	139	111	121	118
A	141	190	84	100	137	105	117	114
M	152	180	88	106	125	99	118	113
J	180	168	87	110	118	100	119	116
J	200	156	86	112	111	105	124	. . .
A	206	155	86	113	111	116	128	. . .
S	195	157	91	117	117	113	129	. . .
O	199	141	91	123	112	116	128	. . .
N	200	123	94	123	112	121	130	. . .
D	200	102	96	124	112	128	128	. . .

APPENDIX — TABLE 31

INTEREST RATES—CUSTOMERS' 4-6 MONTHS COMMERCIAL PAPER

(Charts 54 and 55)

New York

	1919	1920	1921	1922	1923	1924	1925	1926
J	5.875	6.00	7.00	5.50	4.875	5.25	4.00	. . .
F	5.625	6.00	7.00	5.50	4.875	5.00	4.50	. . .
M	5.75	6.00	7.00	5.50	5.00	5.125	4.75	. . .
A	5.75	6.00	7.00	5.50	5.50	5.00	4.625	. . .
M	5.50	6.00	7.00	5.00	5.50	5.00	4.625	. . .
J	5.625	6.00	6.50	5.00	5.29	4.75	4.50	. . .
J	5.375	6.50	6.50	5.25	5.375	4.50	4.50	. . .
A	5.50	6.50	6.50	4.75	5.25	4.25	4.25	. . .
S	5.375	7.00	6.25	4.625	5.375	4.375	4.625	. . .
O	5.625	7.00	6.00	5.00	5.375	4.75	4.625	. . .
N	5.625	7.00	6.00	4.75	5.375	4.375	4.625	. . .
D	5.875	6.50	5.75	4.875	5.375	4.25	4.75	. . .

APPENDIX — TABLE 31

(CHART 54)

INTEREST RATES — CUSTOMERS' 4-6 MONTHS COMMERCIAL PAPER

Simple Average of Prevailing Rates in 22 Branch Cities

	1919	1920	1921	1922	1923	1924	1925	1926
January . . .	6.27	6.28	7.14	6.98	6.47	6.46	5.88	...
February . .	6.26	6.43	7.16	6.84	6.45	6.45	5.86	...
March . . .	6.26	6.51	7.12	6.65	6.36	6.49	5.78	...
April	6.24	6.54	7.21	6.70	6.39	6.57	5.80	...
May	6.20	6.80	7.16	6.66	6.41	6.49	5.88	...
June	6.15	6.92	7.12	6.58	6.37	6.32	5.82	...
July	6.22	7.07	7.10	6.53	6.52	5.98	5.79	...
August . . .	6.21	7.00	7.22	6.52	6.47	5.91	5.88	...
September . .	6.17	7.02	7.04	6.51	6.38	6.00	5.86	...
October . . .	6.22	7.01	7.13	6.45	6.35	5.94	5.93	...
November . .	6.22	7.05	6.95	6.42	6.49	5.94	6.03	...
December . .	6.30	7.08	7.04	6.43	6.50	5.97	5.95	...

APPENDIX — TABLE 31

INTEREST RATES — CUSTOMERS' 4-6 MONTHS COMMERCIAL PAPER

(CHART 54)

Weighted Average of Prevailing Rates in 12 Federal Reserve Bank Cities

	1919	1920	1921	1922	1923	1924	1925	1926
January . . .	5.76	5.98	6.91	5.85	5.19	5.41	4.42	...
February . .	5.70	6.06	6.92	5.78	5.19	5.25	4.61	...
March . . .	5.79	6.12	6.91	5.69	5.33	5.28	4.81	...
April	5.79	6.27	6.93	5.59	5.51	5.21	4.76	...
May	5.60	6.29	6.89	5.31	5.54	5.14	4.76	...
June	5.68	6.41	6.70	5.33	5.39	4.95	4.72	...
July	5.57	6.65	6.68	5.41	5.44	4.81	4.73	...
August . . .	5.62	6.65	6.55	5.12	5.46	4.52	4.59	...
September . .	5.56	6.91	6.45	4.98	5.52	4.60	4.81	...
October . . .	5.68	6.91	6.31	5.16	5.52	4.74	4.85	...
November . .	5.66	6.91	6.22	5.15	5.50	4.56	4.85	...
December . .	5.90	6.90	6.03	5.17	5.46	4.56	4.92	...

APPENDIX — TABLE 32

(CHART 55)

INTEREST RATES—COMMERCIAL PAPER, 4–6 MONTHS PRIME, OPEN MARKET

New York City

	1919	*1920*	*1921*	*1922*	*1923*	*1924*	*1925*
January	5	6	7¾	4¾	4½	4¾	3½
February	5	6½	7¾	5	4¾	4¾	3¾
March	5½	6¾	7¾	4¾	5	4⅝	4
April	5½	7	7½	4½	5⅛	4½	4
May	5¼	7½	7	4¼	5	4¼	3⅞
June	5¼	7¾	6½	4¼	5	3⅝	3⅞
July	5¼	8	6¼	4	5	3⅜	3⅞
August	5¼	8	6¼	4	5¼	3⅛	4⅛
September	5¼	8	6	4¼	5⅜	3¼	4¼
October	5¼	8	5¾	4½	5¼	3⅛	4⅜
November	5¼	8	5¼	4¾	5	3⅜	4⅜
December	6	8	5	4¾	4⅞	3⅝	4⅜

APPENDIX — TABLE 32

INTEREST RATES — CUSTOMERS' 4–6 MONTHS COMMERCIAL PAPER

(CHART 55)

34 Cities — Weighted "Computed Approximation to a National Average"

	1919	*1920*	*1921*	*1922*	*1923*	*1924*	*1925*	*1926*
January	5.88	6.05	6.96	6.11	5.48	5.65	4.74	...
February	5.83	6.14	6.98	6.02	5.48	5.51	4.83	...
March	5.90	6.21	6.96	5.92	5.57	5.55	4.97	...
April	5.89	6.33	7.00	5.84	5.71	5.51	4.99	...
May	5.74	6.41	6.95	5.62	5.74	5.44	5.01	...
June	5.79	6.52	6.80	5.61	5.61	5.25	4.96	...
July	5.72	6.75	6.77	5.67	5.69	5.07	4.97	...
August	5.75	6.73	6.70	5.44	5.69	4.83	4.88	...
September	5.70	6.93	6.59	5.34	5.72	4.91	5.04	...
October	5.80	6.93	6.50	5.46	5.71	5.01	5.09	...
November	5.79	6.94	6.39	5.44	5.73	4.86	5.11	...
December	6.00	6.94	6.26	5.46	5.70	4.87	5.15	...

APPENDIX — TABLE 33

(CHART 56)

FIFTY YEARS OF VARIATIONS IN INTEREST RATES

MONTHLY AVERAGE RATES ON PRIME COMMERCIAL 60–90 DAY PAPER IN NEW YORK CITY

In percentage deviations from 1875–1923 average

THREE MONTHS MOVING AVERAGES. SEASONAL ALLOWED FOR

Years	Jan.	Feb.	Mar.	Apr.	May	June	July	Aug.	Sept.	Oct.	Nov.	Dec.	Average
1875	...	113	116	112	107	99	98	98	106	114	120	126	110
1876	124	129	114	112	113	101	88	80	88	98	106	109	105
1877	108	101	94	90	92	89	97	104	120	122	119	114	104
1878	114	113	112	106	101	89	80	79	86	94	97	94	97
1879	90	92	101	105	104	93	97	99	108	111	114	114	102
1880	113	113	115	114	112	105	100	96	96	97	103	107	106
1881	113	113	114	105	94	86	88	96	105	112	117	117	105
1882	119	117	115	110	111	108	110	111	119	123	119	116	115
1883	114	120	124	123	117	110	107	107	110	109	107	104	113
1884	103	100	100	102	115	124	123	112	103	100	98	96	106
1885	96	95	92	85	82	79	77	72	72	75	81	86	83
1886	86	84	85	86	90	88	92	97	106	110	112	112	96
1887	110	109	109	112	116	122	126	128	123	117	113	113	117
1888	112	110	109	109	107	97	90	90	92	93	92	94	100
1889	96	95	92	89	89	89	95	97	103	106	113	113	98
1890	112	110	110	110	112	112	111	108	108	118	129	132	114
1891	121	111	108	111	118	122	120	113	107	101	96	91	110
1892	86	82	79	75	71	71	74	80	87	93	98	102	83
1893	106	117	123	135	157	199	224	207	160	114	87	75	142
1894	71	71	66	64	66	65	64	62	57	54	53	57	62
1895	66	74	81	75	69	62	65	69	77	80	85	97	75
1896	114	119	115	106	104	102	120	137	153	135	109	80	116
1897	68	67	70	74	75	75	73	74	75	75	72	68	72
1898	67	76	95	107	101	86	75	75	70	67	61	60	78
1899	61	67	74	78	78	78	80	85	90	96	103	105	83
1900	103	99	95	90	86	84	85	83	85	85	88	85	89
1901	84	80	80	83	88	90	91	90	88	88	89	92	87
1902	91	90	90	94	99	100	99	99	103	107	110	109	99
1903	108	108	110	109	111	112	117	114	111	110	110	108	111
1904	105	100	95	89	86	82	79	77	79	79	80	80	86
1905	82	82	83	84	86	88	86	86	86	94	101	106	89
1906	108	107	111	113	118	118	118	118	117	118	117	121	115
1907	125	127	128	124	125	123	124	124	126	132	141	142	128
1908	131	120	108	100	89	84	78	74	72	74	74	75	90
1909	76	75	74	74	75	74	76	76	83	88	95	97	80
1910	97	95	97	99	106	110	111	108	103	102	98	91	101
1911	86	83	82	79	81	82	83	82	82	79	81	81	82
1912	83	82	85	88	91	94	96	99	103	106	110	106	95
1913	106	107	114	117	124	127	128	118	110	105	105	102	114
1914	95	85	81	81	85	90	104	114	122	114	101	88	97
1915	79	74	72	72	74	72	72	69	68	64	62	62	70
1916	63	63	63	63	66	73	77	76	72	69	72	73	69
1917	77	79	83	89	95	98	99	100	105	107	109	111	96
1918	114	117	118	118	119	120	121	122	122	121	119	115	119
1919	110	107	107	108	110	111	112	111	110	109	112	117	110
1920	124	127	131	137	146	154	162	163	163	161	159	159	149
1921	159	156	154	148	143	135	130	124	119	112	107	103	132
1922	101	98	95	91	87	83	81	82	85	88	91	94	90
1923	94	96	99	102	102	102	102	103	104	103	101	100	101
1924	98	96	94	91	87	80	74	68	65	64	66	70	79
1925	73	75	77	79	79	79	81	82	85	87	88	88	81

APPENDIX — TABLE 34

(For chart references for this table, see chart and table index)

INDEXES OF THE TOTAL VOLUME OF TRADE AND OF ITS CHIEF GROUP COMPONENTS

TOTAL VOLUME OF TRADE

	Jan.	Feb.	Mar.	Apr.	May	June	July	Aug.	Sept.	Oct.	Nov.	Dec.
1919	96	96	93	100	105	110	111	109	108	108	108	106
1920	110	105	109	105	105	102	102	100	96	94	93	92
1921	90	90	90	91	92	92	92	94	94	93	91	94
1922	94	95	101	100	102	104	100	100	104	104	104	108
1923	109	110	113	110	110	108	104	104	103	105	108	107
1924	107	111	105	104	102	99	99	101	105	107	107	111
1925	111	113	110	111	109	108	110	107	111	115	111	116

APPENDIX — TABLE 34 A

INDEXES OF PRODUCTIVE ACTIVITY AND PRO-DUCERS' AND CONSUMERS' GOODS

INDEX OF PRODUCTIVE ACTIVITY

	Jan.	Feb.	Mar.	Apr.	May	June	July	Aug.	Sept.	Oct.	Nov.	Dec.
1919	92	90	87	93	95	95	102	103	105	106	103	105
1920	109	106	105	103	100	102	100	98	94	87	83	79
1921	72	78	79	83	81	83	84	88	88	91	86	87
1922	90	92	98	91	98	103	98	102	102	106	113	119
1923	115	118	122	119	116	113	110	113	108	117	116	113
1924	115	125	117	107	102	96	96	98	105	109	105	110
1925	112	115	110	116	108	111	114	109	115	117	113	117

INDEX OF PRODUCERS' GOODS. I

	Jan.	Feb.	Mar.	Apr.	May	June	July	Aug.	Sept.	Oct.	Nov.	Dec.
1919	103	97	90	90	86	89	98	102	99	97	89	96
1920	106	109	108	103	102	105	99	100	100	95	90	85
1921	72	71	68	67	68	68	63	68	69	73	67	75
1922	77	80	85	78	85	87	84	85	90	97	103	106
1923	108	107	111	112	115	110	115	106	103	103	102	96
1924	102	109	99	94	84	75	74	78	87	92	92	102
1925	107	105	101	100	94	93	93	93	97	100	102	107

INDEX OF CONSUMERS' GOODS. II

	Jan.	Feb.	Mar.	Apr.	May	June	July	Aug.	Sept.	Oct.	Nov.	Dec.
1919	106	97	95	107	106	97	101	101	112	110	103	109
1920	113	103	104	99	101	103	101	98	92	84	84	84
1921	81	87	91	96	87	91	94	101	97	96	91	92
1922	93	97	102	87	93	95	95	100	102	101	110	108
1923	107	107	112	109	109	103	99	103	93	104	101	100
1924	104	110	102	104	103	99	104	110	110	103	99	103
1925	108	104	100	104	98	101	107	100	110	105	96	113

APPENDIX — TABLE 34 B
INDEX OF PRIMARY DISTRIBUTION

	Jan.	Feb.	Mar.	Apr.	May	June	July	Aug.	Sept.	Oct.	Nov.	Dec.
1919	98	98	92	112	116	129	118	111	110	102	107	113
1920	113	103	112	103	115	112	114	106	100	96	95	97
1921	95	96	96	98	100	101	99	107	97	94	89	90
1922	91	94	101	99	101	104	100	102	103	101	104	102
1923	103	106	108	109	110	106	106	106	103	102	99	98
1924	101	105	99	101	96	94	93	96	104	107	101	101
1925	98	100	101	102	100	95	99	98	98	96	95	99

APPENDIX — TABLE 34 C
INDEX OF DISTRIBUTION TO CONSUMER

	Jan.	Feb.	Mar.	Apr.	May	June	July	Aug.	Sept.	Oct.	Nov.	Dec.
1919	96	101	100	99	102	101	105	109	106	105	107	103
1920	107	108	108	103	104	100	102	101	96	95	97	93
1921	95	95	97	94	95	97	97	96	94	98	95	97
1922	98	97	98	97	97	98	99	98	101	100	101	103
1923	101	102	105	101	104	104	102	103	104	102	103	103
1924	103	103	99	102	101	102	99	101	103	102	104	106
1925	102	107	101	101	103	102	101	105	105	111	105	112

APPENDIX — TABLE 34 D
INDEX OF FINANCIAL ACTIVITY

	Jan.	Feb.	Mar.	Apr.	May	June	July	Aug.	Sept.	Oct.	Nov.	Dec.
1919	99	96	94	99	134	149	147	118	119	151	125	95
1920	118	105	133	141	112	87	82	78	79	106	99	121
1921	113	99	90	90	95	86	82	70	105	78	96	113
1922	100	85	125	143	144	136	100	83	129	113	90	104
1923	145	124	132	119	120	119	77	71	80	91	138	132
1924	128	115	105	107	121	98	129	117	122	134	153	178
1925	189	183	176	169	160	151	167	127	155	189	179	198

APPENDIX — TABLE 34 E
INDEX OF GENERAL BUSINESS ACTIVITY

	Jan.	Feb.	Mar.	Apr.	May	June	July	Aug.	Sept.	Oct.	Nov.	Dec.
1919	100	97	96	97	105	109	111	112	109	108	112	107
1920	108	104	104	102	99	97	98	99	98	97	98	98
1921	96	90	90	90	93	93	94	95	98	95	97	98
1922	99	100	102	105	104	106	104	103	105	107	100	104
1923	107	109	107	107	106	106	102	98	101	100	101	103
1924	102	105	104	103	103	104	102	107	104	103	107	108
1925	112	110	111	108	112	112	111	111	112	114	114	114

BIBLIOGRAPHY

BRIEF SELECTED BIBLIOGRAPHY ON BUSINESS CYCLES

By LUCILE BAGWELL.

American Telephone and Telegraph Company—"Composite Index of General Business Activity. 1877-1923." Published in F. C. Mills' "Statistical Methods." Holt, New York. 1924.

Ayres, Leonard P.—"Business Recovery Following Depression." Pamphlet, published by Cleveland Trust Company. May, 1922.—"The Prospects for Building Construction in American Cities." Pamphlet, published by Cleveland Trust Company. June, 1922.—Various other articles on interest rates, security prices and trade movements in the monthly Business Bulletins of the Cleveland Trust Company.

Axe, Emerson Wirt, and Houghton, Ruth—"A Bi-Monthly Index of Business Activity since 1884." The Annalist. January 15, 1926. Published by The New York Times Company.

Barber, Joseph H.—"Finding Your Industry's Cycle." Management and Administration. November, 1924. Ronald Press, New York.—"Forecasting the Underlying Cycles." Management and Administration. December, 1924. Ronald Press, New York.—"Budgeting to the Business Cycle." Ronald Press, New York. 1925.—"Economic Control of Inventory." Codex Book Company, New York. 1925.

Benner, Samuel—"Prophecies of Future Ups and Downs in Prices." Chase and Hall, Cincinnati. 1876.

Berridge, William A.—"Employment and the Business Cycle." Harvard Review of Economic Statistics. January, 1922. "Cycles of Unemployment in the United States." Houghton Mifflin, Boston. 1923.

Boody, Elizabeth—"Cyclical Fluctuations in the Volume of Mining, 1913-1923." Harvard Review of Economic Statistics. April, 1924.

Burgess, W. Randolph—"Evidence for the Business Cycle." Administration. February, 1923.

Burton, Theodore E.—"Crises and Depressions." D. Appleton, New York. 1912.

Carver, T. N.—"A Suggestion for a Theory of Industrial Depression." Quarterly Journal of Economics. May, 1923. Harvard University Press, Cambridge.

Copeland, Melvin T.—"Business Statistics." Harvard University Press, Cambridge. 1917.

Commons, John R., McCracken, H. L. and Zeuch, W. E.—"Secular Trends and Business Cycles." Harvard Review of Economic Statistics. October, 1922.

Crum, W. L.—"Cycles of Rates on Commercial Paper." Harvard Review of Economic Statistics. January, 1923.—"Pre-war Indexes of General Business Conditions." (1903-1914). Harvard Review of Economic Statistics. January, 1924.

Crum, W. L., and Vanderblue, Homer B.—"Manufacturing Operations and the Business Cycle." Harvard Business Review. January, 1925. A. W. Shaw, Chicago.—"The Relations of a Commercial Bank to the Business Cycle." Harvard Business Review. April, 1925. A. W. Shaw, Chicago.

315

Day, Edmund E.—"An Index of the Physical Volume of Production." Harvard Review of Economic Statistics. Sept., 1920; Oct., 1920; Nov., 1920; and Dec., 1920. (Contribution was made in November, 1920, by Warren M. Persons and Eunice S. Coyle.)—"Cyclical Fluctuations of the Volume of Manufacture." Harvard Review of Economic Statistics. January, 1923.

Fisher, Irving—"The Business Cycle Largely a Dance of the Dollar." Journal of the American Statistical Association. Dec., 1923.—"Our Unstable Dollar and the So-called Business Cycle." Journal of the American Statistical Association. June, 1925.

Frank, Lawrence K.—"A Theory of Business Cycles." The Quarterly Journal of Economics. August, 1923. Harvard University Press, Cambridge.

Frederiksen, N. C.—"Periodicity of Crises, Liquidations and Expanding Periods." Bankers', Insurance Managers', and Agents' Magazine. Vol. 53. Jan.-June, 1892.

Hansen, Alvin Harvey—"Cycles of Prosperity and Depression in the United States, Great Britain and Germany." (1902-1908). University of Wisconsin Press, Madison. 1921.

Hardy, Charles O.—"Risk and Risk-Bearing." University of Chicago Press, Chicago. 1923.

Hastings, Hudson Bridge—"Costs and Profits. Their Relation to Business Cycles." Houghton Mifflin, Boston and New York. 1923.

Hull, Geo. H.—"Industrial Depressions." F. A. Stokes, New York. 1911.

Kemmerer, E. W.—"Index of the Growth of Business." (1879-1908). Published in "Money and Credit Instruments in Their Relation to General Prices." Holt, New York. 1909.

King, Willford I.—"Business Forecasting. Trends and Cycles in Business." Bankers Statistics Corp., New York. June 8, 1920.—"Business Cycles. Their Cause." American Contractor. March 3, 1923.—"Employment, Hours and Earnings in Prosperity and Depression. United States." Publication of National Bureau of Economic Research. Wm. F. Fell, Philadelphia. 1923.—"Principles Underlying the Isolation of Cycles and Trends." Journal of the American Statistical Association. December, 1924.

Kitchin, Joseph—"Cycles and Trends in Economic Factors." Harvard Review of Economic Statistics. January, 1923.

Macaulay, Frederick R.—"Individual Industries and Enterprises in the Business Cycle." (Chapter II in "Business Cycles and Unemployment." McGraw-Hill, New York. 1923.)

Miller, Harry E.—"Earlier Theories of Crises and Cycles in the United States." The Quarterly Journal of Economics. Feb., 1924. Harvard University Press, Cambridge.

Mitchell, Wesley Clair—"Business Cycles." University of California Press, Berkeley. 1913.—"Thirty Years of World Business Cycles." Credit Monthly. January, 1921.—"Business Cycles." (Chapter I in "Business Cycles and Unemployment." McGraw-Hill, New York. 1923.)

Mitchell, Wesley Clair, and King, Willford I.—"Economic Losses Caused by Business Cycles." (Chapter III in "Business Cycles and Unemployment." McGraw-Hill, New York. 1923.)

Moore, Henry Ludwell—"Economic Cycles: Their Law and Cause." Macmillan, New York. 1914.—"Forecasting the Yield and Price of Cotton." Macmillian, New York. 1917.—"Generating Economic Cycles." Macmillan, New York. 1923.

National Bureau of Economic Research—"Business Cycles and Unemployment." McGraw-Hill, New York. 1923. (See also King, W. I., Macaulay, F. R., and Mitchell, Wesley C.)

Persons, Warren M.—"Construction of a Business Barometer." American Economic Review. December, 1916.—"Indices of Business Conditions." Harvard Review of Economic Statistics. January, 1919. "An Index of General Business Conditions." Ibid. April, 1919.—"A Non-Technical Explanation of the Index of General Business Conditions." Ibid. Feb., 1920.—"Bank Loans and the Business Cycle." Ibid. Feb., 1921. —"An Index of Trade for the United States." Ibid. April, 1923.—"The Revised Index of General Business Conditions." Ibid. July, 1923.— "Cyclical Fluctuations of the Ratio of Bank Loans to Deposits, 1867-1924." Ibid. Oct., 1924.

Persons, Warren M. and Coyle, Eunice S.—"A Commodity Price Index of Business Cycles." Harvard Review of Economic Statistics. Nov., 1921.

Persons, Warren M.; Foster, William Trufant; and Hettinger, Albert J. Jr. —"The Problem of Business Forecasting." Papers presented at the annual meeting of the American Statistical Association in Dec., 1923. Houghton Mifflin, Boston and New York. 1924. (See also Pollak Foundation).

Pollak Foundation for Economic Research—Publication Number Six. "The Problem of Business Forecasting." Houghton Mifflin, Boston and New York. 1924. (*Supra,* Persons, Foster and Hettinger.)

Rogers, J. Harvey—"The Effect of Stock Speculations on the New York Money Market." The Quarterly Journal of Economics. May, 1926. Harvard University Press, Cambridge.

Rorty, M. C.—"Some Problems in Current Economics." A. W. Shaw, Chicago. 1922.

Selden, G. C.—"Trade Cycles and the Efforts to Anticipate." The Quarterly Journal of Economics. Feb., 1902. Harvard University Press, Cambridge.

Snyder, Carl—"Shall We Modify Our View of the Business Cycle?" Administration. May, 1923.—"A New Index of the Volume of Trade." Journal of the American Statistical Association. Dec., 1923.—"A New Index of Business Activity." Ibid. Mar., 1924.—"A New Clearings Index of Business for Fifty Years." Ibid. Sept., 1924.—"Deposits Activity as a Measure of Business Activity." Harvard Review of Economic Statistics. Oct., 1924.—"The Revised Index of the Volume of Trade." Journal of the American Statistical Association. Sept., 1925.—"The Influence of the Interest Rate on the Business Cycle." American Economic Review. Dec., 1925.—"Business Cycles and Business Measures." Macmillan, New York. 1927.

Sprague, O. M. W.—"Bank Management and the Business Cycle." Harvard Business Review. Oct., 1922. A. W. Shaw, Chicago.

Stewart, Walter W.—"An Index Number of Production." (1890-1919.) American Economic Review. March, 1921.

Thomas, Dorothy Swaine—"Social Aspects of the Business Cycle." George Routledge & Sons, London; E. P. Dutton & Company, New York. 1925.

Tice, John H.—"Elements of Meteorology." Published in St. Louis, Mo. 1875.

Tingley, Richard Hoadley—"Business Cycles, Past and Present." The Annalist. Nov. 13, 1922. Published by the New York Times Co.

Vanderblue, Homer B.—"Problems in Business Economics." A. W. Shaw, New York and Chicago. 1924.

Vanderblue, Homer B. and Crum, William L.—"The Relation of a Public Utility to the Business Cycle." Harvard Business Review, July and Oct., 1924. A. W. Shaw, Chicago.

Wallace, Henry A.—"Agricultural Prices." Wallace Publishing Co., Des Moines, Iowa. 1920.

Warren, G. F. and Pearson, F. A.—Various studies of prices and cycles. Farm Economics, Dept. of Agricultural Economics and Farm Management, Cornell University, Ithaca, N. Y.

Warshow, H. T.—"Inventory Valuation and the Business Cycle." Harvard Business Review. Oct., 1924. A. W. Shaw, Chicago.

Wells, D. A.—"Recent Economic Changes." D. Appleton, N. Y. 1889.

Williams, John H.—"The Rôle of Prices in the Business Cycle." Harvard Review of Economic Statistics. April, 1919.

Working, Holbrook—"Prices and the Quantity of Circulating Medium." The Quarterly Journal of Economics. Feb., 1923. Harvard University Press, Cambridge.—Extended in Harvard Review of Economic Statistics. July, 1926.

Wright, Philip G.—"Causes of the Business Cycle." Journal of the American Bankers Association. Feb., 1923.

Young, Allyn A.—"An Analysis of Bank Statistics for the United States." (1901-1914.) Harvard Review of Economic Statistics. Jan. and April, 1925.

Young, Owen D.—"Interpreting the Weather Signs of Business." System. Sept., 1924.

INDEX—CHARTS AND TABLES

INDEX